To My Dear

Fern

From

Hollington Y Tong

Grandson of

Hollington K Tong

7/18/2014

Chiang Kai-shek's Teacher and Ambassador

-An Inside View of the Republic of China from 1911-1958

-General Stilwell and American Policy Change Towards Free China

By

Hollington K. Tong

Edited by Walter C. Mih

authorHOUSE™

1663 LIBERTY DRIVE, SUITE 200
BLOOMINGTON, INDIANA 47403
(800) 839-8640
WWW.AUTHORHOUSE.COM

First published by AuthorHouse 10/21/05

ISBN: 1-4208-3201-8 (e)
ISBN: 1-4208-3202-6 (sc)

Library of Congress Control Number: 2005901102

Printed in the United States of America
Bloomington, Indiana

This book is printed on acid-free paper.

Table of Contents

Introduction

by Mei-li Tong, daughter

My father, Hollington K. Tong, was a devoted Christian, and practiced Christianity all his life. In times of difficulties and dangers, his faith gave him the strength to go on. My grandfather's family was the only Christian home in a small farming village in Ningpo County, Chekiang Province. Later, grandfather gave up farming and became a building contractor in Shanghai.

Father enrolled in a church high school in Shanghai. In his senior year, grandfather died. Father had to take an English teaching job at a school in Fenghua, Ningpo, to support his family. One of his students was Chiang Kai-shek, the future president of the Republic of China.

After father married Sally Chao, also a dedicated Christian, he worked in a publishing company in Shanghai. A missionary friend encouraged him to go to Park College in Parkville, Missouri, for his college education. At that college, students could work off tuition and expenses. It was a difficult decision, because they already had one daughter, plus their parents. Mother would have to support the whole family while father went to America for four years.

After two years at Park College, father decided to study journalism at the University of Missouri. He worked during the summers to pay his way. Through much hard work, he received a B. A. degree and was awarded a scholarship to the Pulitzer School of Journalism at Columbia University in New York. When he was at Columbia, his mother became seriously ill. Being a filial son, he returned to China immediately.

In China, he worked as a journalist and enjoyed a good reputation and success. He once owned a daily newspaper, and later became the chief editor of a large English newspaper in Shanghai. Due to his proficiency in English, his honesty and abilities, high government officers including President and Madame Chiang Kai-shek often invited him to accompany them on their overseas trips and to discuss international problems with them. When Japan invaded China in 1937, which continued through World War II, he was appointed Vice-Minister of Information in charge of the International Department, dealing with publicity and foreign correspondents in Chungking, the war capital of China.

At the end of the war in 1945, he resigned from government service and returned to civilian life. A year later, he was called back by the government to head the Information Office and to be a cabinet minister without portfolio.

In 1949, the Communists overran the China mainland. The Nationalist government retreated to Taiwan, but was in great danger of falling. During those gloomy and difficult years, President Chiang repeatedly sent my father overseas to assess other nations' positions towards Free China. He always gave the president honest and accurate assessments. From this he stepped into the diplomatic service, first as Ambassador to Japan, then as Ambassador to the United States. He did an excellent job in both capacities.

In 1958, he retired at the age of 71 and lived in Taiwan. He became an active lay Christian preacher and wrote several books, including *Christianity in Taiwan–A History, The Preachings of Hollington Tong, The Road to Eternity,* and *An Autobiography.* .

In 1965, my father suffered a stroke and was partially paralyzed. At the urging of family members, my parents lived with me in Monterey, California. Both passed away peacefully; father in 1971 at the age of 84, and mother in 1982 at the age of 92.

Author's Preface

by Hollington K. Tong

I feel a deep reluctance to write a book that includes highly subjective details of my life. Despite this disinclination, I have still written this book; the reason can be found in the insistence of my good wife. She knows my habit of compiling joke books as a form of hobby, and she has served notice upon me that there shall no more book writing until I have put down on paper the facts of my life. When we are in disagreement, she usually wins. She has won this time.

I was a newspaperman for over three decades. Then during the following two decades, it was my privilege to know historical events from the inside: to work closely with Chiang Kai-shek who had made history during our time. It gave me an unusual chance to observe both the greatness and the weakness of historical figures, and to find some thread of meaning in events that were obscure to others.

My wife's contention is that in view of the unusualness of my career, I owe it to our children and grandchildren to record these events while I am still able. My wife knows the struggles and hardships of my life and has cheerfully shared them with me. Because so much of my work has been governmental and confidential, I have not been able to share with her many of my thoughts and experiences. During the years when I was in close daily contact with President Chiang Kai-shek, I was under the tacit obligation to keep much of my information to myself, locking it away even from my wife. This created some areas of secrecy between us. As I near the end of my life, the wife who has stood at my side for half a century deserves to know all.

I believe that it will at least have some value as a reflection of the events and problems of China in the twentieth century. Although libraries of books have been written about China, there are still areas of misunderstanding among people. I have lived through fast-moving and deeply tragic Chinese events. The outcomes of these events are still indeterminate as I write. I believe that I can throw some light upon facts and personalities in modern China which are still not clear. It is with this hope that I have acceded to my wife's request.

Editor's Preface

By Walter C. Mih

After reading Dr. Hollington K. Tong's unpublished autobiography, I was very impressed by his virtuous character and deeds. In addition, I learned about important historical events that occurred in China during his time. It is unusual for a person holding such a high position in the Chinese government to practice Christianity to the full extent that he did. His close association with President Chiang Kai-shek provided him with inside knowledge regarding many historical events that affect us even today. General Stilwell's dispute with President Chiang caused the U. S. to make a major policy change towards Free China. This intriguing situation is delineated and its consequence analyzed.

I respectfully edited this book with the author's original ideas in mind. A small amount of information was added to explain further or to complete the stories that Dr. Tong had already presented.

Acknowledgements

by Mei-li Tong

I and my family members express our sincere thanks to following people:

Dr. Walter C. Mih for taking time to edit this book and encouraging its publication. He did an excellent job of editing. He is an Emeritus Professor of Washington State University and an author.

Dr. Priscilla Wagers for carefully reviewing this book. She is Curator of the Asian American Comparative Collection at the University of Idaho and an established author.

Dr. Martin L. Forst for his detailed review of the manuscript. He is an author.

Mr. Duane Hove for his helpful comments.

Yang-hu and Grace Tong, James and Diana Chen, Myron and Anne Klafter for their reviews.

Chapter One.
Earliest Memories

I came into the world on November 9, 1887. My birthplace was a small village of less than a hundred families, in Chekiang Province, twenty miles southeast of the seaport city of Ningpo, renowned among the American clipper ship traders of the early eighteenth century. It is interesting to note that my native village is just twenty miles northwest of Chekow, the birthplace and ancestral home of Generalissimo Chiang Kai-shek, who was fated to be a close associate in my later career.

My family was poor, even by Chinese standards. We had a small farm of some three acres, four miles outside the village on which we raised rice. Later, my father left farming to become a carpenter. He built houses for the China Inland Mission in Shanghai and in other cities. Unfortunately, my father was not a good businessman; after much hard work, he did not make much money.

What distinguished our family from other villagers was the fact that we were Christians – the only Christian family in the village. My father and mother had both become Christian converts in middle age. As a result, we suffered some unfriendliness from our neighbors. But this did not weaken my parents' faith.

When I was seven I enrolled in a small village school, presided over by one teacher. I went through the ceremony of kowtowing to the teacher on a red carpet. I was not a brilliant pupil. It took me one month to memorize the one hundred characters and two months to write them rather poorly. The teacher was a man who believed in the virtues of bodily punishment to spur the mind. He kept a wooden plank that he used mercilessly to punish pupils who could not recite their characters. When he could not reach the plank in time, he would strike the pupil's forehead with the knuckles of the middle finger of his right hand, or would pull their ears with hard jerks. I frequently suffered such punishment. Whether it helped me to learn, I do not know for sure.

My dread of the schoolmaster caused me to malinger. When the doctor pronounced me sound and well, my mother would recognize that I had been pretending, and she would refuse to speak to me again. My feeble attempts at revolt always resulted in my return to the hated school.

My mother was determined to make me a farmer. When I reached the age of ten, I was introduced to farm work. It was our custom, during the rice planting season, to hire extra workers to help in the planting. They had their luncheon at the farm, four miles from the village where we lived. It was my chore to carry the food in two bamboo baskets, swung on a pole over my shoulders. My second sister prepared the food. One day she was late, and in order to reach the workers in time, I tried to hurry on the weary four-mile trip. My foot became bruised by the stones on the country road and bled profusely. I fainted and dropped by the road. When I regained consciousness, I tore off a piece of my coat to bandage my foot and completed my journey.

This and other unhappy experiences convinced me that I didn't want to be a farmer. Instead, I made up my mind that I would become a scholar. When the planting season was over, I returned to the country school with a new interest in my studies. The schoolmaster found me a more responsive pupil and the beatings began to diminish. I soon found myself enjoying school for the first time.

However, I would probably have escaped from a farmer career anyway, for my father decided to change his career. Despite all the hard work, it had become apparent to my father that our three-acre farm could not support a family of five – my parents, my two sisters, and me. To sustain life even decently we would need at least five acres, and we did not have the money or opportunity to buy the needed two additional acres. All we could do was to lease them from a neighbor for a high fee at half of the harvest, and this proved unprofitable.

When my father received a construction contract from the Inland Mission in Shanghai, he moved the family to that city. I was sent to the Anglo-Chinese College in Shanghai, a Christian school. The title was a misnomer; actually, it was combined primary and high school. Here I came under the instruction of Tsao Sih-keng, a stern disciplinarian but a good teacher. He taught me the alphabet, but I was not a promising pupil. A country boy, I found the Shanghai school a real test. I progressed slowly.

I recall that in the winter of 1899, Shanghai experienced a heavy snow. Because we were poor, I had only one pair of cloth shoes, made by my mother. Excited by the snow, I engaged in a snowball fight with my schoolmates and the cloth soles became soggy with water. When the fight was over, I tried to dry the soles over a fire made out of straw. The soles burned through. I suffered the Spartan punishment of having to attend school with exposed soles for a week before my mother made me another pair.

Our family's finances soon forced me to leave the Anglo-Chinese College for a cheaper one. I transferred to Lowrie High School, in the South Gate area of Shanghai. Lowrie was a Presbyterian school and the tuition including board was just $5 a year, half of the Anglo-Chinese College.

There was the famous Boxer Rebellion. It did not extend to Shanghai, but many feared that it would touch off anti-foreign rioting, particularly against Christian schools. I recalled an episode during the rebellion when the city was in total darkness at night. We were required to sit quietly in our classroom. The American teachers stood guard over the school, with sticks and bamboo poles, and over the girls' school that adjoined it. We students carried our wooden rods, ready to use them unhesitatingly if the Boxers attacked. I was a strong boy of thirteen, and was determined to fight side-by-side with the teachers if there was any trouble. Fortunately, there were no disturbances.

During my second year at this school, I got myself into some trouble that resulted in my temporary expulsion. Our favorite sport was called stick-game, similar to baseball, but played with sticks instead of balls, which we were too poor to afford. One day we broke a window glass during our play. Although we offered to pay for it, the school issued an order forbidding further stick-game contests.

Ten of us boys, moved by the youthful spirit of rebellion, determined to resist the order. We arose early, climbed some trees and cut ten sticks. Since it was necessary to hide these props from the teachers, I volunteered to keep them under my bed. An unexpected inspection by the principal disclosed them. Although my fellow culprits had vowed to stick together, they watched in silence when I was expelled in shame. I left the school with my bundle of belongings. It was my first painful experience of the unreliability of friends when one is in trouble.

I was soundly beaten by my mother when I arrived home. While I was still sobbing, Mrs. George Fitch, wife of the pastor of the Presbyterian Church on Beijing Road, arrived for a pastoral call. Mrs. Fitch kindly offered to speak to the Reverend Silsberg, American head of Lowrie High

School, and request him to give me another chance. Her intercession succeeded and I lost no time returning to school. I have often thought that were it not for Mrs. Fitch's kind intervention at this juncture of my life, my whole future career would have been different. The experience was a salutary one for me. After my return to school, I became a more industrious pupil. I was becoming a serious and ambitious young man.

However, this did not save me from another round of trouble in 1905, when I was eighteen. This was my participation in a boycott movement. An ugly interracial incident had taken place; an American beat a Chinese assessor. Indignation ran through our school, as well as through the city. We students proclaimed a boycott of American goods. We plastered the walls of the school compound with posters urging the boycott. Meanwhile, we cut classes. When our physical education teacher, Chang Ting-yung, tore down our posters, some of us left the school in protest.

As we had nowhere to go, we spent the first night in a temple. The problem arose of getting money to buy food. In this emergency, the principal of the Shanghai High School came to our rescue. He invited some of us to transfer to his school. I was one of those invited. I remained at Shanghai High School for one year, and prepared for graduation.

At this time, to my great sorrow, my father died. Our family was left without a breadwinner. It devolved upon me to go to work to help my mother. I unhesitatingly accepted an offer to return to Ningpo County and to become a teacher of English in Lungching High School at Feng Hua. I remained there for one year.

It was at Feng Hua that I had the fateful experience of meeting the young Chiang Kai-shek, the future president of China. Although he was my own age, he was one of my pupils. (Note: The English education in Shanghai was much more advanced than that in rural schools.) A serious minded youth, his personality made an unusual impression upon the faculty.

Since his room was on the same floor with mine in the school building, I had much opportunity to observe the future president and to note his behavior outside the classroom.

I recall that he was an early riser, and, after his ablutions, it was his custom to stand erect on the veranda in front of his bedroom for half an hour. During this time his lips were compressed, his features were set in determination, and he stood with his arms firmly folded. It is, of course, impossible to say definitely what thoughts filled his mind at such times, but it was fairly obvious that he was thinking of his future. Later it was disclosed in his own diary that he was giving deep thought to the possibility of going to Japan to study military science in order to prepare himself for a career of service to his country.

Another thing that made a deep impression on me was the avidity with which he seized upon the newspapers as they arrived from Shanghai. There was a little reading room for the students, and there during recess he carefully studied them. In those days few newspapers were delivered to rural districts like Feng Hua, and when some found their way there they were highly prized, and no one was as keen to learn of events in the outside world as was the future president.

In the summer of 1906 I visited Chiang's home at Chekou and met his mother, brother and sister. Travelers to the snow-clapped mountains, twenty miles away, must pass Chekou. His mother was a devoted Buddhist, and was kind in receiving us. I was one of several teachers who stopped over on our journey to the famous mountains whose ten thousand feet high waterfall is one of the spectacular scenes in the province. The future President of the Republic of China frequented the same spot. One of his relatives acted as our guide to the mountains. For this trip we had to walk twenty miles from the city of Feng Hua to the Chiang home in Chekou, and another twenty miles to the mountains. It took us one and a half days to cover the distance.

Before the end of the summer semester, an inter-school athletic meet was held in Ningpo. I accompanied the students from Lungching High School to compete. The future President of China ran third in the 100-yard dash. His school felt pride in his showing.

Chiang Kai-shek studied English under me, learning the English alphabet. Japanese was the second required language. I remember him as an apt pupil in his foreign language courses.

I spent my summer vacation with my mother at Tungchiatou, twenty miles away. I remember that I walked the distance, without any thought that I was doing anything unusual. It was flood season, and I had to wade through several streams during my trip. I was nineteen and it was a welcome experience to me. I carried with me a primitive Chinese-made rifle to shoot game on my way. I had a good bag of wild geese and ducks when I arrived home to the delight of my mother.

The year 1907 was memorable in my life, because it was the year of my marriage. I had met my future wife, Miss Sally Chao, while she was a student at the Presbyterian girls' school in Shanghai, adjacent to Lowrie High School. Sally's mother worked as a housekeeper at Lowrie. They lived in a house on the school ground. One day, I purposely kicked a soccer ball into the house in order to meet Sally. I had quickly fallen in love with the bright, vivid girl and we had become engaged to be married before I left Shanghai. Upon her graduation, she went to a nearby city, Sungkiang, where she taught for a year in a women's Bible school while I was teaching at Feng Hua.

I had hoped that we would be married in Ningpo, and that I could remain at my Feng Hua post for another year. But Sally had other ideas. She insisted that I resign my Feng Hua job and come to Shanghai to work. In the end she prevailed, and I reluctantly resigned at Feng Hua.

We were married in Shanghai in January 1907. Reverend Silsberg, the principal of Lowrie High School, performed the religious service. My mother came to Shanghai for the wedding, accompanied by my brother-in-law. An old-fashioned woman, who had been brought up under the old Chinese foot-binding custom, she was shocked by my bride's natural feet. Following custom, I dressed for the wedding in a Mandarin coat, with peacock feathers and high platform boots. My bride was beautifully dressed in a Chinese gown, trimmed according to the elaborate Chinese taste. After the ceremony we followed the custom of kneeling down and kowtowing to my mother three times, then the sumptuous marriage feast.

A married man, I was faced by the problem of earning money to support my family. Through the influence of a close friend of my father, I secured a position with the Commercial Press in Shanghai. For several months, to economize, we lived in a single room in the Mission compound.

Curiously enough, this patron had very nearly become my father-in-law. It had been a family understanding that I was to wed his oldest daughter when I grew up. However, he changed his mind in view of the death of my father and my own notorious poverty. I have always regarded myself as extremely fortunate that I did not follow the Chinese custom of a marriage arranged by the parents. My marriage was one of love and it has proved to be a very happy one.

The Commercial Press, then a comparatively young organization, was later to become the principal printing and publishing house of China. It had been started by former Lowrie High School students and my background at Lowrie stood me in good stead in my new job. I was assigned the task of assisting the manager to write English language letters, as well as of supervising the department of half tone blocks. For this I received 75 Chinese Yuan a month. (Five Chinese Yuan equals one American dollar.) Out of this I had to support my wife, her mother, myself, and my mother plus to pay for my father's debt. One year after our wedding, we were blessed with a baby girl. It was a hard life.

I was an active Christian as I have been all my life. My wife and I attended church and Sunday school regularly. It was in the church that I met the Presbyterian missionary, Paul Montgomery, who was to play a decisive role in my life.

Montgomery took a rare personal interest in me. Noticing my ardent desire to learn fluent English, he generously offering to give me private lessons for free after my office hours at the press. In order to keep my appointments with him, I bought a second hand bicycle. I rode to his home after working hours every day and studied English under him for two or three hours. Only after my lessons did I go home for my supper.

During this period I was haunted by a debt of about 1,500 Chinese Yuan which my poor father had borrowed at the time of my second sister's marriage to give her an adequate dowry. To pay the interest on this debt 10 Chinese Yuan a month, and to liquidate its principal weighed heavily upon me and I could not shirk my responsibility. To increase our scanty income, my wife and I both taught English to ten or more pupils every night. With such a schedule, I worked late every night, and was up again early in the morning to study my English homework before going to the Commercial Press at eight o'clock. To speed up my acquirement of English, I used to snatch time on my job, when there was a pause in my duties, to rehearse myself. I recall committing to memory long passages from the autobiography of Benjamin Franklin at this time. I had the sympathy of an understanding employer. Besides my English lessons, the generous Paul Montgomery also gave me lessons in Latin.

One day, he surprised me by asking if I wanted to go to the United States to obtain a college education. The idea at first seemed fantastic to me. I had no money, and I was weighed down with obligations. At the same time the proposal fascinated me. I had long since come to the conclusion that if I remained at the Commercial Press, I would be accepting a future of white-collared poverty, and would have no certainty of even being able to pay off my father's debt. It seemed to me that if I went to America, my education would lift me to a higher income level upon my return, and my financial problems would be solved.

Montgomery explained to me how it would be possible for me to go there. He himself was a graduate of a remarkable Presbyterian Park College, where the whole student body was given a chance to work their way through by part-time daily tasks. Park College is located near Kansas City, Missouri. He promised to arrange for my admittance and to loan me money for a third class passage to the college.

I decided to take the challenge. There were technicalities to arrange. With the assistance of How Sui-feng, general manager of the Commercial Press, I secured my passport and visa. Then I visited a barber shop for a decisive step. The Manchu emperors still reigned in Beijing and, like all of my generation, I wore the queue. Since I was going to America, I determined to cut it off, even though this symbolized severing ties with China. When I visited a Chinese barber, he fearfully refused to cut it on the ground that it would bring bad luck. Finally, a Japanese barber cut it, charging me double the usual haircut price.

My wife sympathized with my step, but my mother was bitterly opposed. When she heard that I had abandoned my queue and was going to America she threatened to commit suicide in protest. I finally persuaded her to consent. For her support, the Commercial Press agreed to loan me 15 Chinese Yuan a month. My wife accepted a teaching job to support the family in my absence.

Everything was now arranged but my expense money. The Commercial Press kindly gave me a bonus in advance. I was also able to borrow over $100 (U.S.). I outfitted myself with a worn-out suit and an old overcoat, given to me by Mr. Montgomery. I bought two suits of winter underwear. Mr. and Mrs. Fitch gave me a ten dollar gold piece, but my wife pleaded with me so hard to let her keep it as a souvenir that I left it with her. On a cold day in January 1909 I sailed from China on the ship Siberia.

At the Woosung docks to see me off were Mr. Montgomery, my wife and several of her relatives. My young wife wept and I felt like doing likewise but I kept back the tears until the ship was underway. It was a bitter moment for me when, at last alone, I reflected that it would probably be four or five years before I would see my wife and newborn baby again.

In my bare quarters in third class, I passed a sad first night. My pillow was wet with tears. I told myself that it was unmanly to give myself up to grief, but I found it hard to struggle with my heart. I ate my breakfast with strangers and felt very much alone. One day later, the ship reached Kobe, Japan. Two days later it stopped in Yokohama. At both places I disembarked and looked around curiously at this new overseas world that I was now seeing for the first time. After a four-day stay at Yokohama, we sailed for Honolulu, where we arrived after fifteen days.

Before reaching Honolulu, I experienced my first storm at sea. I watched the boiling sea through my porthole, reflecting on the mysterious ways of God, and feeling a deep sense of security with Him. Suddenly the seawater poured in through the porthole nearly choking me. I was seized by a violent seasickness for two days. It was a frightening experience for a new traveler.

Dr. Knaff, a son-in-law of the Fitches, was a fellow passenger on the ship and Mr. Montgomery had asked him to look after me on the voyage. But unwittingly I gave him a great shock. I had left the ship at Honolulu with another third class passenger who had taken me with him to a waterfront saloon. There I gorged myself on lunch, eating chicken, cheese, sandwich and drinking milk. The total cost was only five cents. I was amazed at the cheapness of American life. Meeting Dr. Knaff after I returned to the ship, I told him of my experience. He impressed upon me that when I reached America I must shun saloons, which were frequented only by drunkards and bad characters. His earnest advice has given me a lifelong aversion to saloons.

In San Francisco at last, I was greeted at the pier by Reverend Lawrence, a former American missionary in China. He introduced a Chinese pastor to me in his home. I could not resist one extravagance. I had never possessed a watch in my life and I bought one for $10 shortly after landing.

Two days later I was on the train to Kansas City. Reverend Lawrence packed a brimming basket of food for me to last the four-day rail trip. I hoarded my food to make it last, but I was glad when I finally reached Kansas City. I changed over to the Burlington Railway, and after another nine-mile ride, I was at last in Parkville, Missouri. I was met at the little depot by one of my new fellow students, Newell Preston.

My college days had commenced.

Chapter Two.
College Days in America

Park College is a small school with less than 400 pupils, but there are few parts of the world where its name is not known. At that time, its proudest boast was that over 60 percent of its graduates had entered church or missionary careers. The atmosphere of devout Presbyterianism pervaded the campus. Because I had enjoyed a Presbyterian education in Shanghai, I immediately felt at home. I found genuine warmth among the faculty members and students with whom I was to spend the next two and a half years.

Newell Preston met me at the depot and took me to Woodward dormitory that was to be my home. Shortly afterwards, I was taken to see Dr. Lowell M. McAfee, the president of Park. When he asked me how much money I had brought with me, I counted my slender bankroll and found that I had twenty-five dollars. That will suffice, McAfee told me; we will enter you in Family Three. At the time, I did not know what he meant. Later I was to learn that pupils in Family Three worked four and a half hours a day, six days a week before or after classes, at jobs on the campus that were assigned to them by the college's Labor Department. Had I been able to pay more, I could have enrolled in Family Two and worked only three hours per day.

I had done little really hard manual work in China, but I now found myself running the gamut of fatiguing jobs. Like other new arrivals, I was given as my first assignment, a job shoveling coal in the college powerhouse. It was my first stint with the shovel, and at the end of the day, my hands were swollen and sore. The second day was even worse because my hands were covered with blisters. Unpleasant as the experience was,

I stuck it out. After a few weeks of this, I was transferred to an easier job, this time in the college printing shop. Later, I had other assignments – gardening, picking apples, laying water pipes, and other campus chores. It was an excellent all around experience in physical labor. After the hardship of newness had worn off, I liked it.

On one occasion I found myself assigned to bring milk to the various girls' dormitories, where the students of both sexes had their meals. I had to fetch the milk in a buggy, and en route, I had to drive the buggy across a forded stream. On my first trip, the streambed was dry, but before my return, there had been a heavy shower and the creek was turned into a torrent. Trying to handle the horse, I miscalculated and the buggy overturned. I narrowly escaped drowning. Similar unexpected experiences enlivened my years at Park.

It was not all physical labor; the students were a serious-minded group of typical young American men and women who were ambitiously striving for knowledge. I found the atmosphere especially favorable for study and I progressed rapidly. Living, working, eating and studying with American youths, my English improved dramatically, although I never quite succeeded in eliminating my Chinese accent. It was an excellent vestibule to the life, which lay ahead and filled with warm American contacts.

When my first summer vacation came, I made a strenuous effort to earn money to replenish my depleted reserve. I decided to go to nearby Kansas City to seek work. I knew no one in the city. Arriving at the Union Station, I took a streetcar. There I had a strange encounter with coincidence in life.

On the streetcar was a Chinese couple, Dr. and Mrs. Mong Feng Young, herb doctors. I struck up a conversation with them. When I informed the doctor that I wanted employment, and told him something about my student career, he showed great interest.

Dr. Young invited me to pass the night at his home, saying that he was the owner of the King Joy Lou, a Chinese restaurant of some importance. I accepted his invitation, and the next day he sent me to his restaurant to be a general worker. The hours were exhausting. I worked from nine o'clock in the morning to two o'clock in the afternoon and again from five o'clock in the afternoon to one o'clock the next morning. I received one hundred dollars a month as my wages, plus room and board. I did not get more than five hours sleep a day. However, I did not mind it, for during my six months' stay at Park College, I seldom had more than that amount of sleep.

A close relative of Dr. Young, who was a partner of the restaurant, supervised my work. He would rub his white handkerchief on the floor after I had cleaned it. If the handkerchief showed the presence of dust, I was required to mop it again. He repeated this cleanup with the light bulbs, the chairs, the tables and the surrounding walls. But it was good training. What I learned in the restaurant in 1909 has served me in good stead during my subsequent years. It taught me to practice thoroughness in my tasks, however minor. I endured his drive and his insults patiently.

During the summer, I saved about $300. I sent $200 to Mr. Montgomery in Shanghai with the request that he arrange for my wife to come to Park College and join me as a student, leaving our baby daughter with her mother or my mother. Upon receipt of my letter he called a meeting of all my friends, and considered the advisability of my wife coming to America. All felt that this would not be wise. Eventually, the project was dropped.

I retained $100, out of which I was able to pay the purser at Park College the sum of $75. This entitled me to tuition and board at the cost of only three hours of work a day. It was a welcome relief from the four and half hours schedule that I had worked during my first six months.

I had the good fortune of making a new friend during my summer work. Dr. Mong Feng Young's secretary, Mrs. Wood, she took a personal interest in me and my ambitions. In the succeeding months, she was ready at all times to make financial contributions to my tight budget. She was also an understanding woman whose advice and help was a constant support to me during all my hardships.

At the restaurant my difficulties were compounded by the fact that I did not speak Cantonese (or Guongdong), while Dr. Young's manager did not speak English. I recognized the offensive Cantonese words, which he applied to me, but I could not talk back. Because I needed the job, I endured the rough treatment. I steadfastly kept my troubles from my wife in Shanghai, for fear it would distress her.

When I returned to Park College at the end of the summer, I was admitted to the upper class. Determined to better my status, I studied diligently, and succeeded in being admitted to the class, which matriculated in 1908. I began to adjust myself to the college routine, and I even became fond of American food. When I first arrived, I had found it impossible to eat corn and tomatoes. Now I found that I could relish them.

I was also learning American table manners. When I first arrived, I was seated beside the matron in the girls' dormitory where I had my meals. She made a special effort to acquaint me with good American table manners. For instance, one day she noticed that I was playing nervously with my napkin ring. "It is bad manners, Mr. Tong, to finger your napkin ring while eating," she told me. I obeyed her, but one day I noticed that she was dallying with her napkin ring. "Miss Haney," I said, "it is a poor rule which does not work both ways. Today, you are playing with your napkin ring." Embarrassed, she apologized for the social breach.

On another occasion, my classmates went to Kansas City to attend a concert. An English teacher accompanied us. I paid the streetcar fare for her as prompted by my Chinese sense of propriety. "Mr. Tong," she said, "in this country a gentleman does not pay for the fare of a lady unless he secures her prior approval." I hastily abandoned my attempt to pay, but was greeted with laughter from my fellow students.

Occasionally, there were social affairs at the college and the male students walked with the girls. On such occasions, I found it highly confusing to decide whether to walk on the left or the right of my partner. I solved this problem eventually by deciding always to walk on the exposed side of my partner, thus shielding her from any possible danger.

Often on Sundays the little group of foreign students at Park would be entertained by one of the professors in his home. I particularly remember Dr. Arthur L. Wolfe, professor of Latin, who made a special effort to make us feel at home. Mrs. Wolfe was so efficient a homemaker that she could attend church services in the morning, rush home to prepare dinner, and then be ready to sit down with her guests and entertain them, all without aid from a servant. This was done with a leisurely air that no Chinese woman would have been able to match. It was an eye-opening experience for me in the customs of American family life.

I particularly remember the canning season when fruit from the college orchards was harvested before the winter. The boys and girls of the college worked tirelessly at such times. There was no Chinese equivalent of this fruit season in my experience.

The distinguishing thing about Park was that it was a God-centered college. The Bible was an important study in the curriculum. An inspired man, Professor Mathew Hale Wilson, taught the Bible. I was fortunate enough to make a grade of 94 in his class. This entitled me to enter a Bible contest. The contest required participants to memory the whole book of Proverbs. Ten students entered the competition. All were eliminated in the finals except a Miss Vautres Pruitt and me. I had the thrill of coming in first and winning the prize of $25. At the time I really needed the money. Miss Pruitt, as the second best, received a smaller prize. I enjoyed winning, but I was so sorry that I had snatched the prize away from her.

When the summer of 1910 came around, I decided that I would not return to the Chinese restaurant, but would seek work on a farm. I roughed it while looking for work, carrying with me a small cooking utensil, some rice and some bacon. I used to look for a place near a river or pond to cook my meals. It was a real tramp life and I liked it. Eventually, I secured a job with a farmer twenty miles distant from Park College.

My task was to plough weeds out of the farmer's cornfield. The corn rose ten feet high. I was given a team of mules for the ploughing. I found it hard to keep the mules moving in 103-degree heat. They would stop to nibble at the grass or cornstalks.

At the end of the day, I would return to the farmer's house, dead tired. As soon as I had eaten my supper, I would tumble into bed and sleep soundly until five o'clock, when I had to be up again to grind fodder and feed the mules. Breakfast would be served at six, a hearty meal of bacon, eggs and hot buns. After breakfast, the hard grind of toil would recommence. For all this I received two dollars a day, with board and lodging. I looked forward to Sundays when I could have a day of rest.

I stuck it out with the farmer for one month. Then I quit and I looked around for a different job. I ran into a Japanese Park College student, Seiichi Ikimoto, two years my senior, who was also looking for farm work. We found a job building a dike but Seiichi soon got into an altercation with his fellow workers, who taunted him on his Japanese race. The situation became ugly with the farmhands threatening to bury us in the ditch. We fled precipitately, forfeiting our pay. After this experience, I decided to travel alone, and avoid being involved in the risks of a companion's hot temper.

This Missouri farm experience was a useful experience, although I detested it at the time. It gave me a better understanding of rural American life, its customs and its rooted prejudices.

During this period, I gave much thought to the question of my future. China was then under the yoke of the Manchus monarchy and I was resolved to devote my career to its removal. A military career appealed to me as my best hope for serving China. I was ambitious of gaining admittance to West Point so I wrote a half-dozen letters to Minister Chang Ying-tang, head of our legation in Washington, but received no reply. Undiscouraged, I sent a letter to President Theodore Roosevelt. I was delighted to receive a cordial letter in reply in which the President praised me for my ambition but declared that he could do nothing in the matter unless I obtained an official recommendation from the Chinese Legation. Lacking important family or official backing, I was unable to obtain such a recommendation.

My second choice as a life profession was to become a newspaperman. On one of my trips from Kansas City to Parkville, I saw a newspaperman typing out a story on an Oliver typewriter. I determined that I would become a newspaperman too. I began to study English style assiduously. In this I was aided by a gifted teacher at Park, Professor of English John H. Lawrence. I must have made a nuisance of myself burdening Professor Lawrence with my papers. One day, I read a newspaper article about the school of journalism at the University of Missouri, the first school of journalism in America. From this time, my thoughts were all centered on going to this new school.

I made application for admission to the school of journalism at the University of Missouri. My application was accepted. It was a wrench to leave Park College, which had been my home to me for two and a half years. The faculty strongly urged me to remain until I received my degree in 1912. But my heart was set on journalism.

The University of Missouri is located in Columbia, then a small city of under 10,000, about 150 miles from Parkville. I found the university atmosphere in sharp contrast to the intimacy of small college life. But I was not alone in Columbia. Four other former Park men were also at the University. We constituted a little circle that included Lloyd Boutwell, John B. Peniston and the two Koch brothers. I secured a modest room in the home of a widow, Mrs. Robertson, whose husband had been associated with Dean Walter Williams in the publication of a daily newspaper. I roomed with Boutwell, a youth of great promise, who had come to the University to study medicine after graduating from Park. Both of us were so poor that we could not afford separate beds. Boutwell was something of a practical joker and he used to frighten us by bringing home from the dissecting room gruesome specimens of ears and noses.

Later, in 1917, Boutwell was killed in the First World War. His death weighed heavily upon my spirit. Despite his own hard cramming, he never begrudged time to help me with my early efforts in writing. He was a true friend.

The Missouri School of Journalism was regarded as a bold educational experiment and it had attracted some remarkable men to its faculty. One of these was Charles G. Ross, who later served as White House press secretary to President Harry S. Truman. Ross, for many years, was the Washington correspondent for the *St. Louis Post-Dispatch*. He was the author of a book on newspaper reporting and writing, which he dedicated to his mother. The filial gesture deeply impressed me with my Chinese regard for family ties.

Other teachers at the University of Missouri who made a deep imprint upon me were Dean Walter Williams (later, President of the University), Professors Ross, J. B. Powell and Martin. Dean Williams was a remarkable individual – a largely self-educated man who rose to be head of a great university. He had a warm personality, and he made it his responsibility to know all his pupils and to establish a close intellectual relationship with them. He was a great teacher, sharing some of the qualities of Confucius and Socrates.

I recall Professor Ross's definition of news. It has passed into the public domain of anecdotes now, but then it was new. He asked the class whether it was news when a dog bit a man. Some of us said 'yes,' while others thought that the professor was spoofing us. He then told us that a dog that bit a man was not news, but that a man who bit a dog was a real news story. The lesson stuck.

I remained at the university for a year. I received my B.A. degree from Missouri, in journalism, with credits for courses in international history and law. I was proud of the fact that I had earned a B.A. in just three years of study.

Before attempting to enter newspaper work, I determined to gain some more experience in American journalistic know-how. A rare opportunity to increase my knowledge now presented itself. Joseph Pulitzer, the great publisher of the *New York World* and the *St. Louis Post-Dispatch*, had died and left a part of his fortune to endow a Pulitzer School of Journalism at Columbia University. I applied for admission to the first class, which would open in 1912. I was accepted, and made my plans to go to New York to enroll. Before the school year commenced, I secured some experience in a stringer job on a Kansas City newspaper.

I reached New York in August, and made a frantic effort to secure work on one of the New York papers, which would not only give me experience, but also help me support myself. My experience was disheartening. Refused by the first editor whom I called upon, I decided to offer to work for nothing on my next call. But even this did not get me a job. At the third paper visited, I increased my offer by proposing to pay my own streetcar fare on assignments. The third editor's retort to this was sharp and terse. "There are two kinds of people in the world," he told me, "those who are worthwhile and those who are not. In offering to pay your own car fare, you are admitting that you are worthless. Good day!" It was such a discouraging experience that I lost all appetite for supper that night.

I had found a place to stay in New York in the home of the Rev. Hue. Staying with Hue were Mr. and Mrs. C. P. Ing. All of us were non-paying guests, too poor to find rent money for our kind-hearted host. I recall that on that discouraging night, Mrs. Ing kindly made me a glass of grape juice from fresh grapes, and I began to regain my courage.

If I could not succeed with newspapers, I hoped that I might fare better with magazines. The next morning, I started on the round of magazines, commencing with *The Independent,* a weekly magazine of opinion, which has long disappeared. Its editor was the famous Dr. Hamilton Holt who later had a spectacular career as the President of Rollins College in Florida. I decided to try a different gambit on Holt.

Instead of applying for a job, I told him about my experiences with the daily papers. He was genuinely interested. He then brought me to life by proposing; "Suppose that you work for me without pay for two weeks. If your articles are acceptable and printable, I shall pay you what you are worth." I accepted the offer without a moment's reflection. Dr. Holt then handed me an assignment to write a review of a book by the Japanese writer, Dr. Nitobe, "The *Bushido* (Knighthood) of Japan."

I sat up all night reading the book and then spent three days writing the review. Dr. Holt dashed my hopes by telling me that it was not what he wanted. I asked for a second chance. But when I brought in my second version, Dr. Holt again rejected it.

I talked with Dr. E. E. Slosson, the literary editor of *The Independent,* who was also a professor of history at Columbia. He read both manuscripts and pronounced them good. "I'm afraid you have overlooked one factor," Dr. Slosson told me. "What is it?" I asked. "Dr. Holt was decorated last year by the Emperor of Japan," he informed me, with a wink of the eye.

With this advice, I understood what had been wrong with my articles, too critical of Bushido. On the next try, Holt accepted my review cordially. A month later, he gave me a copy of his own article on commercialism and journalism.

I continued to do part-time work for *The Independent* after the Pulitzer School opened. A sensational news item in all the papers at this time was the suicide of General Nogao and his wife in protest against the declining moral standards of the Japanese people. *The Independent* published an editorial which I wrote approving this deed. Dr. Holt then asked me to write a feature article discussing suicide as a virtue in the Far East. I recall showing the first draft of this article to Miss Iphigene Ochs, daughter of the publisher of the *New York Times,* who was one of my classmates at the Pulitzer School. Miss Ochs read the article with deep distaste. To this day, when we meet, she never fails to remind me of this youthful deed.

Dr. Holt urged me to write an article in the vein of humor, describing some of my experiences on arrival in the Western world. I eventually wrote it, and it received much criticism both toward me and toward *The Independent*. I got a harsh letter from one of my Park College classmates rebuking me for the characterizations of Park College people, which I had included in the article. But there were some balancing letters of approval. If I had it to do over again, I would not be as outspoken in baring my personal feelings to the world.

The Independent gave me the beat of writing all its reviews of books on the Orient. I soon became quite a skillful book reviewer. When, as sometimes happened, I received three or four books for review. I learned to use the old book reviewer's trick of scanning the first and last chapters and then grinding out my reviews. Probably some of my appraisals were superficial but I satisfied Dr. Holt and he began to lean upon me for his judgments of books on the Far East.

My study at the Pulitzer School proved to be one of the most stimulating experiences of my life. I was enrolled in the first class, the class of 1913. There were only fifteen of us. Some of them were to go on to make distinguished names for themselves. One of my fellow students was Carl W. Ackerman, later a distinguished foreign correspondent and for many years the dean of the Pulitzer School. Another was Leon Fraser, later to have an extraordinary career as an international banker, and as assistant secretary of the Treasury. Another was Miss Iphigene Ochs, later the wife of Arthur J. Sulzberger, the president and publisher of the *New York Times*.

The school opened with an inspiring list of teachers. The tone of the new school was ably set by Dean Talcott Williams. Dean Williams was an inspirational teacher, a former missionary in Beirut, Lebanon, and a man of deep culture with broad newspaper experience. He was a spare, wiry little man with a long mustache and large blue eyes. He used to invite me to have dinner with him, and we would discuss at length my plans for a future career in China. One thing which he urged upon me was that I perfect my written Chinese to the point of becoming a Chuangyuan (first in emperor's exam), the recipient of China's highest literary honor. Unless I did this, I would not succeed in making myself well-known throughout China, he told me.

Another teacher who influenced me unusually was Robert L. MacAlarney, former managing editor of the *New York Tribune*. An able writer himself, he was an impressive teacher. He emphasized the importance of news gathering. To sharpen our news sense, he often gave us case assignments.

One such assignment was to the famous Police Lieutenant Becker trial, which was then in progress. To make this a real test of newspaper know-how, he required that members of the class secure admission to the packed courtroom without credentials or admission tickets. Failure to get in would result in flunking.

When I tried to get into the courtroom, the police promptly ejected me. I then hit upon the expedient of following closely behind Mrs. Becker when she entered. This ruse succeeded, then I was recognized by the policeman who had first barred me and he threw me out again without giving me opportunity for explanations. I was downhearted and expected to be flunked. But Professor MacAlarney was impressed by my ingenuity and passed me. Later I received the assignment to cover the trip of the convicted men to Sing Sing prison, on the chance that an attempt at rescue by gangsters might be made. Of course nothing happened on this closely guarded journey, but I felt that I was fast becoming a working reporter.

It was Professor MacAlarney's belief that journalism students should be exposed from the outset to actual crime reporting conditions, so he gave us frequent police assignments. I didn't relish this form of reporting, but I tried my best to master it. I was particularly nauseated when I received an assignment to cover a reported suicide. With the professional newspaper reporters, I rushed to the apartment where I saw the unfortunate man lying in ghastly death in the darkened room. I was shocked by the embarrassing questions that the hard-boiled reporters put to the grieving widow. But when I told Professor MacAlarney that I didn't want any more such assignments, he rejected my plea and gave me an even tougher one.

At the time, the use of cocaine was becoming a public scandal in New York. The newspapers were running feature stories. My teacher told me to go out and get a story on cocaine addicts, preferably about the suppliers. I hit upon the following plan to establish contacts. I hunted up a seedy looking restaurant on East 40th Street where, I understood, addicts were in the habit of hanging out, and I told the proprietor a hard-luck story. I had not eaten for two days, I told him. Would he give me a chance to earn a meal by washing dishes for him? I got the chance. From my obscure position I kept my eyes upon the stream of customers, without observing anything unusual. But about 12:30 p.m., some obvious cocaine peddlers and users made their appearance. One was a shabby looking woman of about forty, who was weeping. When the proprietor was busy elsewhere, I accosted her and asked her why she was crying. She answered readily that she had just experienced a three-day illness, which had prevented her from coming to the restaurant to get her supply of cocaine. She talked freely to me about her craving.

After picking up some more local color, I hurried back to my lodgings and proudly wrote out my story. The next day, Professor MacAlarney praised me highly for my performance and gave me a high grade.

I received other kinds of assignments. Professor Franklin Mathews, who was also city editor of the *New York Times,* gave me a feature writing task. Dean Williams sent us to review plays or to cover art exhibitions. I found such assignments difficult as I had no background in the theater or art field. I hit upon the expedient of questioning other theater goers who appeared to have unusual understanding about the play. Frequently they would give me their reactions to the performance in a form, which I could use in developing my review. At art exhibitions, I would talk to mature patrons, preferably those wearing thick glasses. Their comments on the virtues or faults of the various paintings would give me leads for my write-ups.

Play reviews must be turned in within two hours after the performance, with a clock registering the turn-in time. This necessitated writing the review during the subway ride back to Columbia University. Thus we duplicated the actual working conditions of newspapermen on the New York papers. To get further experience, we worked part-time on the local newspapers. In this capacity, I received an assignment to interview former President Theodore Roosevelt, who was passing through the city.

I sought out Mr. Roosevelt and asked for an interview. With a twinkling eye, he asked me, "Are you a veteran reporter?" "No," I answered, "I am only a greenhorn." The reply must have amused him for he told me to get out my pad and pencil to write down the interview. I complied with alacrity and he dictated a statement to me. I recall that in this statement he used the words, "The United States and China must forever be friends, no matter what changes occur in the world situation." President Roosevelt was himself a great journalist, and he showed his kindness of heart in cheerfully giving his valuable time to such an obvious tyro as me.

But my schooldays were soon to end. In the early part of 1913, I received a telegram from China telling me that my mother was seriously ill and that I must return immediately. Being a filial son, I did not question my decision, even though the return would prevent me from obtaining my M.A. degree. Dean Williams and my teachers were shocked by my announcement of departure before graduation. I was also confronted with the problem of return fare. I had been barely supporting myself by working three hours a day for a bachelor on 80th Street, cooking his dinner and caring for his room. This had given me no opportunity to save anything, and I was virtually broke.

In my difficulty, I approached Dr. Holt. He offered to buy five articles from me in advance, and pay me $200. I worked night and day on these stories and, by the end of a month, they were finished. Dr. Holt paid me the money and I promptly booked a third class passage to Japan. My luggage was light, and I was soon aboard the ship which was to carry me back home.

The return voyage across the Pacific was peaceful and uneventful. In the third class with me was a party of thirty Japanese who made me welcome in their group. Overcoming an initial dislike of Japanese people, I found their companionship agreeable. When we arrived in Yokohama, some of them cordially entertained me in their homes. I spent two days in Tokyo, and then took a train to Nagasaki where I transferred to a medium sized Japanese ship which carried me back to Shanghai.

It was fortunate that I traveled on this boat for one of my fellow passengers was Dr. Sun Yat-sen, father of the Republic of China, which was established in 1911. Dr. Sun, who had been briefly the first President of the Republic of China, was traveling with a large retinue of high Kuomintang (Citizen's Party) officials and important government personages.

This was the period after Dr. Sun had resigned the presidency of the Republic of China in Nanking to avoid a civil war with Yuan Shih-kai, who controlled the Beijing government. Then Beijing became the capital of the new republic. After a stay in Japan, Dr. Sun was returning to China to head the Railway Corporation, for inauguration an ambitious railroad building program in China.

Before leaving New York, I had arranged with one of the newspapers to act as stringer in China. I realized that here was an unexpected opportunity to obtain a major story, and I requested an interview with the great leader. He graciously granted my request, and I was able to secure an important news source. Through this chance shipboard meeting, I was able to establish my first personal contact with the Kuomintang, with which I was to work during most of my future life. This first meeting with Dr. Sun ripened into a closer friendship. I did not recognize it at the time, but I was already launched on the career that was to culminate in my ambassadorship in Washington.

Chapter Three.
Newspaperman in China

It was a joyous experience for me to be reunited with my wife and child after four years. The years of my absence had not been easy years for Sally. In order to aid me in securing a Western education, she had cheerfully assumed the hard role of breadwinner for the family.

She had taken on the burden of two jobs. Part of the day she tutored Chinese to the foreign missionaries and their children. In the remaining hours, she bound books for the Commercial Press as a piece-worker. Her joint income was small: to economize, she used to walk long distances between the homes of her pupils. And yet, without this uncomplaining help of my devoted wife, I would have been unable to go to America. Her letters to me never reflected these hardships that she was facing.

Throughout her adulthood, her life was centered in the Christian Church. Her faith gave her strength to go on. During my absence, she became a close friend of a neighboring Canadian couple, Mr. and Mrs. Mackey. They were missionaries of the Apostolic Church. In their need, she volunteered to act as interpreter for them. Her English training had been limited, but she found that she was able to do this unfamiliar work with great satisfaction to her employers. Her work for the Mackeys cut still further into her time, but she found the hours to perform all her tasks, without neglecting her church activities.

I was immediately faced by the necessity of finding lucrative employment in Shanghai to care for my family. At first, I was met by disappointment in my quest for a job. I then called upon Dr. Sun Yat-sen who introduced me to Ma So, his English secretary. Ma So was also the editor of the *China Republican*, an English-language daily in Shanghai.

On Dr. Sun's recommendation, Ma So gave me the post of assistant editor, under R. I. Hope, a Eurasian British subject, who was editor-in-chief.

Within a week, I was faced by the necessity of undergoing a minor operation. Having no money, I could not go to a hospital and was forced to the expedient of having a male nurse perform the operation, under ether, in a hotel room near the hospital. My strong constitution stood me in good stead, and three days after the operation I was back at my desk.

I had begun my newspaper career at a time of great political turmoil. Two weeks after my return to the *Republican*, I was instructed to cover an event which marked the final break between the Kuomintang (Citizen's Party) and the Yuan Shih-kai regime in Beijing. Much to Yuan's distaste, the Kuomintang had just won a majority in the elections for a new National Assembly. By rank, Sung Chiao-jen, who had succeeded Dr. Sun Yat-sen as the leader of the party, was in line for the premiership. On March 21, 1913, as Sung was about to board a train for Beijing at the Shanghai railway station, a political assassin named Woo Fok-ming shot him. Sung died the following day. President Yuan issued an order to arrest all those implicated in the political murder. In the later investigation, it was revealed that Chao Ping-chun, Premier and Minister of the Interior in Yuan's government, conspired in the assassination. Woo died mysteriously in his cell, but it was plain to all that Yuan himself had ordered the assassination.

The *Republican* covered the assassination and the subsequent investigations under banner headlines. It was an important introduction into the realities of Chinese politics for me, the tyro reporter. All of us sensed that this was the first act of Yuan's scheme to drive the Kuomintang out of the government, and to subvert the revolution of 1911. I had interviewed Sung just before his death, and he had talked to me hopefully of his plans to lead the reorganization of China into a democratic state, similar to that of the United States. After his murder, I attended successive meetings in Dr. Sun's home at which the historic decision was made to launch a drive to overthrow Yuan Shih-kai.

In order to report the coming political struggle, Dr. Sun personally sent me to Beijing to act as correspondent for all Kuomintang's six newspapers in Shanghai. All of them were published in the International or French territories to be safe from Yuan's agents. I recalled that, the day before departure, after supper at his home, Dr. Sun handed me a revolver. "If you are cornered by Yuan's men and there is no escape for you, you can kill yourself," he told me. Such fatalistic advice did not appeal to me in my buoyant mood, as I stood on the threshold of my journalistic career. Nevertheless, I took the weapon with me to Beijing.

This was my first visit to the stately city. I was met on arrival by several Kuomintang members who took me to a hotel. Later I found two rooms in the home of a friend, Wei Ting-tao, who was assisting W. H. Donald, correspondent for the *Manchester Guardian*. It was my duty to send the *China Republican* in Shanghai a few thousand words a day in English. They were translated into Chinese, and distributed among all the other Kuomintang papers. In order to widen my contacts with Kuomintang National Assembly members, I took a position as secretary to Dr. C. T. Wang, vice-speaker of the Senate in addition to my reportorial duties.

One oversight of Yuan was his failure to station a censor at the telegraph office. Hence, I was able to send all copy through without censorship. One day I startled my Shanghai colleagues by sending a news dispatch, based on a leak from the president's office, that Yuan had ordered two Kuomintang generals, one in Hankow and the other in Wuchang, to be shot. The dispatch was met by disbelief in the Shanghai headquarters and the generals were not warned. Both were shot as I had predicted. Fortunately for me, Yuan's agents were never informed of the author of this dispatch.

When the National Assembly met on April 8, 1913, the Kuomintang had a clear majority and was sharply against Yuan. On April 29, they voted down the so-called Quintuple Loan of $25,000,000 which Yuan depended upon to consolidate his rule. The Assembly meetings were riotous. In the heated debates, inkwells were thrown at the Speaker and fist fights flared up among the members. One day a plainly dressed man rose in the balcony and shouted, "Stop all your wrangling, or I will throw down this bomb." I stood only a few feet from him and witnessed the fright of the legislators below. When the police seized him they found that his "bomb" was an egg wrapped in a handkerchief. For a week, the Assembly was deadlocked by the continuous bickering.

While I was still covering the Assembly, the Kuomintang launched a nation-wide revolt. Provincial governors and generals who were favorable to the Kuomintang joined the rebellion. Yuan greeted this by ordering the dissolution of the Kuomintang. He accompanied his order with a purge of Kuomintang members in the Senate and the House of the Assembly.

In the midst of this struggle, I was appointed editor of the *Beijing Daily News*, an English daily. The editorship put me in the journalistic front line of the dangerous political events which then followed.

Yuan, having expelled the Kuomintang members, took a series of bold steps to establish his absolute rule over the disintegrating republic. When he failed to secure a majority Assembly vote, he stationed troops around the Assembly hall and coerced the members into electing him. He followed this by a series of arrests and executions of his opponents. On October 7, 1913, he had himself legally elected president on the third ballot.

In the middle of these counter-revolutionary steps, I tempted fate by publishing one hundred thousand copies of an English translation of an anti-Yuan pamphlet by Wu Shih-hua, an old member of the Kuomintang, calling upon Yuan to quit. Unable to mail the pamphlets, I tried vainly to find storage for them among friends in the foreign legations. No one dared to touch them. In the end, I dug a hole in the backyard of my home and buried the pamphlets and Dr. Sun's revolver in the ground.

Yuan, by stealthy steps, proceeded to destroy all the accomplishments of the 1911 republic revolution. After his purge of the Assembly, he left the vacancies unfilled, thus reducing the legislative branch to impotence. In place of the Assembly, Yuan appointed a political council to advise him in administrative matters. His cabinet, on November 20, 1913 issued a lengthy "Declaration of Policy," authored by Liang Chi-chao, Minister of Justice. This declaration was held back from the press temporarily to permit a few last-minute changes.

Through my friendship with the Director of the Government Printing Office, I was able to scoop out this document from the nation's press. I secured advance copies, quickly had them translated into English, and on the following morning published it in full in the *Beijing Daily News*, both English and Chinese editions. Since President Yuan had issued direct instructions to the Government Printing Office to withhold the release to the press, Yuan was furious. The Director of Printing Office was summarily removed from office. I was proud of my ability to get this exclusive for the *News*, while the *Beijing Gazette*, the rival English-language daily, edited by H. G. W. Woodhead, was left flat-footed.

Yuan, at first, intended to punish me severely. I quickly activated some of my friends in the government to dissuade him. The argument which weighed most heavily with Yuan was that I was well-known in American circles, and any penalization of me would have an unfavorable reaction overseas. Yuan was anxiously cultivating American goodwill, and he decided to overlook my coup. However, I was required to apologize to him in person.

Another factor that gave me some freedom as a newspaperman was that I was not actually a member of the Kuomintang, although I worked consistently in its interest. But until Yuan's wrath was cooled, I was in serious danger, with execution or assassination a real possibility. I did not reveal to my wife how close I had come to being killed until the crisis was past.

I was also able to render desperately needed assistance to my old friend, Dr. C. T. Wang, who had been deposed as vice-speaker of the Senate. During the repressions against the Kuomintang, many of the party leaders had been able to escape Yuan's vengeance by finding sanctuary in the International Settlement and French Concession territories in Shanghai, or the Japanese, French or Italian Concessions in Tientsin. One of those who did not succeed in getting out of Beijing in time was Dr. C. T. Wang. President Yuan secretly planned to execute the brilliant Kuomintang leader. I learned of the plan through a leak in the Presidential Office, and determined to do what I could to save him.

I had not studied American public relations techniques in vain. I consulted R. P. Tenney, counselor of the American Legation in Beijing, who was a good friend of Dr. Wang. He had been a teacher in the Peiyang University when Dr. Wang had been a student. I suggested to Tenney that we freeze Yuan's hand in the matter by cabling a report to the U.S. State Department that Yuan was plan to appoint Dr. Wang as Chinese ambassador to the United States, with a request for approval. Meanwhile, I leaked the story to Reuter's representative in Beijing, who cabled it to London, where it was published conspicuously. United States newspapers picked it up from London and reproduced it.

Dr. Tenney did his part and the State Department replied with an extremely favorable acceptance of Dr. Wang. Through YMCA connections, public statements by prominent American YMCA officials were also hailing the projected appointment of Dr. Wang. I saw to it that the *Shun Tine Shin Pao* published these American tributes to Dr. Wang. The effect was immediate. Realizing the black eye which Wang's execution or assassination would give him in America, he immediately revoked his orders and withdrew the secret police who had been shadowing Dr. Wang. This was one time when I was able to demonstrate what the press can do in an emergency.

It seemed that I was always working for poor newspapers. The *Beijing Daily News* was notoriously poor with little support from advertisers. I had only three editorial helpers. I found myself, in addition to my editorial duties, setting type, running the press and attending personally to all the endless tasks of a small print shop. My training in the Park College printing plant came in handy.

As I have mentioned, we had one English-language competitor, the *Beijing Gazette*. Its founder and editor was H. G. W. Woodhead. He did not stay long, but accepted an offer to go to Tientsin to edit the *Times*. He sold the *Beijing Gazette* to Eugene Chen, a brilliant youth of mixed blood, who was a native of Trinidad. It was I who initiated Chen into newspaper work.

It was frequently possible to secure financial backing from ambitious politicians who desired a newspaper mouthpiece. Chen, who had no money of his own, secured an angel in the person of Chow Tzu-chi, then acting governor of the Bank of China, and the Minister of Communications in Yuan's cabinet. Thanks to this backer, Chen had plenty of money to hire able editorial talent, whereas I had none.

The star on Chen's staff was Ku Hung-ming, a British-educated writer who was the master of a strong prose style. Chen paid Ku a salary of 300 Chinese a month – a fabulous salary at that time. Ku's exceptional articles soon boosted the circulation of the *Beijing Gazette* to a high figure.

But Chen and Ku had a falling out. Ku came over to *Beijing News* and offered to write for me without pay. He attached one condition: that for a period of three months, I must publish whatever he wrote, without editorial corrections. I rashly accepted the offer, thus incurring the enmity of Chen, who threatened to cut off Ku's queue upon sight. Ku, in his turn, carried a dagger with him and threatened to kill anyone who attacked him.

At first, all went well. My circulation languishing at around 800 a day rose to 1,000. My publisher shared my enthusiasm over this accession of new readers. Then Ku and I clashed.

One day Ku brought in a series of articles in support of concubinage. As a Christian, I had definite ideas on the subject. Moreover, I knew the sentiments of my readers, most of them would be outraged by such views. My readers included missionaries, members of the diplomatic corps, teachers with Westernized viewpoints, etc. I refused to run Ku's articles. He then subjected me to a vicious campaign of abuse and annoyance.

The most harmless of the names which he called me was "Babu," the Hindu epithet for "rascal." He made a practice of appearing every evening during the busiest hours and planting himself in the one small room where I worked with my staff. On these occasions he subjected me to a systematic campaign of personal insults and accusing me for a breach of contract. After a few days of this mental torture, I found myself unable to concentrate on my work. My assistants were similarly miserable.

At last, I decided to end the episode by observing my promise to Ku and running the articles. The consequences were disastrous. I was deluged with a flood of protesting letters from missionaries and other Westernized readers. Subscription cancellations came in so fast that our circulation soon dropped from 1,000 to 400. My readers held me personally accountable, some missionaries writing to express their regret that such an unworthy person as I had ever been admitted to the mission schools. It was a painful lesson to me in the danger of ill-considered promises. This ended my cooperation with Ku.

Important historical events were occurring. The most spectacular of these were the Twenty One Demands which Japan served upon China, taking advantage of the World War which was now raging in Europe. These demands, if granted, would have reduced China to the status of a Japanese colony. The demands were served upon President Yuan by the Japanese Foreign Minister on January 18, 1915 in great secrecy. The Japanese were anxious to keep the news out of the press until they could present as a *fait accompli.*

Mr. Frederick Moore was then Beijing correspondent for the Associated Press. He learned from me of the Japanese action and wired the story to New York. Mr. Melvin Stone, the chairman of the Associated Press, doubted the truth of the story and wired for confirmation to the Japanese Minister in Washington. The Minister promptly denied it, and Stone cabled Moore in Beijing to recheck the story. Moore again confirmed the facts. Stone was still unconvinced and again interrogated the Japanese Minister. Once again, he cabled to Moore to recheck. Moore thereupon tendered his resignation.

On April 26, 1915 the Japanese modified their original demands, removing three intolerable provisions, one of which would have authorized the appointment of Japanese police advisers at important Chinese cities. Yuan's government made some counter-demands, which were followed on May 7 by a Japanese ultimatum. The Chinese government, unable to get the support of the western powers as they were preoccupied with the war in Europe, finally capitulated. It was a shameful experience for China, and it plunged us all into a mood of national humiliation.

Against the background of these events, a dangerous agitation for the restoration of the monarchy began to develop. An organization known as the Society of Peace began to circulate the ideas of Dr. Frank J. Goodnow, former professor of political science at Johns Hopkins University and now constitutional adviser to President Yuan. The Society of Peace represented Dr. Goodnow as an advocate of a monarchical system.

Newspaper friends in America, disturbed by the developments, requested me to interview Yuan Shih-kai and ascertain his actual intentions. The interview was arranged through the good offices of Admiral Tsai Ting-kai, who handled press interviews for his chief.

Yuan Shih-kai met me and blandly disclaimed monarchical ambitions:

"I can be China's George Washington," he told me. "Why should I wish to be a Napoleon? I may possess all the qualifications to be China's emperor, but where is my crown prince? My first son is lame and wouldn't make a good crown prince."

I was impressed by the tact and aptness with which the President Yuan parried my questions. Later I learned that it was Admiral Tsai who had coached him in his replies. The admiral had been made a prisoner by the Japanese in the Chinese-Japanese War of 1894 and had been released through Yuan's efforts. The link between them was strong.

Of course, Yuan Shih-kai was putting on an act in front of me, in order to lull the world press concerning his intentions. Shortly afterwards, he ended the Republic and with the sanction of his Council of State had himself proclaimed as Emperor of China under the name of Hung Hsien. His reign was brief and unhappy. In the midst of widespread revolt and insubordination, he relinquished the throne, a broken man. He died on June 6, 1916.

I continued as editor of the *Beijing News*, pursuing stories with the sanction of my publisher, Chu Chih, a man with an outspoken anti-Japanese attitude. I wrote hard-hitting editorials, exposing Japan's plans to subjugate China. Then I was suddenly presented with an impossible situation. Chu Chih sold the *Beijing News* to Wang Yu-ling, who was merely the front man for General Hsu Yu-tseng. Hsu was the right-hand man of Marshal Tuan Chi-jui, who had been prime minister under Yuan Shih-kai, and had continued in that capacity under Yuan's successor, Li Yuan-hung.

The policy of the government was to placate Japan. With my anti-Japanese policy, I found myself out of step. My new owner tried patiently to persuade me to alter my editorial policy but remain with the *Beijing News*. I could not commit this self-stultification and I told Hsu to secure a new editor. So I found myself again unemployed.

I soon found a new post. Hsiung Hai-ling, the former premier, was now director general of the National Oil Administration. Through the intervention of my good friend, Wei Yih, I was appointed secretary of the Administration. At the same the, I retained my contacts with journalism by serving as assistant editor of the *Millard Review*, published by Thomas Millard, a graduate of the University of Missouri, my alma mater. This weekly had a curious later history. Millard sold it to J. B. Powell, one of my old schoolmates at the Missouri School of Journalism, who changed its name to the *China Weekly Review*. After a long and distinguished career under J. B. Powell's editorship, it then came into the hands of Powell's son, John W. Powell, who fell under the influence of the communists after

World War II. The younger Powell remained in China after the communist triumph in 1949, published the *China Weekly Review* as a Chinese Communist propaganda vehicle.

My Oil Administration job was interesting. In February 1914, an arrangement had been made between the Government of China and the Standard Oil Company of New Jersey to exploit the oil resources in the provinces of Shansi and Shensi. Each side appropriated $1 million (U.S.) to finance exploration, with the understanding that if petroleum were found in commercial quantities, a Chinese-American joint corporation would be formed. Fifteen wells had been sunk and things looked bright for Shensi oil production.

Vice President Bemis of the Standard Oil Company was sent from New York to negotiate an agreement. A British lawyer, practicing in Tientsen, named Kent was engaged by the Chinese government to represent it. Kent proved an unfortunate choice. He insisted that so many clauses outside the scope of the original agreement be included that Bemis gave up the negotiations in disgust. In retrospect, it is now clear that this was a misfortune for China. Had the deal been completed, the Standard Oil Company was prepared to build a pipeline from Yenan, in Shensi, to Hankow, a distance of over 1,000 miles. Had this pipeline been built, the later Yenan Communist episode would have been altered.

My Oil Administration service led to my brief return to the United States. V. K. Wellington Koo was then in the United States. One of his missions was to dissuade the United States from loaning Japan one hundred million dollars for the development of Manchuria. He requested my superior, Hsiung Hai-ling, to release me to come to Washington to handle the publicity for China in its fight against this loan. Here I found myself up against the best brains of Japan. Tokyo had sent Baron Shibusawa, known as the Rockefeller of Japan, to seek the loan.

I remained in Washington for ten months also acting as Washington correspondent for the *Beijing News*. I kept in close contact with the fraternity of the Washington Press Club. They were not as numerous as they are today. The Washington Press Club existed at that time, and its influence was much less than that of today.

I wrote numerous articles in the American press, warning against Japanese expansionist plans. The most successful of these was an article in the *Review of Reviews* aptly titled, "Japanese Brains and American Money for the Exploitation of Manchuria."

I did not enjoy my mission, and I was glad to return to China at its conclusion. I was amply rewarded by the failure of Japan to get the money.

Chapter Four.
The Warlord Era

I continued to work with Hsiung Hai-ling, first as secretary of the National Oil Administration, and later on the staff of the Chihli River Commission. But I never permitted myself to become completely detached from journalism. I kept on serving for almost ten years as assistant editor of the *China Weekly Review.* In my official life during the period, which followed Yuan Shih-kai, I became closely acquainted with most of the political leaders in North China. I had the opportunity to observe the careers of now forgotten successive Presidents: Yuan Shih-ki, Li Yuan-hung, Feng Kuo-chang, Hsu Shih-chang and Tsao Kun. I also knew well the colorful warlord, Wu Pei-fu.

My first close contact with Wu was in 1922 when he waged civil war against Marshal Chang Tso-ling, who controlled Manchuria. It was after Wu had defeated Chang's forces at Changhsingti, and was headed for Tientsin along the Beijing-Tientsin Railway, that I joined his train at Lungfeng in order to report his campaign. Here I renewed acquaintance with Upton Close, pseudonym for Josef W. Hall, correspondent for the *Chicago Tribune.* Close spoke very good Chinese.

Wu was fond of Chinese wine, and while drinking, often discoursed freely on events and personalities. In interviewing him, Close congratulated him upon his striking military successes. Wu disclaimed the compliment. "I am not happy over victories over other Chinese," he observed. "There is no glory in this. What would make me happy would be at the head of my army as it entered Tokyo, Japan." I did not expect that Close would file this, but he did so. The next morning the publication of Wu's anti-Japanese statement in Chicago was reported back to us in China. Two days later the

Japanese Legation in Beijing protested against Wu's "insulting" statement and demanded an explanation.

Wu was on the spot and he turned to me for assistance. I called on Mr. Obata, Japanese Charge d'Affaires in Beijing, who was a friend of mine, and assured him that Wu had made no anti-Japanese statement; it was just a small talk after drinking. Mr. Obata was satisfied with my explanation and dropped the issue.

I had an opportunity to observe Wu Pei-fu's military sagacity in a real situation. The train, after leaving Lungfeng, had rolled to a station not far outside Tientsin when we saw several thousand Manchurian cavalrymen approaching. Wu showed no alarm but ordered his artillerymen to fire a noisy salvo at them. The cavalrymen turned tail and fled. When we asked him why such a large body of troops was so easily panicked, he explained that this was always the mentality of troops in retreat after a defeat. They have no heart for a renewal of fighting and they will instinctively avoid a clash. Wu's instincts in waging warfare were almost flawless.

At this time, the communists made one of their early appearances in Chinese history. Marshal Wu was approached by a communist agent named Joseph who offered important Russian aid in the form of munitions, arms and military advisers under certain conditions. Wu unhesitatingly rejected this tender of help, declaring that he had no faith in the promises of communists. Joseph tried to reassure him that the communists had no designs on China because it was an agricultural state, unsuited for industrial collectivization. Wu was unmoved and Joseph departed in disappointment. Wu told me the full details of this episode.

Wu's ultimate defeat by Chang Tso-lin was the result of his betrayal by Marshal Feng Yu-hsiang, who was a secret Communist sympathizer and who died in Russia in 1947. Feng, a faithless ally to all who trusted him, was Wu's ostensible colleague. Both returned to Beijing to report to President Tsao Kun. Wu, distrusting Feng, would not leave the capital as long as Feng remained. Feng tricked him by retiring to Suiyuan, and Wu proceeded to the Shanhaiguan front along the coast. But as soon as he learned that Wu had left Beijing, he came back with his troops and made a prisoner of President Tsao, also seizing Henry Pu-yi, the last of the Manchu emperors. He looted the capital sending away a great amount of priceless treasures.

As I am not writing a history of China, my allusions to historical events must necessarily be sketchy. But since my future career was to be so strongly influenced by the rise of communism in China, I must digress briefly to describe my early contacts with communism. In the early Twenties, on

Dr. Sun Yat-sen's ill-advised agreement with the communists, Russian advisers were occupying posts of authority in Kuomintang-dominated South China. The communists had not been so successful in Northern China where Chang Tso-lin and Wu Pei-fu were disputing for power.

In February 1925, Michael Borodin, the No. 1 Russian adviser in Dr. Sun's camp, came to Beijing on a mission of great secrecy. I was the only newspaperman who learned of his presence. Leo Karakhan was Soviet Ambassador to the Beijing government. I presented myself at the Russian Embassy and sent in my card to see Mr. Borodin. After a wait of about twenty minutes, a secretary came out to ask me whom I wished to see. When I told him Borodin, he denied that such an individual was there.

On the way out, I spoke to the gatekeeper. It was the Chinese Lunar New Year and I tipped the gatekeeper generously. When I asked him where Mr. Borodin was staying, he pointed to a building on the Embassy grounds.

There was no gatekeeper at this smaller building, so I entered and knocked at several successive doors. Finally a heavy foreign woman came to one of the doors and, in reply to my question, said she was Mrs. Borodin. Her husband was having a conference in the adjacent chancellery building, she said, but would return shortly. She invited me to sit down, and talked to me over a cup of red Russian tea. Her English was without accent: I gathered from her remarks that she had been a high school teacher in Chicago where Borodin had managed a private school before returning to Russia. I waited two hours, but the adviser did not return. I was then forced to depart to keep another engagement.

I returned to the house at nine thirty, but found no one at home. I resigned myself to a long wait, and since there was no chair, I perched myself on the stairway. Finally, at twelve, the Borodins appeared. They had been attending a motion picture showing at the Beijing Pavilion, they explained. Borodin readily granted me an interview.

Our talk lasted until two o'clock. Borodin did not look like a Bolshevik: he resembled a cultured professor in a college. His voice was deep and mellow, and he expressed himself carefully, often pausing for the right word. I was deeply impressed by his show of learning and acquaintance with world affairs. Throughout the interview Mrs. Borodin sat with us, pouring tea, and giving perceptible signals to her husband to avoid subjects which might be embarrassing.

We talked mostly about the prospects of China's unification. At this time, the Kuomintang government in the South was assembling the Northern Expedition to subjugate the warlord-ruled North. I expressed the opinion that Kuomintang chances were slight since the Northerners combined had ten times the military forces.

Borodin was not impressed with this view. He declared that they had collected accurate information on the North and that the rivalries between the Northern leaders were so intense that the Kuomintang needed only to divide and rule. "To bring about national unification by military means will not be hard," he told me. "The difficulty will be in setting up an efficient administration." It was obvious to me that the communists were not yet ready to strike out for themselves in China and were doing all their work behind the scenes of the national unification issue.

Afterwards, I learned of the circumstances of Borodin's visit to Beijing. Actually, he was facing a serious dilemma in the South and was on the point of revising his China strategy. The leader who had thwarted his ambitious plans was none other than my old pupil at Lungching, General Chiang Kai-shek. The communists had been admitted into the Kuomintang in 1923 under pledge that they would refrain from subversive activities. The Russian government had sent Borodin to Dr. Sun as a political adviser, and the clever Russian had succeeded in winning the confidence of the Kuomintang leaders by his apparent devotion to Dr. Sun's Three People's Principles, a democratic form of government. After the death of Dr. Sun, Borodin and the Russians whom he brought with him to Guongzhou played a brilliant Machiavellian game in their wooing of the triumvirate of Sun's disciples who succeeded to the Kuomintang rule. The one of the three who was under no illusions concerning Communist designs was Chiang Kai-shek, who had been designated as Commander-in-Chief of the Northern Expedition.

Two attempts had been made to assassinate Chiang with Russian connivance. Chiang had countered by sending troops into Guongzhou and placing the city under virtual martial law. This unexpected action had forestalled a Communist plot to seize the direction of the Kuomintang. Borodin's headquarters in Guongzhou was seized and the Russian advisers were placed under detention. Borodin chose this moment to go to Beijing for further instructions, and thence to Moscow.

Chiang assumed office as the commander of the Northern Expedition for the national unification on July 9, 1926. He issued an historic manifesto citing the fifteen years of civil war the 1911 revolution. He pledged the unification of China through both the overthrow of the warlords who had divided the country, and by stopping the foreign imperialists who supported and encouraged them. That document electrified China.

Meanwhile, Borodin had returned to China from Moscow with apparent instructions to cooperate with the Northern Expedition. Chiang's early advance was crowned with success. The Kuomintang troops captured the cities of Hankow and Wuchang and began a drive down the Yangtse River toward the rich coastal provinces. In the wake of his victorious armies came the Communist plotters. One of those cooperating with Borodin was Eugene Chen, my old newspaper rival in Beijing. Chen had wangled the post of Minister of the Northern Expeditionary Force. After the occupation of Hankow, Chen ordered the seizure of the British Concession in Hankow. Mr. Teichman, the British Charge d'Affaires at Beijing, who was a friend of mine, tipped me off that he had received an order from London to go to Hankow by way of Pukow, where he would board a British gunboat. Foreseeing a British attempt to repossess the Concession by force, I determined to go to Hankow to report this event.

On my arrival, I promptly hunted up Michael Borodin who was ensconced in one of the German owned buildings. He saw me readily and talked freely. He ventured the opinion that the Northern Expedition was premature and would fail – an opinion which later proved baseless. On another question he showed a keen perception of realities. When I told him that I had come to Hankow in anticipation of a British attempt to retake the Concession, he dismissed the possibility as fantastic. He cited the fact that the Yangtse River was low at this season and large vessels capable of transporting adequate attacking forces could not make the up-river trip. He said the British were a cautious people who would not act if there were any risk of defeat. He predicted that after the matter had been debated in the House of Commons, the initial heat would have died down and the Concession seizure would be accepted as a *fait accompli*. There would only be formal protests. Subsequent events confirmed Borodin's accurate appraisal of the situation.

Two months later, I saw Borodin again in Hankow. He told me that he had come to have a low opinion of Chinese officials. He cited Eugene Chen as an example. He related that Chen, emboldened by his successful seizure of the British Concession in Hankow, decided to seize the Japanese Concession in like manner. Borodin heard of the scheme one hour before Chen was preparing to move in on the Japanese. He told me that he rushed to Chen's residence in his pajamas and pointed out to him that it would be folly to give the Japanese militarists this pretext for seizing, not only Hankow, but other key points on the Yangtse which would doom the Northern Expedition. Japan is not like Great Britain, he told Chen. At the last minute, Chen heeded Borodin's advice and called off the attack on the Japanese Concession.

It was during this trip that I went to Changsha to interview Generalissimo Chiang Kai-shek. I went to see him with an introduction from Wu Shih-hua, the same Kuomintang elder whose pamphlet attack on Yuan Shih-kai I had translated ten or more years before, only to be buried in my backyard. Chiang did not recognize me as his teacher from Lungching days: to him I was only another of the swarm of newspapermen who were then following the brilliant young leader in large numbers.

My education in the communist mentality was widened at that time. Shortly after I met Chiang in Changsha, I took a trip into the inland section of Hupeh Province. At Lienling, a town which was then under the control of communist troops, who were cooperating with the Northern Expedition, I talked to a boy of fifteen who had just killed his mother with a kitchen knife. The boy was a recent convert to communism. When I asked him why he had killed her, he replied that she was old and had feudalistic ideas in her head. She should die in order to save food for others. When I asked him his mother's age, he replied, "Fifty."

This was in 1926 and was my first contact with the ghastly effects of Communist teachings on the adolescent mind. Later, I was to witness similar cases of communist child murderers, or parent denouncers. It is a horrifying thought that communism can deaden the moral sensibilities of its addicts to such an extent. The young man at Lienling had no regret or sense of guilt over his deed. He talked to me with icy calmness.

After Chiang's initial successes in his march to the North, Borodin tried to hasten communist control over the Kuomintang. After Chiang curbed the communists in Guongdong, the communists transferred their main operating base to Hankow. The communists inaugurated a reign of terror. Even greater excesses were committed in Hunan, in areas under communist domination. Wealthy men were arrested and stripped of their possessions in order to free themselves from framed charges of espionage and treachery to the revolution. Arrests were a daily occurrence and often led to summary execution, without benefit of a real trial. The fanatic communists disrupted the economic life of the city of Hankow by closing of 27 native banks.

Meanwhile, Chiang Kai-shek was proceeding successfully with the Northern Expedition, despite the communist's knife at his back and the intrigues of foreign powers to slow his advance. In Shantung, Japanese opposition was so determined that he found it necessary to bypass Tsinan, the capital of Shantung, in order to avoid an open clash. Towards the end of 1926, he issued a statement to a foreign correspondent frankly thwarted the interfering foreign powers. He said:

"The imperialists, seeing the opportunity to control our financial arteries, are making desperate efforts to enrich themselves and to lengthen the duration of their hold. ...These foreign elements encouraged Yuan Shih-kai to proclaim himself Emperor, abetted Chang Hsuan in the attempted restoration of the Manchus, supported Feng Kuo-chang and Hsu Shih-chang in their disregard of the Constitution, and assisted Tsao Kun in his theft of the Presidency."

Coincident with Chiang's statement, General Sun Chuan-fang, Governor of Kiangsu, with headquarters at Nanking, illustrated Chiang's warning. He commenced negotiations with a group of British financiers, with the tacit support of London for a loan, which would enable him to halt the advance of the Northern Expedition. I was familiar with the intrigue because Sun asked my friend, Dr. V. K. Ting, High Commissioner in Shanghai, to act for him in the negotiations. Dr. Ting discussed the pros and cons of the matter with me.

In the end, foreign assistance was not sufficient to save the warlords. Having crushed Wu Pei-fu in a series of brilliant engagements, Chiang swung north toward Beijing with only the army of Sun Chuan-fang and the Manchurian army of Chang Tso-lin to bar him. He overcame Sun Chuan-fang, and was preparing to fight Chang Tso-lin's powerful columns. Fate played into his hands by the murder of Chang Tso-lin in a railway train bombing near Mukden in Manchuria. On July 5, 1928 Beijing fell to the Northern Expedition. China was at last unified, although there were still many bridges to cross before warlords had been stamped out in the vast country.

In the meantime I had launched my own Chinese newspaper, *Yung Pao*, which I published at Tientsin. I undertook this venture in 1925, with the savings of a few thousand Chinese dollars. I continued to work for Mr. Hsiung's organization by day and tended to the *Yung Pao* by night. I was happy to have this opportunity to try out my own ideas of newspaper publishing, even though my sleep was soon reduced to four hours per night. I quadrupled in brass, acting as publisher, editor, advertising manager and reporter. Fortunately, I was able to secure some competent Chinese help in getting out the paper.

I introduced one innovation that was to follow American patterns of make-up. I discarded the prevailing Chinese custom of printing advertisements on the first page. I employed American-type spread headlines, with banner heads for extraordinary news. All the popular practices which I had learned in the Missouri School of Journalism and at the Pulitzer School were introduced when practicable.

I found that these American styles of make-up and emphasis were real circulation builders. For instance, when I reported the news of Marshal Chang Tso-ling's murder by a Japanese placed bomb when he was passing over a railway bridge near Mukden, I used banner headlines to emphasize the story. I frankly charged the Japanese with murder, citing the fact that it occurred on a section of the railroad which was under Japanese control. The Japanese in Tientsin were so infuriated that they barred this particular issue from the Japanese Concession. I was becoming known increasingly as an anti-Japanese writer.

While these epochal events were occurring, I was engaged in one of the most risky business adventures of my life. Anxious to produce a better newspaper in Tientsin, I approached Sze Liang-tsai, publisher of the *Shun Pao* of Shanghai, in the hope of obtaining a better printing press. The unification of China enabled me to emerge from the continuous risk of reprisals from the Northern warlords who controlled Tientsin. After years of laborious effort, I was beginning to make a small profit from the *Yung Pao*. But I needed machinery and equipment to expand. I asked Mr. Sze to transfer to me a secondhand rotary press from his Shanghai plant. In return, I would give him a share in the ownership of my newspaper. Mr. Sze agreed to my offer, and we became partners.

I was now drawn into the net of Mr. Sze's involved affairs. He was trying to effect a consolidation of his *Shun Pao* with a circulation 150,000 and *Xin Wen Pao*, another Shanghai daily, with a circulation of 200,000. The hitch was that the majority of shares in the *Xin Wen Pao* were owned by Dr. C. J. Ferguson. Fearing that the staff members of the paper would frustrate the sale, if negotiations took place in Shanghai, Mr. Sze had me to negotiate with Dr. Ferguson in Beijing. I was able to help materially as Dr. Ferguson was a good friend of mine and had been a friend of my father. In the end, Mr. Sze was able to obtain the Ferguson shares at a cost of $400,000 (U.S.).

Unhappily, influential elements in the Kuomintang united to prevent Mr. Sze from exercising his ownership of the *Xin Wen Pao*. False rumors were circulated that I had actually bought the paper for Liang Shih-yi. It was alleged that I had bought the publication through the intermediacy of Yeh Kung-cho. Both of these men were charged with trying to overthrow the Kuomintang. They lived in Hong Kong and were inaccessible for questioning. By preserving complete silence they allowed ugly rumors about me to spread, particularly in the small tabloids known as yellow journals.

We also encountered malevolent attitudes from the staff members. The *Xin Wen Pao* was a real moneymaker, and as a result of Dr. Ferguson's easygoing policies, the staff members had been skimming most of the cream. Mr. Sze asked me to take over the paper in his behalf, and for a week I sat in the office of managing director. The staff did everything in their power to make me uncomfortable. Particularly, the Wang brothers, who had been with the paper for many years, subjected me to mental torture. The Wangs hoped to buy the paper, but they were unwilling to pay Dr. Ferguson a fair price. They had contrived a situation where Dr. Ferguson would be so uncomfortable that he would sell his stock at their price. Mr. Sze's entrance into the situation had stymied this plan.

Finally, the situation became so impossible that I was forced to withdraw from the general manager's office and leave the paper in the hands of the Wangs. A political lawyer, who was a schoolmate of my wife, tried to trick me into signing a statement that I had actually purchased *Xin Wen Pao* for the reactionaries, Liang and Yeh. He had assembled a dossier of my writings in the *Yung Pao* over the years which, taken out of context, implied that I had been against the Citizen's Party. The threat was made that, if these charges were true, Dr. Ferguson's shares would be confiscated.

I was living at the Tai Tung Hotel on Nanking Road in Shanghai. One night four strangers knocked at the door. When I admitted them, they attempted to force me, at gunpoint, to sign a statement admitting that I had bought the Ferguson shares for Liang and Yeh. I protested that it was not true. At the end of two hours of wrangling, I was in such a nervous state that I told them to give me paper to write a letter to my wife and they could then shoot me. They were unwilling to do this but I remained adamant. Finally they told me that they would return the following night and get my answer. If I breathed a word about their visit, they told me, I would be killed. I assured them that nothing would change my mind, but I promised not to tell of their visit. I realized that I had won the first and most dangerous round of this game of blackmail.

That night I could not sleep and the next day I came down with a high fever. I remained in the hotel for two weeks in this condition and then returned to my home in Tientsin. I was sick for several months, and finally convalesced at the seashore at Peitaiho.

In the end we had our way. Mr. Sze held onto the Ferguson shares and continued to publish the *Xin Wen Pao*. To compensate me for my pains, he gave the rotary press to me for free and tore up his articles of partnership. This ended my association with Mr. Sze.

It was an extremely unhappy experience but it taught me the lesson to face danger bravely, even at the risk of death. My faith in God had sustained me in this crisis. It would continue to sustain me in the greater dangers, which lay ahead of me.

Chapter Five.
Touring the World for Navy

An important change in my career took place in the summer of 1929. I was invited to become the managing director and editor of the *China Press*, an English daily in Shanghai.

The *China Press* was founded in 1912 by Dr. Wu Ting-feng, former Chinese Minister to the United States, and by Thomas Millard, an American Far Eastern journalist and author. It had made an important place in China journalism. It shared the English news in Shanghai with another daily, the *North China Daily News*, which was owned by British, and is a small replica of the famous *London Times*. It reflected British Far East viewpoints. The *China Press*, on the other hand, reflected the American standards of journalism.

Once again, my friend, Sze Liang-tsai, publisher of the *Shun Pao*, was behind this new opportunity. Mr. Sze, together with Chang Tso-pang, had bought the *China Press* from a Mr. Ezra, a rich Shanghai merchant of Jewish ancestry. Ezra found he did not have time to manage it. Although there was a scramble to buy it on the part of several foreign interests, notably the Japanese, Ezra preferred to have the newspaper pass into Chinese hands.

I was reluctant to leave Tientsin, where my own paper was doing well, but the new owners insisted so urgently, that I agreed to make the change. I entrusted the management of the *Yung Pao* to a friend, Chiang Kwang-tang, and moved to Shanghai, although my family remained in Tientsin for some time longer.

A few months after I assumed this post Shanghai, my wife arrived unexpectedly bearing an invitation for me to undertake an important government mission. The invitation had come from Admiral H. K. Tu of the Chinese Navy, a warm family friend. The Admiral had been selected by Chiang Kai-shek to surveying the navies of the principal nations in the world in preparation of an extensive program to modernize the Chinese Navy. Admiral Tu spoke limited English and he was anxious to have me accompany him to act as eyes, ears, interpreter, planner and writer, all combined. He offered me the No. 2 man in this naval mission, despite the fact that I had no naval background. It was an extremely attractive offer, and it appealed strongly to my imagination.

Admiral Tu was an important figure, having been the prime minister of China during the presidency of Tsao Kun. His friends included many in my own circle. All insisted that I should accept. Since the duration of the tour was six months, I found that it was possible for me to go. I had put the affairs of the *China Press* in good order, and by November, when we departed, my assistants were able to take over the affairs of the paper during my absence. The mission left Shanghai for Nagasaki, where we were to begin our work by studying the Japanese Navy.

We spent a month and a half in Japan, and visited their naval stations. We were welcomed on inspection tours of all types of naval vessels – battleships, cruisers, destroyers, submarines, minesweepers, etc. I was particularly struck on my visit to the battleships, to see a shrine located in the center of the ship, to which all officers and seamen came twice daily to worship. This combination of modernity and medieval superstition was typical of Japan in that period. I was startled by the incongruity of it.

Towards the end of our stay in Japan, the Emperor of Japan gave Admiral Tu and me an audience. The Admiral had spent almost a fortnight memorizing a five minute talk in English which he was to deliver to the Emperor, since English was the accepted language which foreigners were expected to address the monarch. A Japanese admiral was to translate the speech into Japanese for the Emperor who was to reply in Japanese. The Emperor's words would then be translated back to us in English.

After the first few sentences, Admiral Tu forgot the rest of his address. It was a highly embarrassing moment for both of us. I was standing at the entrance to the huge hall, too far away to prompt him. But the Admiral proved to be resourceful. He said: "Your majesty, I want to thank you for receiving us today." The Emperor gave his reply, which was translated into English.

It was now my turn to walk slowly up to the Emperor and shake hands. I then received a decoration, as Admiral Tu had received one before me. In leaving the Emperor's presence, we had to back out over the polished floor. I had difficulty avoiding slipping, and I had another embarrassing moment when I reached the threshold, unaware that I had to turn right to leave the hall. I had no intimation then that many years later, in 1952, I would be presented to the same Emperor again, as Ambassador from the Republic of China. Between these two presentations was to stretch the deep precipice of the long Chinese-Japanese War.

The most distinguished notable whom we met was Admiral Togo, who had been the victorious naval commander in the Russo-Japanese War of 1904. I recall that during our visit, he spoke only a few words, but these were highly pertinent. "We welcome your study of our navy," he told us. "Pay attention to the spirit of our navy: other factors are of secondary importance."

I recall Admiral Togo's great words at the crisis of the naval encounter with Russia:

"In this battle, whether we are victorious or are defeated, we will determine the glory or the disgrace of our Emperor. You should all exert your utmost and give your all."

The Japanese defeated the proud Russian fleet and won the war.

We next traveled to the United States where our stay was for one month. In New York, Admiral Tu had an embarrassing moment when the whimsical Mayor James J. Walker asked him innocently whether he had traveled to New York on a Chinese war vessel. The Admiral was forced to reply "No." "We have not seen your warship in the Hudson for some time." Mayor Walker rejoined. "I hope that in the not distant future we will have the opportunity to welcome your warship as a guest."

We visited Hollywood and enjoyed a dinner given in our honor by Douglas Fairbanks, Sr. and Mary Pickford at their famed home, Pickfair. The famous couple had crossed the Pacific with us on the same Japanese ship. On shipboard I had an amusing experience. The Japanese barber asked me if I could secure for him Admiral Tu's and my autographs. I jokingly suggested that he obtain the Fairbanks and Pickford autographs instead. His reply revealed the contrast in values between Orientals and Occidentals. "No," he said, "they belong to the class of theatrical entertainers and we do not regard them highly, whereas you and Admiral Tu are representatives of the country of China."

Our next stop was England, always a paramount naval power. China was deeply indebted to the British for its naval know-how; an Englishman had been one of the early advisers to the Chinese Navy and a considerable number of our high naval officers were graduates of the British Naval Academy. His Majesty King George V, himself a navy-trained man, received us. The King, Admiral Tu and I stood in a semi-circle for at least three quarters of an hour discussing our problems. George V revealed that he had an unusual interest in China and its current happenings. With impressive modesty he asked Admiral Tu to explain to him the actual situation in China. Admiral Tu, through my translation, talked to him at length about China's unification and its ambition, now that the era of confusion had passed, to build up a modern navy. His Majesty assured us that Great Britain will give any possible assistance if needed. Later, Prime Minister J. Ramsey MacDonald also gave us a similar assurance.

From Great Britain we proceeded to France, where we were given every courtesy. The next stopover on our tour was Germany, then a republic. We were received by the famous President von Hindenberg. The President was very old and showed his infirmity in his heavy walk. His son acted as his personal aide. I recall that von Hindenberg asked Admiral Tu, "Are you a naval man?" When the Admiral, who was dressed in a morning coat, replied in the affirmative, he asked him embarrassingly, "Why then do you wear civilian clothes?" "I have come to call on a civilian President," answered the Admiral.

One of the most memorable visits on our tour was our reception by Prime Minister Benito Mussolini in Rome. After Admiral Tu and I had made our official call, an official of the Foreign Office visited me at the hotel and asked if I would like to have a second interview with their Duce, this time in my capacity as a newspaperman. Admiral Tu gave me his permission to accept, and the following day I presented myself at the Palazzo Venezia at the appointed hour. I was kept waiting for half an hour and when I was at last admitted I remarked that I had thought our appointment was for the stated hour.

"I have just been seeing a Balkan State prime minister and he stayed far beyond his time," said Mussolini. "Since the situation in the Balkan Peninsula is serious, I could not cut him short." Then, turning to me confidentially, he asked;

"You have just been in the United States. Tell me, what do the American people say about me?"

I answered bluntly:

"Some Americans think highly of you, but I must state that the majority of Americans speculate that one day you may make yourself a Caesar."

He replied lightly,

"Have you seen my yacht, and the yacht of the king of Italy?" I answered "No." "If you had," said Mussolini, "you would have seen that mine is only one half the size of the king's. That would certainly not be the case were I a Caesar."

I asked him if he could accept the invitation of the Chinese Government to visit China.

"The situation in my country is unstable," he answered. "I could not possibly visit a foreign country for at least another two or three years."

Mussolini, always a great showman, put on the performance for foreign visitors. His office was a huge one, and I had a long walk to reach him at its far end. He stood up behind his desk, making the motions of walking toward me, although actually he stood still. When I reached him and shook hands, he talked in a dramatic manner, as if he were a great historic figure. I felt that this interview was a unique experience.

Italy was our last stopover, and I sailed from there by way of the Suez Canal for Shanghai. It took me nearly a month to complete the trip. Admiral Tu and his technical staff had not completed their studies and were to return to France. I was invited to stay with the party until the end, but I had already been away from my responsibilities in China too long. I perhaps missed serious injuries by my departure, in France, the Admiral's car was rammed by a French truck and he suffered broken ribs. Others with him also suffered similarly. I spent the time immediately after my departure to prepare the 200,000-word report which Admiral Tu was to submit on his return. This terminated my connection with naval matters, but the experience gave me a rich background of knowledge as a newspaperman.

An indirect result of the tour was to bring me into closer relationship with Generalissimo Chiang Kai-shek. Shortly before our departure, he had asked Admiral Tu to arrange for me to meet him. The Generalissimo was under the impression that I was a naval man, since I was the second man in the mission. He asked me what I had done previously. I replied that in 1906 I had been a teacher at the Lungching High School.

"Are you the Mr. Tong who was a teacher of English and mathematics at the school?" he asked me eagerly. When I replied in the affirmative, he said: "Then you were my teacher."

I realized this fact ever since he emerged as a national figure, but modesty had prevented me from bringing it to his attention. From this time on our relationship was on a personal basis.

Upon the completion of my tour, Chiang invited me to spend a fortnight with him in his native town, Chikow. I went to Chikow, accompanied by a friend of mine, Chen Ching-han, editor-in-chief of the *Shun Pao*. On our arrival at the Chiang home, Madame Chiang, whom I had met before, remarked,

"You and the Generalissimo are the same age, but you look younger."

It was an embarrassing remark, since her husband was within earshot. I answered tactfully,

"It may be so, but the Generalissimo carries responsibilities which are a hundred times greater than mine."

During this two-week visit I had the opportunity to enjoy an excellent close-up of him. At Chikow he lived the life of a country gentleman and the villagers welcomed him as one of their own. Despite his exalted position, his manner was homespun. I frequently saw him standing beside the swift current of a mountain stream watching the schools of fish struggling upstream against the current. He was especially fond of riding on a bamboo raft in the mountain stream. I was not skilled in riding on bamboo rafts and one day I lost my footing and my foot broke through the strung bamboo and plunged into the water. On my return the Generalissimo loaned me a pair of his shoes. They were cloth shoes made by his relatives and being of a smaller size, they pinched my feet.

On another occasion, we were walking along a very steep mountain path. He rode in a bamboo chair, carried by two bearers. I asked him whether it was too dangerous to ride such a steep path. He reassured me that he had not known of anyone having a fall there. I still hesitated to follow him. Mr. Chen and I decided to climb up the mountain, literally crawling, for a one thousand feet drop was below us.

Later we moved into a cottage at the top of the snow-clad mountain. The cottage, which Chiang rented, was a three-room affair, the center room serving as the drawing room. Generalissimo and Madame Chiang occupied one of the rooms and Mr. Chen and I the other. There was a bathroom behind my hosts' chamber, but we hesitated to use it lest it inconvenience them. The Generalissimo observed this and one day he filled the bathtub with water himself and invited me to bathe. I have always found him considerate of others, as on this occasion.

At night, we would have a bonfire on top of a protruding rock and we would sit and enjoy the silence of the night. The sons and daughters of Dr. H. H. Kung, the Generalissimo's brother-in-law, were other guests. Dr. Kung was then the Minister of Industries. We would talk until late hours, to the accompaniment of the sound from the waterfall. On such vacations, China's national leader built up his strength for the great tasks which awaited him in Nanking.

All too soon, the time came for departure. The Chiangs and the Kungs went to Shanghai on a gunboat. Mr. Chen and I followed on a commercial vessel. This fortnight with the Generalissimo and Madame Chiang on the Snow-Clad Mountains was an eye-opening to me of the modest, unpretentious life of China's first family. It was also a revelation of his kindness to his friends.

One thing impressed me most was his filial attitude toward his mother. She had died before our visit. Always on his vacations at Chikow, Chiang would spend an evening alone in the small cottage adjoining his mother's tomb. During the fortnight of my visit I noted that he visited the tomb at least ten times.

A few years later, the pavilion on the top of the hill, where the Generalissimo lived, was destroyed by the Japanese in a grudge bombing. It was later rebuilt and was the scenic spot of the little village, which has a population of only three or four hundred souls. The villagers are all closely related.

I had been in Chikow before in 1906. When I first saw the village, the future Generalissimo lived in a house with his mother. The pavilion was officially unoccupied and was the showplace of the community. Some Buddhists were allowed to live there. Later, when Chiang returned home and found his old house too small, they voluntarily moved out.

One of the questions Chiang asked me during my visit was whether I had any hobbies. I replied that I had two hobbies: the study of governmental intelligence and chemical warfare. He asked me to submit two memoranda to him on these subjects.

My report on military intelligence interested him. I declared that his army lacked effective intelligence units. To prove my point I cited the fact that in the Northern Expedition, after his army had defeated the troops under General Chang Chung-chong, it failed to move forward because its commanders did not know whether the enemy had suffered a rout or an orderly retreat. Had the commanders enjoyed proper intelligence, they could have pressed forward to Tientsin several weeks earlier than they did, and thus shortened the campaign.

The Generalissimo asked me if I would organize an intelligence service for China's army. But I was so preoccupied with my duties at the *China Press* that I was forced to decline. In my place, Chiang appointed General Tai Li. He was also responsible for intelligence on anti-government activities.

Likewise, after reading my report on chemical warfare, the Generalissimo asked me if I could set up a chemical warfare unit in the army. I also declined the offer. I found newspaper work too fascinating to leave. I had often speculated on where I would have been today had I accepted either of these offers. General Tai Li was killed in an airplane crash after the war, following much cruel smearing in the Western press by pro-Communist writers. His detractors had charged that he was responsible for executing a large number of people. However, the actual number was much less and all of them had been found guilty by due legal process.

Chapter Six.
An Editor in Shanghai

My active editorship of the *China Press* lasted for a little more than five years. Since it coincided with the stirring events, which culminated in the Japanese invasion of China in 1937, it was a period of continuous tension. I had a box seat for the drama of a world convulsion. Shanghai in the thirties was a city of fate.

As an editor of the principal English daily in China, my office was the port of call for the drifting American newspaper talents in the Orient. Some newspapermen who later were to make their mark in American journalism contributed their skill to the *China Press* during those years. Notable among these were Tillman Durdin, now the distinguished correspondent of the *New York Times*; Harold Isaacs, later the writer of numerous books on the Far East; Carroll Alcott, who became a popular radio commenter in the States; Earl Selle, biographer of W. J. Donald; Nevada Chemanza; now the publisher of a daily in California; Joseph Patrick, a top-flight public relations man in New York, and others. I was tempted to refer to my *China Press* office as a house of all talents.

We had to be on our toes, because the militarists who were then dominating Japan were making news almost as fast as we could record it. Probably the outstanding event of my editorship was the coverage of the first Japanese assault on Shanghai in January 1932. Shanghai was sectioned off into (1) the International Settlement, (2) the French Concession, and (3) the Chinese city at Chapei. The fighting took on a bizarre aspect almost unprecedented in warfare. The International Settlement and the French Concession were sanctuaries in the struggle, studiously respected by the Japanese to avoid international complications. The assault was restricted in the Chinese city of Chapei. Here, in full view of the world, in the International Settlement, they vented their ruthlessness and hate upon the swarming unfortunates in the Chinese city. It was as if they wished to impress spectacularly upon China the full frightfulness of what they would be capable to do to us if we spurned their arrogant demands.

The 1932 Shanghai attack was a meaningless operation actually inspired by the bitter rivalry between the Japanese Army and the Navy factions. The Army had just enjoyed the glamour in Japan by its quick conquest of Manchuria in 1931. The Navy was anxious to do something just as spectacular. What gave them an excuse for action was the boycott of Japanese goods, which had been unofficially launched by the Chinese after the Manchuria seizure. Private boycott organizations had sprung up all over China, and although the Chinese government had maintained a perfect diplomatic attitude toward Japan, even to the extent of closing down some boycott offices in Shanghai, the Japanese were determined to retaliate. To give a show of Japanese might, Admiral Shiozawa was in Shanghai waters with two cruisers, an aircraft carrier, sixteen destroyers and a landing force of 3,000 marines.

General Wu The-chen, an elder statesman of the Kuomintang (Citizen's Party), was the Mayor of Shanghai and he carried on earnest negotiations with the Japanese Consul General for settlement of the grievances growing out of the boycott movement. The negotiations were shadowed by rumors that Japanese armed forces were preparing to attack. As a newspaperman, I had to keep vigilant to be prepared for the any news breaks.

The Japanese Residents' Association of Shanghai was issuing a *Daily Bulletin* in English setting forth the Japanese side of the controversy. On the evening of January 28, 1932, at 9 p.m., I noticed in this Bulletin that there was a virtual ultimatum issued by Japanese headquarters to the Chinese authorities to withdraw all Chinese troops from Chapei by twelve o'clock that evening. Failure to do so, it declared, would result in Japanese attack to forcefully drive out Chinese troops.

This statement amazed me since a communiqué of the Mayor and the Japanese Consul General indicating an amicable settlement had been issued only a few hours earlier. I immediately telephoned the home of Mayor Wu, but was informed by the servant that Wu had left word that he was not to be disturbed, since he had retired thoroughly exhausted by the two weeks of negotiations. When I insisted, the Mayor finally came to the phone. He expressed incredulity since, only a few hours before, he had parted with the Japanese Consul General on cordial terms and they had congratulated each other that Sino-Japanese relations would improve.

Nevertheless, he promised to telephone the Consul General, and have an order issued for Chinese officers to be at their stations.

The principal officers of the 19th Route Army, which was stationed in Chapei, had been on the alert for a month. Thinking the crisis was ended, they were attending dinners given by friends. The Mayor sent his representatives to various Chinese restaurants to notify them. In disappointment, they left their dinners half finished and hurried back to their commands.

When Mayor Wu telephoned the Consul General, he was assured that the news was untrue and that he knew of no such ultimatum by the Japanese military authorities. However, I had rushed all my staff reporters to the Japanese military barracks at Hongkow. They had peeped into the headquarters and had noted that the troops were in formation inside, with their tanks ready for action. I relayed this information to the Mayor who again phoned the Japanese Consul General, only to receive the usual denial. But at 11:30 p.m., Mayor Wu received the ultimatum. My office was a beehive of activity. Particularly alarmed was Bang How, managing director of the *Commercial Press,* which was located in Chapei. Because of its anti-Japanese policy, it seemed certain that the *Commercial Press* would be a target if Chapei were occupied.

Our worst foreboding was justified. Precisely at midnight, the gates of the Japanese barracks swung open and, proceeded by tanks, the Japanese troops poured out. The enemy had landed a force of marines for this purpose. Their initial attack on Chapei made progress but was halted by the 19th Route Army. The Japanese followed with an aerial attack on congested Chapei. The bombing caught the defenseless Chinese at 4:30 in the morning. Thousands of civilians lost their lives—at least 250,000 fled to the security of the International Settlement.

This was the beginning of a senseless Japanese coup. But Japan gained nothing from the adventure except a tarnished name. After withdraw of the Chinese army, the united pressure of foreign representatives in Shanghai persuaded the victorious Japanese to withdraw their troops. The Japanese evacuation was completed by May 31, 1932. It was a bloody engagement, Japanese had 634 dead and 791 wounded, and the Chinese total was much greater. The attack was a total failure as an attempt to halt the anti-Japanese boycott. The boycott went on.

But Japan's principal loss was in the realm of the imponderable. The slaughter of defenseless Chinese civilians in Chapei horrified the world and solidified world opinion against the Japanese militarists, some thing not even the Manchuria seizure had done. And the example of the heroic stand which Chinese soldiers had made in Shanghai against the mechanized Japanese sent a spark of pride through the Chinese population. It stiffened the confidence of Chinese everywhere to stand up against the aggressors.

My own staff worked night and day giving coverage to the fighting. It is not often that a newspaper can report on a big war taking place within the confines of its own city. Tillman Durdin was the city editor and Harold James the night editor. They worked tirelessly to keep our readers informed of every development.

It was fortunate for us that the *China Press* offices were located in the International Settlement. Had we been in Chapei, the Japanese, in view of the outspoken policy of the paper, would undoubtedly have arrested all our Chinese employees and molested those who were American. As it was, we were able to print the war news under display banner headline and to write unsparing editorials denouncing Japanese aggression and misdeeds. The ordeal was so nerve-wracking that by the time of the Japanese withdrawal some of us were near a stage of collapse.

After the paper was put to bed, usually as late as four or five o'clock in the morning, the staff used to retreat to the Jimmy Kitchen for refreshments. From the Kitchen we then walked home, for no transportation was available at that hour. Despite the hard work and the ever-present danger, I think all enjoyed the experience because we were young enough to welcome the challenge. Also, we were sustained by pride in what we were doing. The *China Press* easily topped our competitors in its coverage and its imaginative handling of the news. We were conscious that we had done a standout newspaper job.

The unfortunate side of the Shanghai campaign was the distorted sense of importance, which was given to the commanders of the 19th Route Army. During the fighting, the 19th Route Army had been built up colorfully in the press for its heroic resistance. The admiration went to the heads of its leaders. In the fall of 1933, they began a heady dream of overthrowing the Chiang Kai-shek government and they united with a group of disgruntled politicians to precipitate what was known as Fukien Rebellion.

The revolt started with a mass meeting in Foochow, the Fukien capital. The mass meeting issued an anti-Nationalist government manifesto. Chiang replied by giving the 19th Route Army a week to disband the new Fukien rebel regime. Failing this, he served notice that he would "destroy the jade and the stone alike."

The revolt was short-lived. The Generalissimo took personal command of the suppression campaign. It was the first military effort in China in which air forces played an important role. Temporary airports were established in Wenchow and Chuchow and from these the bombers made repeated flights over the rebel lines, and the rebel headquarters, dropping bombs. This speedily wrecked the morale of the Fukien junta. It was a heartening test of China's new air power. The collapse of the rebellion was hastened by the fact that most of the 19th Route Army officers were lukewarm in their sympathies with the rebellion and welcomed the chance to go over to the Government side.

The *China Press* gave full coverage to the Fukien hostilities. Unfortunately we made a bad mistake, which involved me in an unpleasant situation with the Generalissimo. In a Sunday supplement, we published a picture of a school in Foochow being destroyed by aerial bombing. The mistake had been made by Harold Isaacs, who was in charge of the supplement, and it had escaped my notice. A week after we ran the photo, I received a telegram from Chiang Kai-shek calling my attention to the picture and asking me to come to Nanking to explain why I had published it.

My staff was in a panic, fearing that I was going to be punished. Isaacs, after urging me in vain to ignore the telegram and to remain in the security of the International Settlement, told me that he and the staff would make an international issue of it if I were detained. They declared that they would force the hand of the Generalissimo by publicity.

I did not see it this way. I felt that it was my duty to go to Nanking and explain to the Generalissimo the overworked conditions under which we got out the newspaper, and which had resulted inadvertently in this blooper.

After an unhappy night trip to Nanking, I presented myself at the Generalissimo's office. Late in the morning I was ushered into his presence. He demanded to know why I had permitted the publishing of a picture, which was so damaging to the good name of China's air force in a paper that was widely read by foreigners.

"Do you think it is wrong to have such a picture published in Chinese-owned English daily?" he asked me reprovingly.

Knowing his mind, I answered, "Yes, it is wrong."

He thereupon brushed aside the subject, remarking that it would not be mentioned again, and adverted to other matters. The *China Press* got off with this mild rebuke. In this instance, as in all my future relations with him, I found the Generalissimo a reasonable and understanding superior.

Both in China and abroad, during the desperate Chapei fighting, the 19th Route Army was allowed to hold the spotlight for its gallant defense. The part played by other Chinese armies in the Shanghai crisis was not publicized. But those of us who were close to the picture knew that others played an outstanding role in these events. Although the facts were in our hands, the Generalissimo was unwilling to dull the luster of the 19th Route Army. He did not permit us to tell the true story of his own immense efforts behind the scenes in the conduct of the Chapei defense until two years later, in 1934.

What prompted Chiang to break his silence was the untruthful propaganda, which was put out by General Tsai Ting-kai, commander of the 19th Route Army. After the Fukien Rebellion, General Tsai went to the United States where he openly accused Chiang of engaging in a series of acts to destroy the 19th Route Army. Tsai charged that not a single soldier had been sent to reinforce him and that the Nationalist government had even held up his supplies.

When the *China Press*, with Chiang's permission, published the true facts in 1934, we revealed that the picture, which had been presented to the world, was distorted. The 19th Route Army had not stood alone. Actually, the 87th and 88th Divisions, which had been personally trained by the Generalissimo, bore the brunt of the fighting. One third of their strength had been wiped out by the Japanese. The Generalissimo did not personally command the fighting. Shortly before the Shanghai attack, in disgust with the intrigues of some of his political ill-wishers in the Government, he had submitted his resignation, and had even secured a passport to go abroad. The crisis came when he was a private citizen, without official authority to issue an order or make a decision.

Despite his personal feelings, when the country was in danger, he laid aside his passport and remained to aid the defense as a behind the scenes adviser. All he could do was to use his personal influence with the commanders. He was in daily communication with General Tsai, as well as with the commanders of the 87th and 88th Divisions.

When the crackup of the resistance came, it was the direct consequence of a 19th Route Army blunder. Chiang had warned that Chinese troops should be stationed at Liuho on the Yangtse, to prevent a Japanese landing of reinforcements. General Tsai ignored the advice and the Japanese made this precise move. This misfortune was followed by an order of retreat given by the 19th Route Army commanders – an order issued without prior advice to the Fifth Army. The latter continued to fight through the night, its flank exposed by Tsai's withdrawal, and it suffered staggering losses. Two days later the reinforcements, which Chiang had promised, arrived. They were too late to affect the outcome. I knew these facts when they happened, but the Generalissimo forbade me to publish them. I kept his confidence.

In addition to my post as editor of the *China Press*, I had accepted the managing directorship of the *Tai Wan Pao*, an evening paper edited by a personal friend, Tseng Hsueh-pai. I had known Tseng since my Tientsin days and had found him an able writer and a keen newspaperman. This newspaper followed American make-up customs and it was popular in Shanghai because of the novelty of its appearance.

In the winter of 1935, I became ill and was obliged to relinquish the editorship of the *China Press*. I had sold *Yung Pao* in Tientsin to the Red Swastika Society (not the same as Hitler's Swastika Society, although the names were the same). The sale had been negotiated by Chiang Kwang-tang, my business manager. It later became known that the Society was acting for the Japanese in the sale. When this fact transpired, it was too late to do anything about it.

Chiang Kwang-tang turned out to be a rapacious associate. He appropriated most of the proceeds of the sale. My share amounted to little more than what I had invested in the paper, with no compensation for the years of grueling labor, which I had put into the publication.

As I look back now, I realized that I would probably have been better off financially if I had never gone to Shanghai but had remained with the *Yung Pao* in Tientsin. But the whole future course of my life would have been different. Certainly, my life has been enriched as a result of my experience at the *China Press*. It brought me in prominent contact with influential Chinese and foreigners, both in public and in private life, whose friendship has directed my life into new and wider scopes. Life is more than making money; it is also the accumulation of vital experience. Unquestionably, my editorship of the *China Press* was a vestibule to a fuller and more meaningful career.

It is interesting to recall that while I was with the *China Press*, the Soviet government invited me several times to take an expense-paid trip to meet Marshal Stalin and other key Soviet officials in Russia. The Shanghai correspondent of TASS, the Russian news agency, made the offer to me. I was frankly interested in the offer and stipulated that I would write a series of articles for the *China Press* and would submit them to Stalin for review before publishing them. It was a fair offer, but apparently it did not interest Stalin.

Later, I got the impression that Stalin did not want me to visit Moscow as a correspondent, but as a prospective convert to Communism. I lost interest in the proposal. Although the Chinese government was suppressing the Chinese Communists, it was carrying on correct diplomatic relations with Communist Russia. Apparently the overtures to me were connected in some way with the devious relations between the Russian and the Chinese Communists in the mid-Twenties.

Chapter Seven.
I Become a Censor

While convalescing in Shanghai, I received a message from W. H. Donald, the famous unofficial adviser to Generalissimo Chiang Kai-shek, that in the interests of patriotism for China, I should consider the possibility of becoming the censor of all outgoing press dispatches. I had maintained a cordial friendship with Donald ever since 1913 when I first went to Beijing as correspondent for the Shanghai Kuomintang press. At that time, he was acting correspondent for the *London Times*. He was also editing a monthly, the *Far Eastern Review*, which was devoted to commercial Asian news. Our first joint work was to expose Japan's notorious Twenty One Demands.

In 1928, Generalissimo and Madame Chiang invited Donald to join them as unofficial adviser. He was then living in the Palace Hotel in Shanghai, and we were in the habit of breakfasting together. He discussed with me his misgivings concerning Chiang's invitation, but finally decided to accept because he was convinced that China, now unified, was on the threshold of becoming a world power. He believed he could do a great work for the Chiangs in winning favorable overseas publicity.

When I sat down with Donald to discuss the proposed censorship task, I asked him to explain specifically what he meant by the words "I should accept the post for patriotic reasons." He explained that China was beginning to suffer from a very bad press abroad because of inefficient censorship of outgoing news. He felt that, with the Japanese situation worsening, China would need international understanding as never before.

He pointed out that foreign correspondents were making constant complaints to Generalissimo and Madame Chiang Kai-shek about the way their dispatches were being treated. Censorship was being so indiscriminately applied that the telegraph editors in America and other countries were actually receiving dispatches from China with nothing but the punctuation marks left in them. The *New York Times* cable desk is said to have received a dispatch from its China correspondent which reads: "*New York Times:* Stop. Stop. Stop. Signed James Wood." This was hurting China.

I agreed with Donald that something must be done. Soon after this meeting, Generalissimo Chiang invited me to join him at Chengtu in Szechwan, to discuss the whole censorship problem with him. He was in Chengtu, later events disclosed, to make preparations for the establishment of a wartime government should Japan wage war on China. This was in 1935, when the province of Szechwan was still under the control of warlords. A distance less than 150 miles between Chungking and Chengtu was controlled by three warlords, and everyone had to obtain special permission to travel in their territories.

Even at that early date the Generalissimo was well aware that when the Japanese forced a war, the government would have to be moved into the interior. The best place was Szechwan. It was necessary for him to conciliate the political influences in that province. When I visited him there in 1935, it seemed a remote hinterland. By 1939, it had become the hub of our war-torn nation.

Although I disliked censorship as much as any newspaperman, the job of improving it appealed to me. I considered it an opportunity to contribute my share toward building foreign goodwill through the press. I accepted the appointment and soon found myself installed in an office in Shanghai, exercising censorship over all outgoing foreign press dispatches.

I looked around for qualified assistants to work with me in the censorship office. I selected my old friend, F. L. Pratt, a veteran Australian journalist; Z. B. Toong, an English scholar; and Miss S. C. Chu, who was conversant with the Russian and French languages. Dispatches in English, Russian and French passed through my office. Japanese correspondents evaded censorship by sending their dispatches to Tokyo directly over a special Japanese telegraph line in the International Settlement.

A test of our new censorship facilities came in 1936 during so-called Xian coup d'etat. A brief sketch of this dramatic incident is necessary to convey understanding of our difficulties in the censorship office.

In 1936 the political atmosphere in China was electric with tension due to civil war between the Nationalist government and the communist party, and the threat of Japanese invasion. There was a pervasive feeling that events were building up to a decisive climax. The climax came on December 12 when the Generalissimo was seized and made a prisoner by disloyal subordinates in Xian, in the northwest province of Shensi.

At that time, the Chinese Communists were holed up in Shensi, a dwindling but still defiant band of rebels. In a series of campaigns, Chiang Kai-shek had driven them out of central China. Their remnants, after a wearisome ten-month migration, had found a remote spot of security in and around Yenan, Shensi.

Late in 1936, the Generalissimo in Nanking received urgent messages from Chang Hsueh-liang, the 'Young Marshal,' and son of Chang Tso-ling, who was stationed in the Northwest. It said that the communist agents had infiltrated the government troops in Shensi. The Chinese Communists were fearful of further attack by Chiang's army. They were spreading propaganda among the government troops, which surrounded the communists, telling them that they were fighting the wrong enemy. They should be fighting the Japanese, not fellow-Chinese who happened to be communist. This propaganda was softening up the government troops, the 'Young Marshal' told Chiang.

There was another armed force in Shensi, the provincial Shensi army under the command of Yang Hu-cheng, a former bandit. Yang's troops were supposed to be cooperating with Chang's troops, which had been driven out of Manchuria when the Japanese occupied it in 1931.

Chang's army, composed of men whose minds were primarily set on the prospect of return to their Manchurian homes through expulsion of the Japanese, proved responsive to the communists' pleas for immediate war with Japan. Disturbing rumors of fraternization between Chang's officers and their communist counterparts reached the Generalissimo. He flew to Loyang, in adjacent Honan province, and conferred with Chang. The Generalissimo took the unyielding attitude that the communists must be suppressed first, before China went to war with Japan, in order that there would be no treacherous elements behind his lines, while he was fighting the foreign enemy. Had the communists been suppressed at this time, and they were so weak that the Nationalist government could have done so, all the future disasters, which came upon China would have been avoided. Later, the government learned that the communists were so discouraged in 1936 that they were contemplating disbanding their party. Mao Tse-dong himself was preparing to go to Russia for study.

Against warnings, the Generalissimo proceeded to Shensi, and with an entourage of only 20 bodyguards and 60 gendarmes, installed himself at Lintung, a famed hot springs resort, 15 miles from the provincial capital

Xian. The house he occupied was located at the foot of a mountain. One of those who warned Chiang not to trust Chang Hsueh-liang was General Chen Cheng, later the vice president of the Republic of China in Taiwan.

On the evening of December 11, the Generalissimo planned to entertain both Chang and Yang at a dinner. Yang declined, but Chang was present. At 9 o'clock the dinner was over and Chiang spent the rest of the evening drafting a plan for an offensive against the Communists by Chang's and Yang's armies.

At 5:30 a.m., Chiang was awakened by an attack on his Lintung headquarters by some of Chang's troops. More than 40 of his bodyguards and gendarmes were killed. Simultaneously, in Xian, Yang's forces were making prisoners of Chen Cheng and 16 other high Nationalist government officials. Chiang Kai-shek was seized by Chang's lieutenants at Lintung and made a prisoner.

The grave news became known in Nanking at 3:30 in the afternoon. Half an hour later, General Ho Ying-ching, Minister of War, received a telegram from Xian signed by Chang, Yang, and numerous others (12 of the names were forged). The telegram announced that the rebels wanted an 8-point program, which included a coalition government with the Communists, and cessation of the government attacks upon the Mao Tse-tung followers.

There followed a strange psychological event, which could only have occurred in an Asian nation. Chang, after talking exhaustively with the Generalissimo, and reading his diary, in which Chiang had set forth his actual ambitions for China, reversed himself on the third day. He decided to extricate the Generalissimo from the dangerous situation in which his insubordination had caused him. Meanwhile, W. H. Donald, who had formerly been Chang Hsueh-liang's adviser, and had influence on him, flew to Xian to dissuade his former chief from this mad venture. On the fourth day, Chang invited Madame Chiang Kai-shek to fly to Xian to be at her husband's side.

Meanwhile, back in Nanking, the Central Political Council of the Kuomintang appointed Ho Ying-ching commander-in-chief to suppress the rebels and liberate the Generalissimo. It was an ill-advised move since, in the hostilities, the Generalissimo's life might have been lost. Nanking's planes commenced bombardment of Hwahsien, a point between Loyang and Xian, killing some of Chang's soldiers. Chang sent a message to Ho Ying-ching, signed by the Generalissimo, asking for a suspension of the bombardment. The message was conveyed by Ting-wen, one of Chiang's lieutenants.

In Nanking, where the government officials were in the dark concerning actual conditions in Xian, this letter was mistrusted. It was decided to inform the 'Young Marshal' that the Government would not call off military operations, but to notify him that bombing would be suspended until the deadline date, December 19. T. V. Soong, the Generalissimo's brother-in-law, flew to Xian and conferred with Chiang. At Madame Chiang's request, the deadline date for renewed bombing was suspended. Soong accompanied by Donald then flew back to Nanking to inform the government that a peaceful solution was possible, although the situation was still dangerous. He then flew back to the Generalissimo's side accompanied by Madame Chiang, Donald and Chiang Ting-wen. It was generally realized that this was the decisive moment. Upon the success of the four depended the life of the Generalissimo. By December 24 it became evident that Chang Hsueh-liang was willing to release the Generalissimo, but was fearful of what Yang Hu-cheng might do in the moment of departure. The Generalissimo spurned the Chang suggestion that he depart in disguise. It was decided that Chiang and his wife should leave openly by air the next day, which was Christmas.

His departure was unopposed. Chang Hsueh-lieng volunteered to return to Nanking with the Chiang party, to accept whatever punishment might be meted out to him. This quixotic act was taken by him, without anyone's suggestion. The party arrived in Loyang safely, to be greeted by cheering crowds. All China had been holding its breath during the crisis, and the return of the Generalissimo released a wave of rejoicing, which swept the nation. At 6:15 p.m., the happy news reached Shanghai, and the city went wild in celebration.

My own part in these occurrences, as China's censor, was nerve-wracking. It is not surprising that my hair turned almost white. The duty of the chief censor was to prevent the wiring out of false news or rumors. It was necessary to keep in touch with Nanking, from the Shanghai offices, by hourly long distance calls. It was necessary to communicate with the highest authority, which was Madame Chiang, or Dr. Kung, Dr. Soong or General Ho. If, in the event of the Generalissimo's actual death, the censor should delete the truth from the dispatches, however, he would be doing an injustice that would infuriate the press of the world.

I lived in fear and trembling throughout the fortnight. It was necessary to maintain a 24-hour watch, and even when I attempted to snatch a little sleep, a telephone was placed under my pillow to connect me with my assistant, Mr. Z. B. Toong. Some of the correspondents, like Hallet Abend of the *New York Times*, made a practice of calling me very late at night. He would often inform me that he had gotten word that the Generalissimo was dead, and he would ask me accusingly why I was suppressing the news from the press. This necessitated wearisome calls to Nanking, and call-back to inform Abend that I had official assurance that he was mistaken.

To my great pride, I succeeded in preventing any false news from leaving Shanghai from any of the accredited correspondents. But I could not do anything about the rumor mongers in the States. American newspapers printed much misleading news material on the incident, most of which was received by way of Japan. After the coup d'etat, the Japanese Minister to China, at a public dinner, sarcastically remarked: "You are an American-educated Chinese and you have given much help to the American correspondents by briefing them on the Xian happenings. Unfortunately, you have not been friendly to the Japanese correspondents, and they have reported the Generalissimo's death at least ten times. This has caused much prestige damage to the Japanese newspapers."

I replied that the Japanese newspapermen had never submitted their news reports to me for censorship. The other nations had done this willingly, and I had been able to check their accuracy. The Minister seemed satisfied.

As the world now knows, good came out of the agony of this Xian coup d'etat; China emerged a united nation. An object lesson had been given to the world of the deep emotion Chiang Kai-shek had upon the people of the country. Until 1936, the Japanese had been deluding themselves that China was hopelessly disunited. Japan had poised its armies to move into an easy conquest of a weak nation. Now the Japanese knew the unwelcome fact that China was strong and united. The militarist faction decided that if they were to win China, it must be now, before it became any stronger. Most likely, the Xian incident hastened the Sino-Japanese war.

Six months later on July 7, 1937, the blow fell. In the trumped-up Marco Polo Bridge incident and the Japanese armies moved in to take Beijing and Tientsin. The Sino-Japan war began. The incident started by a false claim that a Japanese soldier was murdered. The soldier was drunk and failed to return to his camp on time. After his return, the Japanese commander quickly sent him back home and covered it up. In August 1937, when the Japanese insolently demanded that China withdraw its garrison troops from the Shanghai area, I went to Nanking to be briefed on the Generalissimo's intentions. To my question of whether he would remove his troops to avert all-out war, Chiang replied, "Positively no!" Shortly afterwards, Japan attacked Shanghai.

I inopportunely fell seriously ill. An operation was necessary. I was recommended to an excellent American surgeon. But just then the unfortunate blunder of a Chinese aviator dropped bombs on the International Settlement, and the surgeon was commandeered to aid the wounded. Finally, I secured Dr. Dana Nance, son of the former president of Soochow University. Dr. Nance, upon examining me, discovered that I had peritonitis, an extremely dangerous condition. Within two hours I was on the hospital operating table. Dr. Nance gave me just three chances out of ten to survive. But I did survive, although it was with a feeling that I was now living on borrowed time.

While still in the hospital, another censorship crisis broke. An American passenger ship, *S. S. Hoover*, docked in Woosung near Shanghai, was hit by a plane-delivered bomb. The question was, whether the plane was Chinese or Japanese. China desperately needed American support. It would be extremely hurtful publicity-wise should news of Chinese bombing of an American vessel reach American newspaper readers.

I contacted Madame Chiang, then head of China's air force, by telephone. She admitted that the offender had been a Chinese plane. On the theory that it was better to admit the blunder, and end the publicity, than to try to conceal it, I sadly gave the order to my staff to pass the news stories. The situation was saved by an immediate Chinese government apology to the American Embassy at Nanking with the promise to pay for the damages to the *S. S. Hoover* and to punish the guilty pilot. With the traditional American spirit of fair play, the American press did not place blame on China.

After I was released from the hospital, I set up a cot in my office and resumed my duties, with frequent rests on the cot between censorship decisions. With the Japanese invasion at its explosive stage, this required an almost round-the-clock vigil. Perhaps it was just as well that I found myself temporarily replaced in the chief censor's job by Dr. H. H. Chang.

Dr. Chang's tenure was short and not sweet. A scholarly man, he had little conception of the importance of time to the working newspaperman. He would hold up cables for several days while he gave leisurely consideration to their contents. Eventually, he stubbed his toe badly.

On September 22, 1937, the fateful news broke that the Chinese Communists had announced the reorganization of their former Red Army as a unit of the Chinese National Army. This was a tremendous story, as it meant that the last autonomous faction in China was about to merge with the nation. But when the foreign correspondents quoted this news development from the Chinese *Central News*, Dr. Chang mistook the release for a eulogy of Communism and he killed it. His ruling created much unfavorable talk among the foreign correspondents, and he was soon asked to retire. I found myself reinstated.

However, my return did not indicate that most of China's political leaders had a clearer concept of press relations. I was confronted by Chinese incomprehension of western journalistic habits. Many government leaders could not understand my painstaking activities to win goodwill among American publishers and editors. I frequently felt that I was struggling against insurmountable odds.

I was also handicapped by the Chinese traditional trait of politeness. Chinese as a people dislike dispute. The Chinese capacity of compromise is almost limitless, because they do not enjoy verbal collisions. This often resulted in agreement for the sake of peace. Because I was temperamentally a direct and not a devious person, this made by tasks harder. I could not always agree with my colleagues who thought of my job primarily as a sort of government peacemaker.

I was not an ideal censor because my natural inclination usually led me to sympathize with erring human nature. I was a censor who was not censorious. In my own mind I had worked out a fairly specific philosophy of censorship. I believed that it must restrict itself to serving the good of the nation or "national security" while giving writers all possible free reign. I think it was because I sincerely held this philosophy that I was able, so successfully, to work with the foreign correspondents. Certainly there was no truth in the charge that I succeeded because I was westernized.

What was the punishment for rebellious Chang Hsueh-liang of the Xian incident in 1936? He was under house arrest for 23 years, in Nanking and other places, finally in Taiwan. In 1954, Madame Chiang asked Sally and me to visit Chang Hsueh-liang and his companion Chao Yi-di, to teach them English. We used English Christian books for teaching and introduced them to Christianity. Sally's genuine and intense Christian love deeply touched them. After six months, they became devoted Christians. Shortly afterwards, they were married. Both Chang Hsueh-liang and Yi-di wrote many articles on their new faith and translated a Christian book from English to Chinese in collaboration with me.

When we were leaving Taiwan for the ambassadorship to the U.S. in 1956, Chao Yi-di confided to Sally, in tears, that they had a son Lu-lin, in the U.S., but had lost contact with him for many years. In 1940, she was in Hong Kong and decided to voluntarily join Chang Hsueh-liang under house arrest in Quichou Province. Before she took this fateful and risky step, she brought her five-year old son Lu-lin to San Francisco to entrust him to a family friend, Mr. Jacob and his wife Anna. Chao Yi-di asked Mr. Jacob not to reveal the boy's parentage for fear that the political turmoil could affect his safety. It was a gut-wrenching decision. She knew that once under house arrest, there would be no way to contact her son again. There is a Chinese phrase for this sad situation for the mother known as "Tuo Gu" which means "Entrusting the Orphan."

After we arrived in the United States, Sally tried her best to find Lu-lin but failed. I, as an ambassador, asked the U.S. State Department who enlisted the FBI to look for Mr. Jacob. After considerable effort, they found Mr. Jacob in Los Angeles. Through him, Lu-lin was located. We sent the good news along with photos of Lu-lin and his family to the Changs in Taiwan, which brought immense joy to them. Lu-lin was an engineer and married to a Chinese girl. They had two sons. In 1959, the Changs received their freedom and traveled to the U.S. to meet their son Lu-lin and his family.

Chapter Eight.
As Vice-Minister of Information

I had not been back in the censorship office two weeks when I was notified that I had been appointed Vice-Minister of the Fifth Board of the National Military Council. Stripped of its confusing title, this meant that I had been chosen to set up a propaganda organization to tell the Chinese side of the story to the world. I was no longer to be tied down to the purely negative job of telling foreign correspondents what they should not print. I was now to have the creative task of supplying them with news, which we wanted them to publish.

It was mid-October of 1937 when I returned to Shanghai by automobile from Nanking with my instructions. There was continuous peril of strafing by the Japanese planes that watched the highway with hawk-like intensity. Farmers along the highway told us that one section, a half hour's ride outside Shanghai, was constantly watched by enemy planes, which strafed both cars and pedestrians indiscriminately. But, one farmer told us, there was a two-hour period between twelve and two when the pilots apparently grounded for lunch and the road was safe. We followed this suggestion and got through safely.

I learned that it had been Madame Chiang, as well as the Generalissimo, who had urged my appointment as Vice-Minister. More than anyone else in the Government, Madame Chiang was awake to the imperative need of a good American press in the desperate crisis period. American-educated herself, and enjoying a wide circle of important American friends, she clearly understood American thought processes. She regularly read to a large number of American periodicals and studied intently for their opinions on China. Knowing me as a Chinese newspaperman who had enjoyed top

American newspaper training, she felt that I had unusual qualification for interpreting China to the Western world. The appointment of such a propaganda specialist was unprecedented in Chinese government. But with Madame Chiang's insistence, the program was instituted.

There was another reason why I was appointed. The post of Minister of the Fifth Board was then held by Chen Kung-po, who belonged to the Wang Ching-wei faction of the Kuomintang. Both Chen and Wang were later to defect to the enemy and to become heads of the Japanese puppet government in occupied China in 1941. But this was in the future, and none of us could have foreseen this culmination in 1937. But Wang Ching-wei, who had been one of Dr. Sun Yat-sen's intimate associates, had never forgiven Chiang Kai-shek for thwarting his burning ambitions to succeed Dr. Sun as the leader. On the surface, he maintained friendship with the Generalissimo, but he was always an uncertain factor. As early as 1937, Chiang had reason to suspect Wang's lukewarmness in the war against Japan. The presence of Wang's henchman, Chen Kung-po at the head of China's propaganda was a disquieting situation. I was placed in the ministry as second in command to forestall any equivocal action. After my appointment, Wang Ching-wei himself made it a point to discourage me in my new task. But I refused to heed his warnings.

Chen was under no illusions about the reason for my appointment. He gave me the cold shoulder, and it was quickly apparent that we could not effectively work together. I took steps to detach my work from the rest of the activities of the Fifth Board. During the first few weeks, I made it a point to carry on my activities in Shanghai while Chen worked in Nanking.

Chen had become a close friend of Count and Countess Ciano, Mussolini's son-in-law and daughter, while Ciano was stationed in Shanghai as Italy's Consul General. Believing that he could influence the Italian government, Chen secured the Generalissimo's permission to go to Italy to enlist Mussolini's support for China's cause. It was a foolish mission, in view of China's close friendship with the United States and Great Britain. But it fitted into Wang Ching-wei's devious plans to end the Japanese War, even at the cost of accepting Mussolini as a mediator. Just before leaving, Chen requested me to make a large sum of money available in Shanghai for him to take to Rome along with a Shanghai woman who had influence on Ciano, who was now Italy's Foreign Secretary. I rebuffed the suggestion telling him that China, though hard-pressed, would not stoop to what is called by Chinese "the intrigue with women." This embittered Chen against me still further. Chen failed in his efforts in Rome and returned to Nanking only to find his post abolished. With Chen's departure, I became acting minister with control over both domestic and foreign information activities.

Four years later, in 1941, he defected to Japan. He became puppet mayor of Shanghai, and succeeded Wang Ching-wei as head of the puppet government in Nanking after Wang's death in 1944. At the close of the war, he was made a prisoner by the United States Army, turned over to the Chinese for trial, and died by the firing squad.

But I soon learned that Chen was not my only headache. I also quickly found myself confronted by an impasse of Kuomintang politics. Seniority in Kuomintang membership was a jealously guarded requirement for government ministerial positions. Although I had worked with the Kuomintang since my return to China in 1913, I had not actually become a member until 1934, when the Generalissimo asked me to join. Some government leaders had been party members for a quarter of a century, I, with my three-year membership, seemed a crass junior.

The problem confronted me in acute form when, shortly after my appointment, the Fifth Board was abolished and its functions transferred to the Ministry of Information. This Ministry, unfortunately, was a subsidiary of the Kuomintang party, rather than of the Nationalist government. I was re-assigned as Vice-Minister of the Ministry of Information. I found myself the only party officer of this rank who was not a member of the Kuomintang General Executive Committee, or Central Supervisory Committee. It was a difficult spot for me and it required frequent compromises with suspicious Kuomintang leaders. But since I had the unique distinction, in a national emergency, of being better qualified by experience for my post than any possible successor, I held on. But there were difficult moments.

The battle of Shanghai was still raging when I returned from Nanking in my new post. There was no time to be lost in setting up an efficient news distributing organization. Japan was spending large amounts of money to place a distorted, Japanese-slanted picture of its war against China in the columns of the world press. China, new to the propaganda field, had to build from the ground up. And we built in the midst of fast-moving news of war.

In the crisis, I believed that my first job was to reach the Shanghai community of foreigners. The news, as seen through their eyes, would shape the opinions of their fellow-countrymen across the seas. Particularly, it was important to reach the English-speaking residents.

When I commenced my work, I found that the Japanese had already either corrupted or gained control of a large segment of the Shanghai foreign press. But two of the English dailies had taken an unreserved attitude in support of China. These were the *Evening Post and Mercury*, edited by Randall Gould, and the *China Weekly Review*, edited by J. B. Powell, on whose staff I had once been assistant editor. Both papers were outspoken in their denunciation of Japanese aggression. Both Gould and Powell had been threatened with death by the Japanese and were forced to carry pistols for their personal safety. One day a bomb wrapped in a newspaper was thrown at Powell. Fortunately it proved a dud.

The other two newspapers in Shanghai were not friendly to us. The *North China Daily News*, British-owned, was disappointingly cautious and non-committal in dealing with the Japanese aggression. It was the mouthpiece of the Municipal Council of the International Settlement, on which the Japanese were strongly represented. It tried to pursue a safe middle course. The other English daily, the *Shanghai Times*, though edited by British fronts, was virtually owned by the Japanese and openly defended Japan. Unfortunately for us, these two non-cooperative papers influenced a larger number of Shanghai foreigners than did the pro-Chinese press. The *Shanghai Times* was edited by R. I. Hope, a British subject, who had worked under me in Beijing on the *Beijing Daily News*.

To combat the neutralist and even pro-Japanese spirit of much of the Shanghai foreign community, my staff prepared pamphlets, wrote letters and made broadcasts over small privately owned stations. A committee of Shanghai citizens who supported the China cause was organized, and worked closely with our official agencies. It took the name of "Anti-Enemy Committee." Its membership was mostly Chinese, and it comprised men of the highest caliber. Among them were Dr. C. L. Hsia, president of the Anglo-Chinese Medhurst College, Dr. Wen Yuan-ning, editor of *Tien Hsia*, a monthly English magazine of important influence among Shanghai's intelligentsia, Dr. Herman Liu, president of Shanghai University, and H. J. Timperly, correspondent of the *Manchester Guardian*. The danger to the committee members was demonstrated when Dr. Liu was assassinated by Japanese hirelings at one of the bus stops in Shanghai. Later, most of the officers of the committee became members of my staff. Dr. C. L. Hsia eventually became the director of all our activities in North America.

At this early stage of our work, we began to use the device of the press conference. We arranged for the Mayor of Shanghai, O. K. Yui, to hold daily press conferences with the foreign correspondents. Mr. Yui, a former newspaper reporter, and a man who respected factual accuracy, proved an inspired choice for this task. Correspondents accustomed to the evasiveness of the old style of Chinese official were pleasantly surprised by Mr. Yui's candor and directness. The press conference became an influential channel to overseas public opinion. I also visited the battlefront and arranged with the four commanding generals to relay daily war communiqués to my office. These generals were Ku Chu-tung, Chen Cheng, Chang Fah-kwei and Chu Shao-liang.

I was also fortunate in securing the cooperation of Hsu-pei Tseng, who became my principal assistant. Tseng had been a colleague of mine for twenty years in the newspaper field. At the time I enlisted him, he was editor-in-chief of the *Ta Wan Pao*, the Chinese evening daily. A man of the highest ability, he remained with me throughout the war, and was afterwards my chief assistant in the postwar Ministry of Information. He later headed the *Central News Daily* in the Republic in Taiwan.

As the Shanghai battle began to turn against us, I addressed myself more and more to the task of strengthening the main operation of the Ministry in Nanking. I was preoccupied with the problem of providing more and better news, both spot news and features, to the Nanking foreign correspondents. There were Americans, British, French, German and Russian correspondents permanently stationed in the capital. I established cooperation with the Central News, the unofficial Chinese news agency, which was then headed by T. T. Hsaio, who was a veteran of the Chinese revolution and a patriot. He agreed to place his news gathering facilities virtually under government control for the duration of the War. The Central News was a comparatively young organization, with limited resources. It could not be compared with the Associated Press, United News or Reuters. But it was still China's largest news source and had developed a wire service to reach into all parts of the country.

Mr. Hsaio impressed me the necessity of producing more and better written human interest stories, to supplement the news. Few of my staff was qualified to do this kind of writing, but I succeeded in developing two writers, Frank Liu and Hawthorne Cheng, who were soon turning out highly competent feature articles. Similarly, my association with Hsaio led to the setting up of an effective photographic division. This division started with only one truly professional press photographer, H. S. "Newsreel" Wang. Possessed of a rare news instinct, Wang turned out some war pictures which were widely reproduced in the world press. His picture of a lonely weeping baby sitting amid the ruins of the bombed railway station in Shanghai became the most famous picture of the war from China.

There was much experimentation in this attempt to create from scratch a working news organization in the midst of shattering war, but we made progress. By the time we reconsolidated our activities in Chungking,

China had a foreign information operation which was fast approaching professional effectiveness.

The changing fortunes of the war continuously impinged upon our activities and handicapped us immensely. During the first two years of the hostilities, we were an information agency in transit. The Shanghai battle ended on November 11, 1937, when the main forces of China's army withdrew from the Shanghai area and the National Military Council issued a farewell message to the people of the city. Shanghai was such a symbol to most foreigners that its fall seemed to many the signal of the loss of the war. The Japanese conquerors respected the International Settlement and the French Concession and these enclaves became listening posts for our operations until 1941 when Japan declared war with the West and occupied these enclaves.

Fortunately the wave of defeatism did not encompass the Chinese people as a whole. Ours was still a vast country. The loss of Shanghai did not spell disaster to the scores of millions of Chinese in interior China who had never regarded this Western-built city as a part of real China. Throughout the agonies which were ahead, the Chinese people were sustained by an unfailing faith in the unconquerability of China. This faith, in the darkest hours became a mystique, which baffled all foreign observers. Compounded with this faith was an abiding confidence in the leadership of the Generalissimo. In the hour when China's fortunes were at their nadir, the prestige of Chiang Kai-shek reached its pinnacle. Chinese people had an unshaken confidence that somehow, he would bring them through to victory. In the end they found that their confidence had not been misplaced.

The end of the Shanghai fighting meant that the activities of my organization must now be concentrated in Nanking. We were under no illusions that Nanking could be permanently held, but for a few months, all of China's official efforts pivoted about this city. There was an influx of foreign writers and correspondents, eager to supply a news-hungry world with the dramatic China story. Nanking's Metropolitan Hotel seemed crowded with itinerant reporters, each carrying his inevitable portable typewriter. It was my responsibility to see that these, for the most part, cynical writers sent home a truthful picture of our heroically resisting China.

I soon found that Nanking was going to be a much more difficult place for an effective information operation than Shanghai. Here there was no competent Mayor O. K. Yui to cooperate with us by helpful daily news conferences. Government officials, unconvinced of the importance of public relations, were unwilling to take on the additional work of press releases and press conferences. To all my requests there was one uniform answer: the necessity of concentrating upon the conduct of the war was so pressing that there was no time for such fringe activities as propaganda. There was a deplorable failure to recognize that in time of war, propaganda can be as powerful a weapon for a hard-pressed nation as airplanes or tanks. All through Nanking and Hankow resistance periods, I encountered this heartbreaking difficulty in making my government colleagues understand the need for propaganda.

Moreover, I was handicapped from the start by the problem of personnel. I had inherited, from the old Fifth Board, an incompetent staff of subordinates, few of whom had actual newspaper experience or knew any other language but Chinese. For an office which was charged with the handling of foreign publicity, this was a hopeless situation. When I contemplated making a sweeping cleanout of dead wood, I found myself stopped by the political factor of the Kuomintang. I knew that if I should be too aggressive in my changes, I might easily be displaced.

I brought my troubles to the Generalissimo. He was at first persuaded that the Fifth Board should be continued, and promised me larger authority in the Board. I explained to him that it was not my own status which was at stake, but the effectiveness of our efforts. I urged him strongly to abolish the Board and to create in its place a smaller organization to be staffed by young men who were good newspapermen or who had enjoyed some experience in public relations. My arguments must have influenced him because, on November 15, 1937, I received the welcome word that the Supreme National Defense Council had abolished the Fifth Board, alone with other sweeping Government reorganizations. As I have mentioned, the functions of the Fifth Board were to be transferred to the Ministry of Information, which would be a Kuomintang organ. The Ministry would contain an international department with authority over overseas publicity. As Vice-Minister, I was to head this department. I retained this authority until the end of the war. Ministers of Information came and went but I remained in my International Department.

I had an opportunity to bring some new blood into the organization. I operated on the rule that new appointees must have the qualification of actual experience in newspaper or public relations work. Well-meaning amateurs were discouraged. The Chinese Civil Service has a long waiting list of very able young men trained in philosophy and cultural subjects, but bitter experience had taught me that few of them had any sense of news values.

The reorganization coincided with a moving program. All of us realized that Nanking could not be permanently held against the Japanese forces, which were now approaching from Shanghai. At most, we could conduct a holding operation while a stronger defense line was prepared further west. The real fight, it was anticipated, would be at Hankow, a thousand miles to the west, where the Yangtse River bends southward. As a precaution, many of the government departments, with their records, were being moved to Hankow and its sister city, Wuchang, or even to the more distant Changsha or Chungking. At the Information Ministry, we worked exhaustingly, night and day, packing the records that we wanted to save, and arranging for their shipment into the interior. I had decided that I would send the whole administrative staff to Hankow, and that only Hsu-pei Tseng and I would remain behind. The staff work would be done in Hankow, while Tseng and I would remain in Nanking to handle the foreign correspondents, as long as the city was held.

Most of the correspondents stayed in Nanking until the end. My relationship with them was purely informal, since I had no staff to oversee and no press releases to issue. I formed the habit of meeting them almost daily, either at lunch or at the Metropolitan Hotel. I was able to help them with their dispatches, and most of them gave China an extremely fair presentation in their stories.

On November 19, 1937, my *China Press* colleague, Tillman Durdin, who was correspondent for the *New York Times*, came to my office with the disturbing news that the city of Soochow had been lost. This was a blow to our hopes for it meant that Nanking would soon be invaded. On the following day, the Generalissimo instructed me to leave for Hankow immediately. I made reservations for Tseng and myself to leave on the up-river boat that night. Just before my departure, I received a summons from the Generalissimo. He wanted me to help him in the preparation and translation of a statement for the *New York Times*. As a result, we missed our boat, and remained in Nanking for another week. The Generalissimo's statement contained stirring words:

> "When the enemy reaches Nanking," he said, "we will defend it. Even when the enemy attacks Szechwan, we will defend Szechwan. As long as the enemy's invasion lasts, we will continue our resistance. . . The enemy never realizes that China's territory is not conquerable. She is indestructible. As long as there is one spot in China free from enemy encroachment, the Nationalist government will remain supreme."

This statement was an effective answer to those Western observers who had assumed that China was on the verge of surrender. It was a statement which will go down in the history of the war, with the best utterances of Winston Churchill.

The old Kuomintang leader, Shao Li-tze, had been appointed Minister of Information, as my immediate superior. Unlike Chen Kung-Po, I found him an understanding and sympathetic colleague. The Generalissimo asked Shao to proceed immediately to Hankow to organize the offices there. Tseng and I felt it best to remain in Nanking to maintain contact with the correspondents until the end.

In this final hour at Nanking, General Chang Chun, Secretary General of the National Military Council, agreed to meet the press daily to keep them advised of the fast-moving events. As General Chang's English was not perfect, I acted as translator in all these conferences. The General, an old intimate of the Generalissimo's since student days in Japan, could speak with authority since he enjoyed the full confidence of Chiang.

On November 25, I was able to arrange a reception for the foreign correspondents by Generalissimo and Madame Chiang. The occasion was saddened by the receipt of a telegram advising the Generalissimo that the Western Powers had just postponed indefinitely any action on the request to invoke the Nine Powers Treaty against Japan's attack on China. Great hopes had been entertained that the Western Powers would intervene in behalf of China. Now, in an excess of political caution, they had closed the door. China was left alone to deal with the Japanese aggressors. But no reflection of his bitter disappointment escaped the Generalissimo in his conversation with the correspondents. He accepted his lonely responsibility with stoicism.

While the reception was in progress, the air raid alarm sounded. There was no dugout available. We all stepped out into the garden to await the end of the raid. Later, we were to take these air raids more seriously.

But my vigil in Nanking was now to end. The fall of the city was imminent and unavoidable. The following day, November 26, the Generalissimo ordered me to depart by boat for Hankow together with Tseng and Chen Pu-lei, the chief secretary of the Generalissimo. Chen told us that during the day, Chiang had visited the mausoleum of Sun Yat-sen to say his farewells. To us, this meant that the Generalissimo was preparing to leave the capital immediately. The act of paying respect to the revered founder of the Kuomintang signified clearly that there was no longer hope of holding Nanking.

However, it turned out that the Generalissimo and Madam Chiang did not depart until December 7. The city was held until December 13 when Chiang gave the order to the remaining Chinese troops to withdraw. The Japanese then swarmed into the city, starting an orgy of murder, looting and rape that horrified the world. Fortunately, a little handful of foreigners, including 18 Americans, remained behind after the city fell to witness the atrocities. Among these was Tillman Durdin who succeeded in getting through a dispatch to the *New York Times* describing the horrors. There was no immediate reaction by the western powers, but from this point forward, world sympathy swung to the Chinese side in this barbaric Japanese attempt of conquest.

Chapter Nine.
Hankow Ordeal

The early days in Hankow were shadowed by doom. The two successive defeats at Shanghai and Nanking had been dishearteningly costly to China. Not only had we lost the nation's capital and its richest seaport, our window to the world, we had also lost the flower of our trained troops, and most of our weapons and munitions. We retreated over a thousand miles to the interior of China holding precariously to a city which we had little hope of saving.

But one asset we still possessed – unshattered morale. It was to maintain the morale of the Chinese people that Generalissimo Chiang had fought the two agonizing battles of Shanghai and Nanking. With the Great Powers dishonoring the Nine Powers Treaty, which agreed not to further fracturing China's territory, we had no tangible hope to receive foreign aid. Chiang and his associates were able to communicate the electric spark of confidence to the fleeing Chinese people. We believed unquestioningly that somewhere – if not in Hankow, then in Changsha, or even distant Chungking – we would make a stand and hold. It was in that unflagging assurance that we held firm in Hankow through eleven distressing months.

Few of us believed that we could hold Hankow for more than six weeks. My first act was to rent a two-room building for my offices. The owner exacted three months' rent in advance. I was certain that I had paid double for the period we would be in Hankow. I worked and slept in one of the rooms. My colleague, H. P. Tseng, occupied the other. But I also had my thirty employees to house. Reluctantly, I followed the practice of the other ministries and expropriated a Japanese-owned building to house them.

In those first days of insecurity, I speculated on where we would go after Hankow. The safest refuge from the Japanese was the ancient city of Chungking, over a thousand miles inland on the Yangtse. It was in Szechwan province, surrounded by mountains, but one of the few spots in China which had not been brought under the full authority of the Nationalist government. It was still controlled by predatory warlords. To transfer China's capital to such an uncertain city would be a veritable leap into the dark.

The feeling of fatality was so strong in Hankow that I even appointed a replacement in my office in case I should fall into Japanese hands. I designated Dr. Wen Yuan-ning, then the director of my Hong Kong office, to succeed me in an emergency and to keep open our overseas offices in the United States, in England and in Australia. I provided him with funds for such contingency.

Fortunately, we had extracted too much Japanese offensive power. The weeks passed and their armies made little progress toward Hankow. It was apparent that the enemy was more exhausted than we had realized by its first two campaigns and needed time for rest and regrouping. Besides, the Chinese armies even won a victory over the Japanese in a clash at Taierhzhuang near Hsuchow, 150 miles north of Nanking. Here the Generalissimo laid a trap for the over-confident Japanese and they walked into it. Of 62,000 Japanese soldiers who started the engagement, only 20,000 survived. Chinese losses were also heavy, but our armies had proven that they could beat the Japanese. At Hankow the news was received with jubilation. Morale skyrocketed. There was even irresponsible talk that Hankow itself could be held.

A full corps of foreign correspondents was now in Hankow and my office spared no effort to give them all-out cooperation in getting facts. Japanese, to minimize their defeat, had let the story trickle to the foreign press that they were still holding the town. With General Chen Cheng's help, we put a party of correspondents on a military plane and sent them over the area to see for themselves.

Infuriated by their setback, the Japanese made a fierce attack on Hsuchow. After a sharp fight, we yielded the city. Japanese propagandists tried to turn the success into a major victory by claiming that General Li Tsung-jen and his army had been trapped. Actually they had escaped, crossing the Tientsin-Pukow Railroad and rejoining the main Chinese armies. I was able to turn the Japanese publicity boasting into a serious loss of face.

At Hankow I began to get excellent cooperation from high government officials in my daily contacts with the foreign correspondents. Gone was the skepticism about the value of publicity, which prevailed during the months in Shanghai and Nanking. Everybody was eager to get the story of China's resistance before the world audience. I had little difficulty in getting high government officials to speak. General Chen Cheng, then the Minister of Political Training, was especially helpful. General Chen was liked by the newspaper group because he did not indulge in the Chinese traditional weakness for giving out exaggerated figures. Correspondents knew that when General Chen Cheng told them something, it was the truth. His policy helped to win more confidence in Chinese publicity among editors overseas. General Hsu Pei-kong, who was in charge of military intelligence, was similarly conscientious in his official releases. I had often been humiliated by the clumsy attempts of some Chinese generals to magnify their successes and to conceal their reverses. At Hankow we succeeded in halting this self-defeating nonsense.

One reason why our publicity moved more smoothly at this stage was that for the first time over a decade, we were enjoying an era of goodwill with the Communists. The Hitler-Stalin Pact was still a year ahead, and the Communists were nominally giving full support to resisting the Japanese. The influential New York and London cliques of pro-Communist writers had declared a moratorium in their criticism of Chiang Kai-shek.

It seemed that we had achieved a united front in China. Of course, the united front was full of cracks: the Generalissimo knew the Communists too well to trust them implicitly. Already, he was beginning to receive disturbing dispatches from the North that the communists were up to their old game of infiltration and anti-government rumor-mongering. But publicly, all was sweet harmony.

In the Hankow days, I saw much of Chou En-lai, the future Communist Premier, who represented the Communists at the capitol as Vice-Minister of the Board of Political Training. Chou had a gift of natural charm which he could turn on at will. Also, unlike the other Chinese Communists, he spoke English fluently. Until the later break, he worked cordially with my office, and assiduously building up the friendships with "Liberal" writers and correspondents who were to stand him in such good stead when, later, the Communists broke from the Government.

The advent of Shao Li-tze in the Information Ministry had also ushered in a period of liberal censorship, which proved extremely popular among the correspondents. Shao, who later was to be China's Ambassador to Moscow, was known as a left-winger in the Kuomintang. His conciliatory attitude made him an appropriate Information Minister during this period of attempted friendliness with the communists. Later, when the Communists seized power in 1949, Shao was one of the small Kuomintang minorities who defected to them. He later lived in Beijing, an uncritical supporter of Mao Tse-dong's regime.

No intimation of these future events was in our minds as we worked together in Hankow. My relations with Shao were cordial and pleasant. He had set up his Ministry offices in Wuchan, across the river from Hankow, where most of the Government agencies were clustered. My International Department, now called the Central Publicity Board, maintained its offices in Hankow, where we could be close to the correspondents and the diplomatic offices. For all practical purposes, mine was an autonomous operation.

During the Hankow period, we experienced the first tide of pro-Communist foreign writers and correspondents who began to fill the American and British magazines and newspapers with puff stories about the virtues of the Chinese Communists. They were Anna Louise Strong, Agnes Smedley, Israel Epstein, and Ilona Sues. Not all visiting writers were pro-Communists. Other important journalists popped up in Hankow during the eleven months to report the war. The world was waking up to the fact that events of a major historic magnitude were taking place in China.

One of those who came was John Gunther. The famous author was collecting material for his later book, *Inside Asia*. One day, after Gunther had interviewed the Generalissimo, I accompanied him to the offices of the Central Bank of China to see Dr. H. H. Kung. By a slip-up, the Generalissimo had an appointment to see Dr. Kung at the same hour, but arriving and finding Gunther in the midst of his interview, he walked away without announcing himself. Gunther looked out of the window and saw the first man of China unconcernedly strolling down the street, with no thought of personal danger. The author expressed the greatest surprise in this confidence of Chiang in his people, in view of the elaborate precautions, which were routine in other countries to protect their leaders.

Another visitor was Edgar Ansell Mowrer, the columnist. It was my first meeting with this gifted journalist who has been such a staunch friend of Free China through the years.

During the Hankow months, arrangements proceeded to prepare Chungking for the eventual national capital. The breach with the Szechwan warlords was eased. For better security, government departments including the Ministry of Foreign Affairs were moved up to the river to Chungking. Some of the legations and embassies had already moved to Chungking. This resulted in the anomalous situation for Madame Chiang Kai-shek who exercised virtually all the functions of the Foreign Office in Hankow. As a result of my close personal relationship to Madame and Generalissimo Chiang, I supported her as a Vice-Minister during this period. Because Madame Chiang was able to make quick decisions, she was able to avert a number of threatened disasters in China's foreign relations.

The worst of these involved Colonel Joseph W. Stilwell, then U.S. military attaché, who was later to play an important role in China's mid-war crisis. A report had reached the Generalissimo that Stilwell had filed a report in Washington advising that China's resistance to Japan would collapse in a fortnight. Highly displeased, the Generalissimo asked me to speak to the American Consul General in Hankow.

I was aware of the delicacy of the situation, and sought the assistance of Madame Chiang. I suggested that she receive Colonel Stilwell at a tea and sound him out. She agreed and I contacted the Colonel. It happened that Stilwell was an old acquaintance of mine from Beijing days when I had met him as a student learning Chinese. An interview was arranged.

Madame Chiang asked me to be present at the interview. After an hour of informal talk, she was convinced that Stilwell was not unsympathetic to China, or to the Generalissimo. Upon her assurance, Chiang was satisfied and asked me to drop the matter. Later, when Stilwell's acid-penned memoirs were published, with his unrestrained insults to the Generalissimo, I wondered if he had been altogether truthful in that afternoon in Hankow.

Signs began to accumulate in June 1938 that the long lull in the Japanese drive to Hankow would soon begin. The enemy signaled his coming offensive by moving gunboats up the river from Nanking. In anticipation of severe fighting, the authorities began to move women and children out of the 1,000,000-population Hankow-Wuhan cities. Refugees began to be evacuated at the rate of 20,000 a day.

To our surprise, the British Charge d'Affaires delivered to us a statement of the ten conditions which the Japanese had drafted as their price for the setting up of a neutral zone in Hankow from which Chinese soldiers could be evacuated. The terms were humiliating. But what displeased the Generalissimo most in the incident was the fact that the British should allow themselves to be used as messengers for the Japanese in this virtual ultimatum. He received the British Charge d'Affaires at an interview in which I acted as interpreter, and expressed his resentment in blunt terms. Later, he asked me to release his statement to the foreign correspondents that had not yet been told of the Japanese ten points.

I felt that this would be a bad mistake, and I attempted to dissuade the Generalissimo. He remained adamant. In this dilemma, I asked Madame Chiang, who agreed with me, and tried to change her husband's determination. His mind was so firmly made up, that they quarreled angrily when she opposed his plan. To strengthen our case, I persuaded Chen Pu-lei, his trusted secretary general, to intervene. The unfortunate Chen was subjected to a severe rebuke. Next, the Generalissimo called me in.

"You cannot be a diplomat," he told me. "Your action has made me very angry."

In the end, the Generalissimo acceded to our request, but the whole incident rankled his mind. I came out of the incident with considerable loss of prestige. But my dissuasion of Chiang was in vain. A *United Press* correspondent, who had learned of the Japanese demands and the Generalissimo's reaction, violated his pledge of secrecy to me, and filed the story. It was published in Shanghai. The harm was done.

Another key city, Guongzhou, fell to the Japanese. The Japanese now had their foothold in the south. The loss of Guongzhou started a chain reaction of discouragement in Hankow. Anticipating the early arrival of the enemy, my office began in earnest to pack its records and supplies. A steam launch was placed at our disposal for the up-river trip. I made it a point to salvage some things discarded by other offices, which I thought might be useful in Chungking. By a happy inspiration, I secured the essential parts of a radio transmitting station, which was headed for abandonment by order of Mayor K. C. Wu. I sent it on to Chungking. Subsequently, it proved a priceless possession in beleaguered Chungking.

By an oversight, I left behind a cache of 500,000 silver dollars, obviously owned by the Japanese owner of the house where we were holding our press conferences. A former Chinese servant revealed its hiding place. We located the treasure but I was reluctant to seize it. We left it behind, and it undoubtedly fell into the hands of the Japanese.

I found, in the same building, one hundred cases of indigo which were owned by Japanese. In a country where 80 percent of the people wore indigo-dyed cotton garments, such a supply was certain to be extremely valuable, as war shortages continued. It would have been easy for me to pack it on the steam launch and take it with me. I estimated that it could eventually be worth a billion Chinese dollars. But I had no heart for looting, and I left the indigo behind.

It was decided that all the principal office buildings owned by Japanese would be dynamited when the last government official left Hankow. We had placed explosives in the fireplace of my office, and in other locations. During my last few days in Hankow I had the unpleasant feeling that I was perched over an active volcano. A few days before the end, I sent H. P. Tseng and the other members of my staff to Chungking to set up our new office. One staff member, J. A. MacCausland, better known as Ma Ping-ho, declined to go.

MacCausland was one of those strange expatriates whom one meets only in Asia. An Oxford man, he had become interested in the Chinese classics while still at the Christ College. When he arrived in China, he abandoned his western garb, his name and many of western ways. He adopted a life of ascetic poverty. I had engaged him for his extraordinary ability as a translator. Some of the best known English drafts of the Generalissimo's wartime speeches were the work of Ma Ping-ho. At last I persuaded him to depart and for three days I was alone in my offices with the exception of Jimmy Shen, a University of Missouri journalism school graduate.

Those three days were full of excitement. The Generalissimo had asked me to stay to the last and leave with the last soldier group. It was necessary that I do so as we had arranged a final press conference in which I was to present prepared statements explaining the reasons for our withdrawal. Admittedly, those were anxious hours.

The Generalissimo was to call me, after he and Madame Chiang had departed, giving me the exact zero hour. It was understood that if I did not hear from him before 10 a.m., October 25, I was to go ahead with the press conference. With the Japanese on the point of entrance, every hour counted. At midnight on the 24th, Chou En-lai, the Communist representation, called me repeatedly to advise that his last truck was leaving at 1 a.m. and urging that I join him to avoid capture by the Japanese. I declined. Every hour, Jimmy Shen called me from the garrison headquarters, telling of the steady thinning of the people. I had to instruct him to wait. At 4 a.m., Jimmy called me from the garrison advising that the last of the staff members was departing. I instructed him to leave with them. I was now alone.

Sleep was out of the question, and I sat in my office chair until 9 a.m. Still I had not heard from the Generalissimo. I thereupon called the press conference for 10 a.m. Since telephone service was now cut off, Tillman Durdin was so kind as to go around in his jeep and inform as many of the correspondents as he could reach. When I met the correspondents, we were all overcome with emotion. Among the words which I read was the following ringing message of confidence:

"The shifting of our armed forces on this occasion marks a turning point in our struggle from the defensive to the offensive. It also makes a beginning of a change of tide in the war. It must not mistakenly be viewed as a military reverse or retreat. For the key to victorious conclusion of our war of resistance lies not in what happens in Wuhan but in the conservation of our strength for continuous resistance."

The story of the next fateful six years of our struggle against Japan was in those valedictory words of mine in Hankow.

Now that I had held the conference, I was released from the Generalissimo's instructions to wait for his call. I began to address myself to the problem of getting safely out of the falling city. My own car had been sent to Changsha and I had no transportation. I walked to the garrison headquarters, a distance of two miles. Japanese planes were hovering overhead, refugees were streaming hysterically out of the city and those who were to remain had barricaded themselves against looters. In this hour of danger, I visited William Baker, an English missionary, who had been my close friend. Mr. and Mrs. Baker and I joined in prayer. I have always believed in the efficacy of prayer. The brief prayer which Mr. Baker spoke that day asking for my safety was miraculously answered before the day was over.

At three o'clock in the afternoon, an officer friend invited me to go with him in his car to Changsha. I was about to go when I was suddenly struck by a splitting headache. Thinking it was caused by hunger, I ate something. The headache increased to the point of the unbearable. My condition was so appalling that my friend decided that he would have to go without me. And here is the miracle. Less than three hours later, the car which I was to have taken was machine gunned on the road by Japanese planes. The car was blown to pieces and all its occupants killed. My life had been preserved by the headache.

At seven o'clock, word reached the garrison headquarters that Japanese cavalry had already entered the Japanese Concession from the east. Only one way of escape was open to us. We had to leave Hankow on foot. Together with General Lin Wei-wen, the garrison commander, we crossed the Han River over a pontoon bridge, which we dynamited behind us to prevent pursuit.

The next ten days were nightmares of exhaustion with ever-present danger. We headed for Changsha, where the Generalissimo had set up temporary headquarters. With Japanese planes hovering over the road by day, ready to bomb any living object, we did all of our walking in the dark of the night. Stumbling over unpaved, rutty roads, with only the light of a Chinese paper lantern, we often fell into mud holes or ditches. It was the life of moles. By day we always found some place to hole up. I should have been miserable, but so resilient is the human spirit that after the beginning, I found myself enjoying the experience. For the first time in years, I had ten days to myself away from telephones, free of responsibilities. I had nothing to do but walk and I learned to saver every hour of the trip.

Meanwhile, the Generalissimo, not knowing of our fate, was telegraphing anxiously to the various commanders asking if they had seen us. Before we reached Changsha, he had given us up for lost.

On November 5, 1938, we at last arrived in Changsha. The Generalissimo was deeply moved to see us again. He invited General Lin and me to dinner. We did not know that it was his birthday. Sir Archibald Clark Kerr, the British Ambassador, was the principal guest. Generalissimo Chiang was in an excellent mood and although he abstained from taking wine himself, he urged all of us to "kan pei" (bottoms up). All of us with the exception of the Chiangs drank to excess. It was a relief from the terrible tension we were living under.

For a time I had little to do, as the correspondents were scattered and my staff were in distant Chungking, or elsewhere. By the end of 1938, our whole organization was reestablished in Chungking. We were at the beginning of a new and frightening stage of this long war.

Chapter Ten.
Stand at Chungking

When we withdrew to Chungking in late 1938, few of us foresaw that we would stay there for over seven years.

There are many reasons why Chungking is poorly suited to be China's capital. The first, of course, is its inaccessibility. It could not be reached by railway or by modern highways. Throughout the seven years, we were dependent upon river boats navigating through the Yangtse gorges, and limited air transportation for the movements of our supplies and personnel. While these factors made us secure from Japanese land attack, they placed logistic burdens upon the Government.

The outside world could only be reached, until 1942, by plane to Hong Kong, or by a tortuous road to Burma. Even these contact points were later to be cut off when the war became global. Living in Chungking gave one in a different world feeling, as if one were living in a fictional Hilton Shangri-La.

The climate was also depressing to one who had lived in the sunshine of the coastal cities. For nine months of the year, Chungking is mantled by intermittent fogs, which hang over the city like a suffocating blanket. When the fogs lift during the summer three months, the heat of the city is enervating and unrelieved.

The government officials and the swarm of refugees who poured into the city in the winter of 1938–1939 felt unwelcome. Szechwan province was then parceled out between three warlords. There was little national consciousness among the people, who looked upon the newcomers as little better than invaders. The task of organizing civil government in Szechwan was given to General Chang Chun, the Generalissimo's loyal friend from youth. Chang Chun was an able and honest administrator and with unfailing patience; he gradually won the Szechwanese to a new spirit of unity with the rest of the nation. But it was not an easy task, and there were many unpleasant encounters in the beginning.

My scattered staff found its way to the new capital during the month of December 1938, by various modes of transportation. I made the trip from Changsha by plane. We immediately resumed our work. I secured for the International Department the building of an old middle school, known as Pa Hsien School, located on a hilltop on the outskirts of Chungking. It was a large rambling structure made of mud and plaster, roofed with loose tiles. It was a dilapidated building with doors which didn't lock or close snugly, was infested with rats, and the roof was always threatening to collapse over our heads in a storm. To house my staff and their families, we had to build a row of shacks in the compound behind the main building. My family and I moved into the ruins of an old pavilion nearby.

Almost immediately we were confronted by the problem of a change of ministers. Shao Li-tse was transferred to the ambassadorship in Moscow. The Generalissimo tried to persuade Ku Meng-yu to take the post. Ku, who had been Minister of Railways, had no heart for the job. Even after I took a special air trip to Hong Kong to urge him, he evaded me and would not be drafted. At last, the Generalissimo's choice was Chow Fu-hai as the acting Minister of Information. It was an extremely ill-advised appointment.

I was distrustful of Chow from the outset. He was an opium smoker who had intrigued with the Communists, during the attempted Communist takeover in 1926. He had been arrested in Shanghai when his guilty activities became known. Only through the intervention of Dr. Wang Shih-chieh was he freed. After this experience, he had lost interest in Communism. But there were indications that he had recently flirted with Japanese.

Chow Fu-hai did not like me and he began to attempt interference with my policies and department. At the risk of being replaced, I defied him. A weak man at heart, Chow accepted the situation.

Fortunately, Chow's term of office was brief. My suspicion of him grew when, after we relocated in Chungking, he volunteered the information that he had initiated talks with important Japanese. He became a member of a little ring of traitors who followed Wang Ching-wei into the Japanese camp early in 1939. Chow suddenly departed from Chungking, leaving behind a memorandum appointing me Acting Minister of Information, an action which he did not have the authority to take. When we next heard of him, Chow was in Nanking, behind the shelter of the Japanese army, serving as Minister of Finance in Wang's puppet regime.

The Wang Ching-wei defection struck us with sadness during our first difficult months in Chungking. Apparently, the Japanese believed that the winning over Wang would start a chain reaction of defections that would destroy us from within. But they had foolishly underestimated the patriotic fortitude of the Chinese people.

Wang, when he defected, was nominally the No. 2 man in the Nationalist government. A man of heroic revolutionary record, a trusted intimate of Dr. Sun Yat-sen, he might have risen to the summit in China had he not been marked by moral defects which led him astray in every crisis of his life. At Chungking he was alternate chairman of the Supreme War Council, presiding in the Generalissimo's absence. For some time, he had differed with the Generalissimo on the conduct of the war. He had urged that China rely upon the Fascist nations – Germany and Italy – to persuade the Japanese to call off the war, and that we should disassociate ourselves from the democratic nations. He had become a center of defeatism in the Government. How he made contact with the Japanese has always been a mystery. But on December 18, 1938, he fled from Chungking to Hanoi, Vietnam, having stopped over in Yunnan en route in an unsuccessful effort to win over Lung Yun, the Yunnan chief, to the Japanese side. At Hanoi he released a statement calling for peace with the Japanese on their terms.

Only a few important people followed him, including two of my former superiors in the Information Office, Chen Kung-po and Chow Fu-hai. Later, Wang showed up in Shanghai where he proclaimed himself the legitimate head of the Kuomintang, after holding a bogus 'Sixth Kuomintang Congress.' In 1940 he set up a puppet regime, with Nanking as capital, where he flourished ingloriously until his death in 1944. Wang's betrayal was a bitter experience for the resisting Chinese nation, but contrary to enemy hopes, it did not weaken our purpose to go on with the war until the day of victory.

Chow Fu-hai was succeeded in the Information Ministry by Yeh Chu-tsang, who headed newspapers in Shanghai during the first few years of the Republic. It happened that I had served as his Beijing correspondent during that period. He was highly regarded as a journalist, although he belonged to the old school of scholarly Chinese writing. As one of the older and more influential members of the Kuomintang he was able to persuade the party to allow us to conduct the Information Ministry in enlightened ways.

Our first few months in Chungking, when the city was shrouded with clouds and fog, gave us a false sense of security, because Japanese bombers were unable to penetrate the overcast. But with the arrival of sunny weather, our peril began. The first heavy raids were staged on May 3, 1939. The bombing was indiscriminate. The International Department suffered heavily; our radio facilities were almost completely destroyed. For a period of a fortnight, we were unable to transmit any press messages from the city.

Since we could expect repeated raids, I determined to set up a transmitter in a dugout. In the face of warnings by engineers that this was technically impossible, I persisted. For this project I had the equipment, the old 6-kilowatt transmitter which I had salvaged in Hankow, dismantled and sent up the river. I still had to secure parts and it was not until two summers had passed that it was really set up for use. But eventually, this transmitter was the link keeping the foreign correspondents in touch with their home newspapers overseas.

Next day, May 4th, there was a more terrifying bombing. The Japanese were obviously trying to paralyze our defense by leveling Chungking to the ground. Expecting the worst, we at the International Department attempted to spread the risk. Three mat sheds were built at scattered points in the compound and supplies, both office and personal, were divided between the three. It seemed inconceivable that a bomb, if it fell, would demolish all three, so we could hope to save something. Later we were to have dugout shelters, but at the beginning, we were exposed to the enemy's attacks. With office and dormitories in the same area, there was always the danger of a complete wipe-out, if the bombers got our range.

While the bombings continued, the correspondents had acceptable stories about the terror. By the fall of 1939, when the returning mists halted the raids, the correspondents found themselves with nothing newsworthy to write about. It was difficult for them to cover the fighting at the front lines, where news was being made, as they had done in Shanghai and Nanking. Knowing how correspondents gripe when they are idle, I feared to risk the demoralization of inaction. I decided to do something about it.

At the time, the Japanese were making the first of their three costly attempts to conquer the city of Changsha, a strategic station on the only north-south railway between Beijing and Guongzhou. It seemed to me that the heroic stand of the Chinese defenders would seize the imagination of the world, if properly reported. I decided to go to Changsha personally and set up facilities. I agreed to take a party of correspondents with me.

At Changsha, General Hsueh Yueh received the correspondents and gave them an uncensored briefing on the fighting. The correspondents at last had a story that they could get their teeth into. They learned that Chinese soldiers could give good account of themselves, even when opposed by the best troops of the enemy. General Hsueh's frank, likeable personality made a real hit with the correspondents.

Against the General's advice, the correspondents decided that they wanted to see some actual fighting. Lacking other transportation, we hiked. After three days of continuous walking over the difficult terrain, broken only by occasional lifts in sedan chairs, some of my companions were ready to quit. It was a matter of considerable pride to me that, although I was almost twice the age of most of the correspondents, I endured the hardship better than they.

One particularly miserable night, we had run into a rain and were plodding through a mountainous region. We could hear wolves howling in the distance. We finally reached a farmhouse, and finding my charges scattered, I shouted in the darkness for them to assemble at that place. After a meager meal of rice, we spent a wretched night, trying to sleep in our wet clothes on the mud floor of the farmhouse.

The correspondents decided that the trip was too hazardous and they turned back. However, they were able to report that the Japanese had suffered a major setback. The Japanese troops, who had first advanced fifty miles toward Changsha, were forced to fall back to a point even behind their takeoff point. Their losses had been crushing. When this news reached the world, many Westerners who despaired China's cause, regained confidence.

One truth was brought home to me by this experience. I realized that foreign correspondents, not speaking Chinese and unaccustomed to adapting themselves to primitive Chinese village conditions, could not safely visit outlying battlefronts without an escort. They were likely to be caught between the lines, and unable to converse, to be in acute danger. In later years, I came in for some criticism because I did not allow foreign correspondents to cover the fighting fronts as they were accustomed to do in Europe. While it was difficult to convince self-confident reporters that they were incapable of solo coverage of China fighting, my refusal was grounded in painful experience with the western correspondents.

Our first two years in Chungking were a nightmare of savage Japanese bombings, whenever the weather permitted. The bombings during the summer of 1940 were perhaps the hardest to endure. Our International Department fared much better than other offices. During the first year, we had built a press hostel, just across a narrow alley from our office building. The hostel housed the foreign correspondents and gave them easy access to information, censorship and telegraphic facilities. During the first of the heavy bombings of 1940, the enemy hit nothing squarely in our compound except the kitchens. Later, however, our luck ran out.

One day, a raid made a direct hit and partially destroyed my office buildings, together with our library. My own house, which was built under the roof of the five- cornered pavilion, was shaken to its foundation, although it was not destroyed.

On another occasion, when an air raid alarm sounded late in the evening, we drove to the Chialing River for safety and crawled into a dugout along the riverbank and near the water edge. On the slippery, muddy floor of the dugout, I lost my foot hold and slid rapidly down towards the river. At the last moment, I succeeded in breaking my slide, and was saved.

Apparently the Japanese had gotten our range after the heavy bombings of June 28, 1940. For a protracted period, we experienced a daily ration of half a dozen bombs. It became increasingly difficult for us to carry on our work. We spent a long time in dugouts. We were without telephone service for over a month, and our water supply was unpredictable. But the health of our staff, under these trying and dangerous conditions, held up wonderfully. We did not halt our work, our daily releases went out. We even launched an additional project, a monthly magazine, *China at War*, which at first was printed in Hong Kong and forwarded to the United States for distribution.

If the Japanese thought that they could crush our morale, they were about to have a rude awakening. There is an innate heroism in men and women, which only reveals itself in supreme moments of crisis. They tap some hidden spring of unsuspected strength. The hardships which we endured during the three summers of the bombings merely hardened our will to resist. The question on everyone's lips in Chungking was not whether we could hold out, but whether the enemy could keep up the strain of the offensive. The Japanese had spread out too thinly over the occupied regions; the fine edge of their initial offensive had become blunted. They were learning the sad lesson which other would-be conquerors had learned before them – a united China was virtually unconquerable.

An intercepted Japanese announcement in July 1940, claiming that they had razed the International Department to the ground, revealed to us that we had become a major target for the raiders. We were glad to learn it; because it disclosed that our publicity work overseas was really hurting the Japanese and they considered it a prime war target to put us out of business. Stepping up the rate of their bombings, the Japanese in August began to stage moonlight raids. These raids, on an average, lasted three hours. We had to stay in the dugouts longer. Fortunately, none of my colleagues broke under the strain.

During the early hours of August 3, a near-hit almost wrecked the house of Tillman and Peggy Durdin. They had the famous Edgar Snow as their houseguest. Snow, a brilliant writer, was the man who first introduced Mao Tse-dong to Western readers through his widely read book describing the communist's 10-month trek from Kiangsi to Yenan. His bias was consistently in favor of the Chinese Communists. Despite the sharp divergence of our political views, we had maintained friendly relations ever since I had first met him, while I was the censor in Shanghai and he was a correspondent. He was the first of a long procession of big name writers who began to appear in Chungking to write books and magazine articles about the dramatic Chinese stand.

In 1941, the Japanese tried out some new techniques in order to make the Chungking bombings more unendurable. They were called 'attrition raids.' The bombings lasted even longer so as to induce the maximum in physical suffering and nervous exhaustion. But the determination of the defenders was so unshakable, that these torturous raids had no more effect than their predecessors.

Our compound had one bad day on May 28, 1941; five bombs fell near the entrance of our dugout. Miraculously, none of them exploded; all of them landed in a wet paddy field. But another bomb struck the kitchen and killed two of our faithful servants who had not gone to the dugout.

Madame Chiang Kai-shek made a visit to our compound shortly before dusk to view the damage and to make certain that those who had lost heavily were being provided for. During the worst of the raids, she was unfailing in her care for the sufferers.

On July 5, 6, and 7, 1941, we were the target of three successive days of bombings. The damage was devastating. The radio studio, which had been hit before and repaired, was demolished by a direct hit. Next day, two other offices, the annex to the press hotel and the dining room, were completely destroyed. My own house was damaged during the three days, and when I emerged from the dugout on the final day, I found one of the walls of my house entirely gone.

The next day was Sunday. Frank Price of the Nanking Theological Seminary dropped in to accompany us to church. We invited him to breakfast in the ruined house, although we had hastily to send out to procure the food. While waiting for the meal, we heard a terrific crash. My wife ran from the house while Price quickly slid under a bed. Fortunately a cupboard held the roof and saved me from being buried alive. After this experience, my wife readily moved to the mat shed.

Throughout all the hardships and dangers which I endured in these early Chungking days, the presence of my brave wife beside me was a sustaining strength. Through out the worst of the bombings, her spirit never faltered. There was one period that summer when the bombings were so continuous that we had to spend from ten to fifteen hours in the dugout. It was difficult to work under these inhuman conditions, but we managed to carry on.

Late that summer, the press hotel was completely destroyed. The correspondents were forced to move to Chialing House, the government guesthouse for distinguished visitors, or to find shelter in private homes. This made contact with our offices difficult, so we erected a large mat shed on our grounds, as a temporary expedient for the correspondents.

All in all, the Japanese in the third summer of intensified raids dropped more than 10,000 bombs. They admitted the use of 1,000 planes for 150 consecutive hours. The drain on their resources was tremendous, but all this effort proved not enough. At the end of the third year, Chungking still stood firm. Our heads were bloody, but unbowed.

This was to be the last summer of the blitz. The enemy recognized his failure and turned to other adventures. By December 7, 1941 a Japanese attack on Pearl Harbor had happened, and the Japanese were too busy with their war against the United States and the British to resume their costly Chungking raids. For the rest of the war, Chungking was safe.

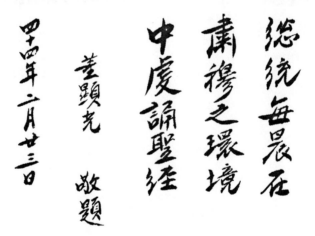

Photo 1. President Chiang Kai-shek reads the bible.

The note below the photo was handwritten by Hollington K. Tong. It says that President Chiang reads the Bible every morning with reverence. Tong affixed his signature and seal to the note dated February 23, 1955. (Photo credit: All photos in this book are from personal collection of Mei-li Tong.)

Photo 2. President Chiang Kai-shek gives a gift to Hollington Tong

From left: President Chiang, Madame Chiang, and Hollington Tong

Photo 3. Sally and Holly Tong when he was at the age of 70.
(Hollington was well-known as Holly among his friends.)

Photo 4. A reception for Madame Chiang at the Chinese Embassy
in Washington, DC, 1958.

From left: Madame Chiang, Mrs. Walter Robertson, Hollington Tong and
Walter Robertson, Assistant Secretary of State for Far East Affairs.

Photo 5. Madame and President Chiang in a garden in Taiwan, 1959.

Photo 6. Hollington K. Tong with Premier Chiang Ching-kuo (Right),
1956.

Premier Chiang Ching-kuo carried out ten major construction projects
in 1960s, which boosted economic growth in Taiwan. He often
visited common people, and brought in many native Taiwanese to the
government. People liked him and elected him to be the President of the
Republic of China after the passing of Chiang Kai-shek in 1974. He was
son of Chiang Kai-shek.

Photo 7. Wedding photo of Mrs. and Dr. Sun Yat-sen, 1915.

Dr. Sun Yat-sen was the founder of the Republic of China in 1911.
Chiang Kai-shek was Dr. Sun's right-hand man and a faithful follower
of his democratic ideas. Hollington Tong also worked for Dr. Sun as a
journalist in 1913. Mrs. Sun was a sister of Madame Chiang.

Chapter Eleven.
The World Comes to Chungking

As long as Russia had feared Japanese aggression against her, she had encouraged and even aided China. Japan was Russia's historic enemy, and was always a potential military threat against Russia's sprawling Siberian provinces. Hence, the Moscow policy, from 1937 to 1939, had been to keep Japan so occupied in China that it had no offensive strength to hurl against Siberia.

With this in mind, Russia had aided China materially during the early stage of our struggle against Japanese aggression since July 7, 1937. After the signing of the Sino-Russian Non-Aggression Pact on August 21, 1937, Russia actually loaned China $50 million (U.S.). Thanks to this loan, China had been able to equip ten divisions with Russian arms. Stalin also supplied badly needed planes to China, and maintained five wings of Russian aircraft in China, manned by trained Russian personnel. He also supplied Russian military advisers to Chungking, the most notable being Georgi Zhukov, later the celebrated Russian Marshal in World War II.

Russia also immobilized the Chinese Communists. Under Russian pressure, they had temporarily abandoned their rebellion and had placed their Red Army under the Generalissimo's command. As long as Russia was anti-Japanese, the Chinese Communists fought effectively against the Japanese invaders in the northern areas which Chiang Kai-shek had assigned to them.

Soviet Russia, which had hitherto been the target of Hitler's and Mussolini's Anti-Communist Pact, suddenly joined her enemies. By the Hitler-Stalin Pact of August 23, 1939, Russia turned her back upon the democracies and became a virtual ally of Hitler. Since Germany and Italy had a close understanding with Japan, Russia could now depend upon Germany's good offices to restrain Japan from action against her. It no longer needed China. The Russian advisers and fliers were called home. Russian supplies to Chungking ended. Taking the cue from Stalin, the Chinese Communists now turned from guerilla attacks on the Japanese to territorial seizures in North China at the expense of Chungking. Our situation, bad as it had been before, now became worse.

On September 15, 1939, Russia and Japan, which had been engaged in border hostilities in both Manchuria and Mongolia since 1938, signed an armistice in Moscow and appointed a border commission. In addition, the signing of the Russia-Japan Pact of 1941, the Japanese were emboldened to withdraw their crack Kwantung (East of the Great War) Army from Manchuria, where it had been used as a shield against the Russians. This released 100,000 fresh Japanese troops to be thrown against China. The Chinese Communists' depredations against the Nationalist government in the North became so widespread that Chiang was forced to deploy some of his already inadequate forces from the front lines and send them north to prevent the communists from occupying Central China.

To make matters worse, the British, fearful of involvement with Japan while fighting against Germany for survival in Europe, appeased Japan at China's expense by closing the Burma Road in July 1940. This road, built through almost superhuman efforts, had become China's main source of supplies from the outside world, after Japan had shut off the whole coast. When Britain closed the road, Chungking had no other link with the outside world save by air.

This was the disheartening international background of China's resistance during the bitter period between 1939 and 1941. Literally, China was hanging on by her fingernails with her extraordinary resolve.

I was especially concerned during this period with the tendency of many correspondents who were covering the war to remain in the comfort of Shanghai or Hong Kong, instead of coming to Chungking. In Shanghai their principal news sources were the Japanese, while in Hong Kong, the British were maintaining an attitude of neutrality which actually worked in Japan's favor.

I had no other choice but to visit both cities and to establish channels through which more news favorable to China could reach the outside world. In January 1939, after we had moved to Chungking, I paid a secret visit to Shanghai. To avoid capture by the enemy, I disguised myself as a farmer and entered Shanghai unquestioned on a British ship sailing from Hong Kong. I found the Chinese who enjoyed the security of the International

Settlement and the French Concession still staunchly supported the central government. I was happy to see Chinese and Kuomintang flags displayed openly. I also found more support in the foreign colony for China than hitherto. On a previous trip in 1938, I had set up a secret informational and contact office in Shanghai, right under the noses of the Japanese. This office was manned by two brave people – John B. Peniston, a former Park College classmate and a newspaperman who had worked under me on the *China Press*, and Mrs. S. T. Chu. Although Mrs. Chu was imprisoned and questioned by the Japanese for five days in the Shanghai Japanese torture chamber known as the Bridge House, she had allayed their suspicions and been released.

I now set up another information office in Hong Kong, this under the direction of Z. B. Toong, F. L. Pratt and Jimmy Wei, all highly trusted colleagues. Through the Hong Kong office, we were able to maintain helpful relations with the correspondents and news services and to get our point of view into the foreign press. The Hong Kong office was a beehive of activity until the Japanese conquered the city after the attack on Pearl Harbor in December 1941.

In Shanghai, I tried to persuade Sir Archibald Clark Kerr, the British Ambassador, to move the British Embassy to Chungking. He showed no interest in the suggestion, but later the Japanese turned Shanghai into a virtual war base, and the British found it advisable to come to Chungking.

I did not get out of Shanghai without having a nerve-wracking narrow escape. I telephoned Hallet Abend, correspondent for the *New York Times*, for an appointment. He replied hesitantly and asked me to come an hour later. When I saw him, he informed me to my dismay that the admiral commanding the Japanese naval forces at Shanghai had been with him when I had called. When I left Abend's office, I encountered a Japanese acquaintance, Mr. Horiguchi, a graduate of the Missouri Journalism School, who was the assistant editor of *Domei*, the Japanese news service. I knew Horiguchi as a ruthless man, who would not have hesitated to send me to my death. Fortunately, he brushed past me without looking. Upon such narrow threads does life depend in time of war.

I was still not safe. I succeeded in boarding a British ship for Hong Kong without questioning. But at Shanghai's suburb of Woosung, the ship was stopped by the Japanese who boarded it and remained for an hour talking to the ship's officers. I was in a state of acute nervous apprehension during this seemingly endless hour.

At Hong Kong, I encountered a difficult problem for China. Strange as it may seem, there was an influential body of opinion in Great Britain, which questioned whether Chinese victory in the struggle against Japan would be in Britain's interest. Hong Kong, a Crown colony, reflected this sentiment in varying degrees. The censorship office in Hong Kong was pursuing a policy of such strained neutrality that it did not even permit the use of terms "enemy" or "puppet" in newspapers when referring to Japanese aggression.

Such restraints would not have been important if the British had been equally severe in censoring the pro-Japanese press. They were not. In Hong Kong, there were five daily newspapers which were controlled by the Japanese and their agents. There was also a large Japanese propaganda, designed to undermine Chinese morale and spread defeatism. The Hong Kong censorship office handled these pro-Japanese papers with kid gloves.

Realizing that we needed a man in Hong Kong of first-rate ability, I appointed Dr. Wen Yuan-ning to head our Hong Kong office. Dr. Wen had been editor of the magazine *Tien Hsia*, and had been one of the active members of the original Anti-Enemy Committee in Shanghai. He was particularly skillful in getting along with the British. Dr. Wen quickly improved our relations with the Hong Kong authorities. His office also served as the distributing point for our informational material to our overseas offices until December 1941 when Hong Kong was occupied by Japanese.

Of course, our big propaganda target during these pre-Pearl Harbor years was the United States. Here the Japanese had set up an extensive and costly propaganda operation, which tried to buy out American magazines' opinion. This was done by the widespread distribution of elaborately printed pro-Japanese booklets, the constant exploitation of the anti-Communist stand which appealed to many Americans, and the unsparing use of bribing funds. Our American operations, although conducted upon a shoestring, were guided by a better understanding of the American mentality than was exhibited by the heavy-handed Japanese. They soon began to yield rich results.

We set up an office in New York to coordinate all pro-Chinese activities, at first under Earl Leaf, former United Press correspondent, and later under Dr. C. L. Hsia. In our initial American activities, we received help from H. J. Timperley, who had been working with me ever since the days of the Shanghai Anti-Enemy Committee. I used Timperley to survey public opinion in both Great Britain and the United States, and to aid in setting up our propaganda effort in both countries. He never failed me. Simultaneously, we set up an office in London, which soon established ties with important British individuals and groups.

Meanwhile, in Chungking, I was rounding out an organization of both Chinese and Americans who were capable of conducting a worldwide propaganda operation. My Chinese staff members were placed under the able direction of H. P. Tseng. In 1938, I engaged W. A. Farmer, an Australian newspaperman, as our English editor. Under Farmer's direction, we launched a monthly slick-paper magazine, *China at War*. This was an illustrated history of the war in China, rich with human interest stories. It was circulated through our offices in both England and the United States. When Farmer left us to join the *China Press* in Shanghai, I engaged Maurice Votaw, dean of the St. John's University School of Journalism in Shanghai. Two brilliant younger men also joined my staff: Theodore H. White and Melville Jacoby. White was later to join the China staff of *Time*, and he went on to become a best-selling author in America. Jacoby unfortunately was killed in the war.

The Pearl Harbor date found us with an able team, both in Chungking, and at our various offices overseas. All this I was able to do on a budget of $5,000 a month. In contrast to this, reliable estimates of Japanese public opinion expenditures in the United States alone aggregated over $250,000 a month.

During 1937 to 1941, I was fully occupied with this tremendous propaganda task. I felt like a man who had been caught up by the great winds of history, and was moving with those winds toward whatever destiny lay ahead for my country. But we lived each day to its limit of effort. As I look back, I realize that never before or since have I lived more intensively, or more enjoyably than during this dangerous interlude.

While we were extending our propaganda reach throughout the English-speaking world, the representatives of major magazines and newspapers were beginning to come to Chungking to report China's side of the war. My time was increasingly taken up in their reception and assistance.

Our visitors included James R. Young, a correspondent of the *International News Service*. Young had been given permission by the Japanese to visit Japanese-occupied China. Instead, he chose to come to Free China. He arrived in the fall of 1939, just after we had passed through a summer of harrowing air raids. Young wrote twenty widely quoted articles on what he saw in Free China. His outspoken reporting had an eye-opening effect upon American readers who had concluded that China had lost the war.

There was a sad aftermath to Young's visit. When he returned to Tokyo, he was placed under arrest by the Japanese police who accused him, under the Army Code, of sending thirty-eight "extremely slanderous news items" concerning the Japanese forces in China, and of spreading false rumors in the Imperial Hotel. Young was kept as a prisoner for sixty-one days, thirty of which were spent in a dark police cell. He then underwent a farcical trial and was sentenced to six months' imprisonment and three years of probation. So intense was the pressure from the American government that he was permitted to leave Japan after his conviction. Back in the United States, he attracted wide attention by his writings and lectures. The Japanese revenge boomeranged unexpectedly against them.

In the fall of 1940, Roy Howard, head of the Scripps-Howard newspaper chain, and of the *United Press*, visited Chungking. Howard had been on a tour of the Orient, accompanied by ten other top American newspapermen. The Japanese were so anxious to have the distinguished publisher getting their side of the war story, that they placed a special plane at his disposal. I persuaded Dr. Wang Chung-hui, Minister of Foreign Affairs, to issue a special invitation to Howard to visit Chungking. Howard came, thus securing a scoop over his fellow travelers.

The Generalissimo had recently announced a policy of granting no more exclusive interviews. But in the case of Howard, an embarrassing situation arose. Together with Dr. H. H. King, Dr. Li Wei-kuo and I, he had breakfast with the Generalissimo the day after his arrival. The talk was very frank and lasted for over an hour. But when Howard asked Chiang if he could report the interview, the answer was "No."

The publisher never did get to Japan on this trip, even though Foreign Minister Matsuoko was his personal friend. When he got back to the United States, he wrote a series of widely-read articles. They did China much good in clarifying the Far East issues.

Later when Arch Gunnison of the *North America Newspaper Alliance* visited Chungking, the Generalissimo reversed his ruling and granted Gunnison an exclusive interview. Gunnison's account was very favorable to China and was carried by 45 important American dailies.

The significant visitors were not all journalists. Mr. Jawaharlal Nehru, an important leader of the Congress Party in India, arrived in Chungking on August 23, 1939. Nehru expressed a desire to improve relations between India, Burma and China. I was detailed by Generalissimo Chiang to look after him. The British confidentially expressed to me that if we and Nehru should arrive at any working agreement to counteract Japanese aggression in both India and Burma, they be kept informed and their views sought.

Nehru visited the Generalissimo and Madame Chiang at their mountain home at Huangshan, across the Yangtse, on August 28, and I was with him. Under the difficult conditions of an air raid they talked about the whole range of Asiatic problems. While Nehru was bathing, reports were received that 54 enemy planes were coming. I asked him to hurry up and have supper before we would go to the dugout. Immediately after the meal the urgent alarm was sounded. Nehru, the Generalissimo, Madame Chiang and I went to the dugout. For three hours they remained in the dugout. I interpreted the conversation.

The Generalissimo's quest for information concerning the kind of organization which the Indian peasants have was the starting point for a lengthy conversation which did not end until 12 p.m. Nehru referred to the refusal of the British government to prevent Indians from becoming independent. Its standing army of 200,000 Indian soldiers was commanded by British officers. He cited an instance how these soldiers could turn against the British. He said:

"A few years ago, when one of their regiments was ordered to fire upon a mob, the regiment refused, and this movement of disobedience was rapidly spread to other regiments. Some of the officers were court-martialed, but this incident showed the temper of Indian soldiers under British control. We are conducting propaganda among them through their relatives, wives, sisters and brothers. These soldiers must return home now and then on leave. During such occasions they have been indoctrinated with the national spirit.

In preparation for the day of independence, students in universities are required to go through a regular course of military training. Other volunteer movements for such training have been promoted. The majority of the peasants have already pledged their support to the National Congress Party because of the individual efforts of Gandhi and me. I know at least 1,000,000 of them. For this reason, I alone am powerful enough to counteract all propaganda efforts of the Indian Communists in capturing the hearts of the peasants."

While waiting for enemy bombings in the dugout, the mountain air at night became chilly. Generalissimo and Madame Chiang each put on their light overcoats. Nehru put on his Indian cloth, and the Generalissimo turned to me and asked whether I needed something heavy to protect against the increasing cold, and being a strong man, I politely declined.

The next morning, the Generalissimo discovered that the guest wore a heavy winter coat. Nehru said that his friends told him China is a cold country so that he did not bring lighter clothing. Madame found a lighter linen long gown belonging to the Generalissimo to give him to wear. Before he left, five long gowns were made; two linen and three silk as gifts for him.

On August 29, 1939, Nehru reminded me that he would like to go to Yenan, the headquarters of the Chinese Communists in Shensi, to see the Indian medical unit at work and to report to his colleagues in India. He wanted to understand what the Communist corner of China was like and what its leaders stood for. He added:

"This seems to me important to a proper understanding of the situation in China. A great deal has been written about it in Europe and America, and the name of the Eighth Route Army is well known. In Europe, they generally consider that Chinese Communists are not real Communism, but would be considered as liberal or radical democracy. I have no information other than these vague reports and I should like to be clearer in my own mind. I think that recent developments in the international sphere indicate that the Communists and the Third Communist International will lose all strength in countries outside Russia, provided of course that a situation does not develop to help them. It is just possible that if I went to Yenan and saw some people there, I might be of some service to China."

Because of the lack of time, however, he did not make the trip to Yenan. During his stay in Chungking Nehru came to my humble home several times to have dinners prepared by Sally, and we became quite intimate. Both Sally and I thought that he would remain a staunch friend of Generalissimo and Madame Chiang, and of Free China.

In the spring of 1940, Sir Stafford Cripps, British Labor Party leader, who was later in both the Churchill and the Atlee cabinets, visited us. So anxious were we to cultivate British goodwill that W. H. Donald made a special trip to Rangoon to meet Sir Stafford and escort him to Chungking. Sir Stafford, a man of austere character, made a real effort to acquaint himself with the tarnished facts about beleaguered China. He displayed a sincere friendship for China's cause and I had an opportunity to discuss with him our problems with the British press, that the London newspapers gave inadequate coverage of Free China. When I explained that only Reuters maintained a Chungking correspondent, he was obviously disturbed. Whether it was his efforts, or by mere coincidence, we began to enjoy more space in the major British dailies after his return to England.

A sign of the changing attitude was the appearance of a *London Times* correspondent in Chungking.

In May 1941, a notable husband-and-wife team came to Chungking. They were the famous publisher of *Time*, *Life* and *Fortune*, Henry R. Luce and his equally famous wife, Clare Boothe Luce. Mr. Luce was the son of a missionary in Shantung Province, China. He always had a ready willingness to help the Chinese people, and his magazines had been supportive of China. Just before coming to China, Mr. and Mrs. Luce had been active in the United China Relief drive in New York.

The Luces were particularly anxious to visit the front and to see for themselves the actual conditions of the fighting. The nearest active front that could be reached by plane was Xian, in the northern province of Shensi. Since no commercial planes were flying, the Luces persuaded the Generalissimo to assign a military plane for their trip. Chiang asked me to accompany them.

It was a thrilling trip. In our first attempt to surmount the mountains which lie between Chungking and the Northwest, we ran into a storm and the pilot found it so difficult to get elevation that he was forced to turn back to Chengtu, the capital city of Szechwan province. After a short stay at Chengtu when the Luces visited the missionaries and invited their point of view on China events, we took off for Xian again. It was a hazardous flight, but the Luces were restricted to a five-day schedule and they were willing to take chances. Narrowly avoiding a crash landing at Xian, we found that we had arrived in the midst of an air raid. We were rushed to a neighboring wheat field and instructed to lie down. We remained in our prone position until the three strafing Japanese planes had disappeared.

The visitors' desire to visit the actual front lines was gratified by a trip to the divisional headquarters, about ten miles from the Yellow River. From there, we had to ride ponies to the Yellow River front. From this front, it was only a few hundred yards to the Japanese lines. Only a few days before, the Japanese had heavily shelled the spot where we stood, and ruins were everywhere. However, we did not encounter any action. The Luces visited the soldiers in the barracks and at their stations, talking to them through interpreters. They were deeply impressed by the Chinese spirit.

Their actual reaction to this difficult China trip was expressed in Mr. Luce's own dispatch to his office. He said in part:

"Serious battle now develops Yellow River. . . Army of Generalissimo was the best thing for China. Morale was magnificent against appalling difficulties."

During the Luces' visit, I was the unwitting agent in advancing the career of a man who was later to become a damaging enemy of the Chiang Kai-shek leadership in China. My staff member, Theodore H. White, met the Luces and succeeded in ingratiating himself with them. Not wanting to stand in the way of his advancement, I spoke highly of White to Mr. Luce. When they left, White accompanied them, and shortly afterwards materialized as a *Time* reporter.

However, when the vicious foreign smearing campaign against the Generalissimo began, Theodore H. White became one of its promoters. In 1945, in collaboration with Anna Lee Jacoby, widow of another of my staff members, White wrote, "*Thunder over China*," a bitter and one-sided 'expose' of the Chinese government. The book was distributed by the Book of the Month Club in New York and had an immense sale. It had a poisonous effect upon American public opinion when American post-war policies toward China were being worked out. White was a brilliant writer, but his mind had an unwavering left-wing slant.

Another visitor in 1941 was Ralph M. Ingersoll, from the left-slanted *New York P.M.* Ingersoll revealed none of his critical attitudes while with us. I arranged an interview for him with the Generalissimo. I recalled that he made the flat prediction that America's showdown with Japan would come in three or four months. History confirmed his forecast with uncanny accuracy. It is not often that a newspaperman is willing to risk his reputation by such frank speech, but we all found Mr. Ingersoll's personality refreshing.

The Japanese were not happy at the news of the distinguished visitors who were making the long journey to Chungking. Their dismay reached its height in October 1941 when the United States sent a military mission to China headed by Brigader General John Magruder. This act by Washington was the most overt act of friendship for China, which the Roosevelt administration had yet taken.

I flew to Hong Kong to meet Gen. Magruder and his party. I arranged a much publicized function in Hong Kong to receive the visitors. At this function, Gen. Magruder delivered a public address which made no concealment of his serious intention to help the Chungking government. Gen. Magruder came when our military resources were almost touching bottom. The Japanese were making preparations for a second assault on Changsa and we seriously doubted if we could withstand them. Magruder gave off-the-record assurances to the Generalissimo, which encouraged us to go on.

So many correspondents had now collected in Chungking that I was under continuous pressure to arrange interviews with Chiang. On November 7, 1941, I arranged a mass news conference of 23 visiting reporters with Chiang. The news conference was the Generalissimo's first open meeting with correspondents since the beginning of the war. Madame Chiang served as the interpreter. An aggregate of no less than 10,000 words was filed by correspondents after the news conference.

Shortly after this, I gave a dinner for correspondents. I talked to them in a friendly vein, deploring the fact that some correspondents were unwittingly giving China a bad name overseas by emphasizing the friction between the Government and the Chinese Communists and predicting a resumption of a civil war. I recalled that the only correspondent present who seemed offended at my words was Vincent Sheean, the noted author of *"Personal Story."* Later, to my dismay, Sheean wrote a damaging series of articles in the *New York Herald Tribune* charging that democratic processes in China had been suspended by the "dictatorship of the general." He also directed innuendoes against Chiang Kai-shek. It was a malicious series, and set the tone for much of the slanderous reports, which were later to fill American newspapers and magazines.

I came in contact with the Communist problem in another form in the dark months just preceding Pearl Harbor. In early February 1941, the Generalissimo asked me to go to Hong Kong to meet Launchlin Currie, who was then a White House administrative assistant to President Roosevelt. He was accompanied by a Harvard graduate, Emile Despres.

When we reached Chungking, Currie explained the objective of his visit to the Generalissimo. He had been asked by T. V. Soong in Washington to come to China and make an on-the-spot study of the Chinese economy. President Roosevelt, he said, had approved the trip.

During his interview he gave the Generalissimo what he claimed was a verbal message from the President concerning China's Communist problem. He said he had recorded the Roosevelt message verbatim. It was:

"It appears at 10,000 miles away that the Chinese Communists are what in our country we would call socialists. We like their attitude toward the peasants, toward women, and towards Japan. It seems to me that these so-called communists and the Nationalist government have more in common than they have differences. We hope they can work out their differences and work more closely together in the interest of the common objective of fighting Japan. When two parties differ in the proportion of say 70 to 80, it is very difficult to find a common ground. If, however, the differences are only in the proportion of, say 40 to 60, it is very much easier to get together."

I interpreted the conversation. The Generalissimo took sharp exception to this opinion, and warned Mr. Currie that the Communists were skilled and unscrupulous liars who had misrepresented the China situation to the world in nearly every aspect. He cautioned against taking their claims at face value since, he said that International Communism controlled the Chinese Communists completely, a fact which foreign commentators did not realize.

Mr. Currie expressed a desire to talk to Chou En-lai and the Soviet ambassador, a request to which the Generalissimo acceded readily. But he cautioned the envoy that the International Communism, which controlled Chinese Communists, would do everything to prevent close cooperation between China and both the United States and Britain. He warned that Currie would find that the Communists would work in cooperation with China's Central Government only so long as China's policies did not conflict with those of the International Communism. When they conflicted, the Chinese Communists would do everything in their power to thwart the government.

In subsequent talks with Chiang, Currie continued to raise the Communist question with almost suspicious insistence. He returned home, but in 1942, after the United States had entered the war, he reappeared in Chungking and again referred to his theme of cooperation with the communists in his confidential talks. I felt that if Currie were a true interpreter of President Roosevelt's mind, the latter must be receiving some extremely untruthful advice about China. It was at that time the idea formed in my mind that communism may have planted men close to the President to mislead him on Asia. In 1941, we had no information that the Institute of Pacific Relations, in which Currie was then an important figure, was already honeycombed with communist sympathizers.

It was through Currie that another incongruous figure was introduced into the China picture. This was Owen Lattimore, an official of the Institute of Pacific Relations. Lattimore's employment came about as a result of a chance remark of the Generalissimo. On February 22, 1941, Chiang asked Currie to invite President Roosevelt to recommend to him an American political adviser who enjoyed the full confidence of the President. Chiang suggested William C. Bullitt, former American ambassador to Russia and later to France. Currie gave three reasons to the Generalissimo why he believed Bullitt would be a miscast.

Shortly afterwards we learned that President Roosevelt, on Currie's recommendation, had appointed Owen Lattimore. I was sent to Hong Kong to greet Latimore and escort him to Chungking. The Generalissimo was surprised to learn that President Roosevelt did not even know Lattimore before he recommended him.

Stanley K. Hornbeck, then in charge of the Far Eastern Division at the State Department, told the strange story of the Lattimore appointment in his testimony before the Senate Judiciary Subcommittee, which filed its report to the Senate on July 2, 1952. In the report the Subcommittee summarized Hornbeck's testimony as follows: (1) Hornbeck, who should normally have been consulted, was told by Currie that it was he (Currie) who had made the recommendation. The request by Hornbeck to reconsider was impossible because the appointment was already an accomplished fact; (2) Currie admitted that he had not even consulted the Secretary of State on the selection; (3) Lattimore left for Chungking in July 1941, in the company of Chi Ch'ao-ting, who had been made the secretary general of the American-British-Chinese Currency Stabilization Fund. The record shows that Lattimore knew that Chi was a Communist. Later, Chi held an important position in Red China.

When Currie was sought by the Senate Internal Security Subcommittee for questioning after the Korean War, he was hiding in Columbia in South America out of reach of the Subcommittee. In its report, Currie was characterized as "a conscious articulate instrument of the Soviet conspiracy." Furthermore, he was identified by Elizabeth Bentley, former chief of the Soviet spy ring in Washington, as one of the government officials who aided her in supplying information to Russian military during the war. Currie was the evil genius who ruined the wartime relationship between China and the United States.

It has been often asked why China's officials were fooled by such men as Launchlin Currie, Owen Lattimore, and others who aided the communists in China during the war years. It must be remembered that these individuals were sent to China by President Roosevelt himself. It would have been ungracious of us to question the good faith of the President. It was not until after the war, and the fall of mainland China, that all the facts about the horrible Institute of Pacific Relations conspiracy became known to the world. Then it was too late to rectify the betrayals.

Chapter Twelve.
My Wartime Overseas Missions

December 7, 1941 was a fateful day for China, as it was for the United States. Although the appalling Pearl Harbor attack ushered in an immediate period of greater hardship for us, it also assured our final victory. We now became allies with the United States and Great Britain. China's war against Japan, so long conducted in lonely despair, now became a theater of the global war with the entrance of the Americans, the great democratic power. The free world's fence-sitting in regard to China was at last ended.

The incredible news of Pearl Harbor reached us in Chungking through Mike Peng, who was in charge of my radio programs. Owing to the sixteen-hour time discrepancy, Mike did not pick it up until 1 a.m., December 8. Disbelieving his ears, he hesitated to report to me. Once he did so, I immediately telephoned the historic news to the Generalissimo. On the same day, December 8, China officially declared war on the Axis powers. On December 9, the Generalissimo sent the following messages to President Roosevelt and Prime Minister Churchill:

"To our new common battle, we offer all we are and all we have,
to stand with you until the Pacific and the world are freed from
brute force and endless perfidy."

Shortly after this declaration, Chungking was the scene of a United Nations conference to reconsider the whole problem of Far Eastern strategy. Sir Archibald Wavell, head of the British Command in India, and Major General George A. Brett, chief of the U.S. Army Air Corps, flew to Chungking to confer with the Generalissimo. Major General John and British General L. E. Denys sat in on these conferences. I acted as interpreter at all sessions, relieved sometimes by Madame Chiang Kai-shek.

While these conferences were taking place, the intensified war was striking my own International Department organization throughout Southeast Asia. The Japanese swarmed south immediately following Pearl Harbor and conquered Hong Kong by Christmas Day of 1941. My two Hong Kong offices, under Dr. Wen Yuan-ning and Z. B. Toong, were in the Crown Colony when it fell, and I feared the worst. Fortunately, both men escaped, although it was two months before Wen reestablished contact, and five months before I learned of the safety of Toong.

My next concern was over our Singapore and Rangoon offices threatened by the onrush of Japanese. On January 19, 1942, I received a message from George Yeh, our Singapore director, asking permission to proceed to Batavia in company with Robert Scott, chief Far East representative of the British Ministry of Information. I gave him this permission and he got out of Singapore just three days before the enemy captured it.

From this point in the war, I found myself called upon to make official trips outside China in furtherance of our relations with our allies. Without attempting to follow chronological order, I will tell the story of these journeys.

The first trip was to India in 1941. I accompanied the Generalissimo and Madame Chiang on a visit to Mahatma Gandhi and the other leaders of the Congress Party in an attempt to induce them, with their great influence over India masses, to support wholeheartedly the British war effort against Japan.

The idea of the trip was not enthusiastically received by the British. India, in February 1942, was in danger of a Japanese invasion. Some nationalist elements in India, headed by Ghose, were actually supporting the Japanese. The Congress Party was then at a low ebb in its long struggle with the British for Indian independence. The Generalissimo feared that the Japanese with their demagogic 'Asia for Asiatics' propaganda would win Gandhi and his followers to their cause. Because he was himself a man of Asia, he felt that he could talk to Gandhi more convincingly than could any Englishman or American.

He made it clear that he was not coming officially, but only in his personal capacity. At his request, the visit was unannounced to the press, the party traveling without passports to keep it secret. The Chiangs had been in India for five days before the outside world knew that they had left Chungking. Our first stop was in Calcutta, then to New Delhi by train.

Pandit Jawaharlal Nehru was Gandhi's first lieutenant. Nehru, returning courtesies for his visit to Chungking three years before, invited the members of the Generalissimo's party to a picnic on the rolling lawn of his home. After the preliminaries were over, Nehru gave us an exhibition of informality by taking off his coat and executing a series of somersaults on the turf. Later, I learned that this somersault act was his public relations stock in trade: he repeated it before all important foreign visitors to emphasize his common touch. I recall that his daughter, who was close to him throughout his political career, registered extreme embarrassment at her father's antics. To demonstrate that our Chinese group was also free spirited, Chang Tao-fan, later President of the Legislative Branch of our Parliament, peeled off his coat and joined the Indian leader in the somersaults. However, Chang was not adept in acrobatics and he could only roll on the lawn.

That evening, we attempted to return the courtesy by inviting the father and the daughter to a Chinese dinner. Pandit Nehru arrived promptly but without his daughter. After we had waited an hour, I telephoned the daughter. Her reply was crisp. She told me, "I am sorry I cannot join your party. I am afraid my father might do his somersault trick again and I just couldn't stand it." I had no reply for this declination.

At Calcutta, we met Mahatma Gandhi. I was the interpreter for about half hour, and then Gandhi told the Generalissimo:

"It is all right for you to have an official interpreter when you see the king or emperor of a foreign state. But I am a humble man and I suggest that Madame Chiang interpret for you. Besides, I like to hear her sweet voice while I listen to the unfolding of your thoughts."

I was excused for the session, which was a welcome respite for me.

There was no doubt that the Generalissimo's coming in the face of danger made a moving impression upon the Indian people. Generalissimo and Madame Chiang received more than 1,000 messages of welcome from Indian political and civic organizations, from high society to common people expressing the Indian point of view.

Realizing the controversial atmosphere in which he found himself, the Generalissimo made no public statements until the final day of his visit. Then, he delivered an address over the All-Indian Radio Station in which he expressed his deep sympathy with the Indian people's struggle for liberty. He suggested that Great Britain grant real political power to the Indian people at the earliest possible date and that the Indians, on the other hand, permit nothing to interfere with their wholehearted support of the struggle against the aggressors.

Unfortunately, stubborn British policies resulted in the jailing of both Gandhi and Nehru within a few months of our visit, but the Generalissimo had made a gesture that he was behind their anti-colonial hopes. He had frustrated the plan of the Japanese to establish a tie with the Congress Party. During the rest of the war, Gandhi was at odds with the British, but unlike his former disciple Ghose, he was never deceived by Japan's Greater East Asia Co-Prosperity rhetoric.

On the return trip from India, the Generalissimo received the unpleasant news that the situation in Burma was becoming more serious. He decided to fly to Lashio in Burma to confer with Generals Wavell and Stilwell, leaving Madame Chiang in Kunming. Lashio was the beginning of the Burma Road which led to Kunming and Chungking to the north. A railway connected Lashio to Rangoon, a major sea port in the south. This was the only land link of China to the Free World. The Generalissimo had asked British General Wavell whether or not any assistance would be needed in Burma from China. Wavell thought assistance would be unnecessary. However, when Rangoon had fallen to Japanese, at Gen. Wavell's request, Chinese assistance was given. But it was too late.

On the day of our arrival in Lashio there was an air raid. The Japanese had apparently received intelligence reports that the Generalissimo was expected. Before the enemy raiders arrived we had a few emotional crises among ourselves. We had arrived at luncheon time. After lunch the Generalissimo customarily took a half hour's nap. After he had gone to his room for a nap, I told my colleagues that I had to go to the city to buy some much needed handkerchiefs. They agreed to stand by. When I came out of the haberdashery, I was astonished to see all of my colleagues also roaming the streets of Lashio. The lure of the city had been so great they had followed me.

I knew there would be trouble, and hurried back. I found the Generalissimo in a rage. He had been left with only his servant who could not speak English. The insistent ringing of the telephone had awakened him. He had answered, but he could not understand the person at the other end of the wire. He had the impression that it was urgent. "You know that Heng Teh and I cannot speak English," the Generalissimo said to me angrily. "You are all thoughtless."

General Shang Chen, the principal military member of the accompanying party, received extreme criticism. We felt as though a bomb had dropped in our midst. But we felt worse when the telephone rang again and we discovered that the call the Generalissimo had answered was to warn us that Japanese bombers were approaching. We had to scramble into a car and get out of town to a safe place before the raiders arrived.

The Generalissimo never mentioned the incident again, and in 1944 General Shang Chen headed the Chinese Military Mission to Washington. The Generalissimo was a forgiving man.

A few weeks later the Generalissimo went again to Burma, accompanied by Madame Chiang. I was again in the party, since I was often needed for interpreting. We flew to Lashio, and motored from Lashio to Maymyo, summer capital of Burma. Two days after our arrival at Maymyo, more than twenty Japanese bombers arrived without warning. The air raid warning system in Maymyo had not been properly installed, nor had any dugouts been built. The Generalissimo and Madame Chiang simply stood quietly in the garden watching the enemy bombers releasing their bombs one by one. One landed only fifty yards from where they stood, but by good fortune, it was a dud.

The next morning we went to Lashio. There the Generalissimo was urged to leave by air immediately for Kunming. The Japanese had a well-organized spy system, and it was feared that even a stopover of a few hours would attract the bombers. The Generalissimo held the military conferences which he had arranged, and we took off, with China's famous pilot, Moon Chin, at the controls.

But apparently we had stayed in Lashio too long. Ten minutes after the takeoff, we received a radio warning that eighteen Japanese pursuit planes, in three squadrons, were in the air, searching for the Generalissimo's plane. There followed an anxious period. There were only four parachutes in the plane for twenty people. Death seemed very near. But one hour later, we were met by a squadron of fighters from Kunming and we were safe.

It was after the Burma trip that China won an objective, which she had been working for since the revolution of 1911. This was the abrogation of the unfair territory treaties with the United States and Britain. The idea that the Western powers should have enclaves of political control within Chinese territory, in the form of the foreign settlements, had tortured the pride of the Chinese people. They were holdovers from the days of the declining Manchu empire. Chiang, before the Japanese attack, was negotiating for their abrogation, but he had encountered a great reluctance, particularly on the part of the British. Now, at the initiative of the United States, China's war allies had decided to make this gesture to show their appreciation of China's wartime contributions. It was a proud day for

China. More than 30,000 people packed the public square in Chungking to celebrate the announcement.

At this time, Madame Chiang, who had been maintaining a killing schedule of work, was incapacitated by a rare nervous ailment which took the form of a painful skin disease known as urticarea. Although the Generalissimo was loath to be separated from her, he realized that she must have better medical care than she could secure in beleaguered Chungking. It was decided that she should go to the United States and the Generalissimo asked me to accompany her. Making the trip with us on the plane was Owen Lattimore, who was concluding his service with the Generalissimo.

We left Chungking under the strictest secrecy and immediately upon our arrival in New York, Madame Chiang entered the Presbyterian Medical Center for examination. Arrangements for her hospitalization were made from Washington by Harry L. Hopkins, President Roosevelt's adviser. Two of America's leading medical specialists, Robert F. Loeb and Aschlen, personally supervised her treatment. From November 1942 to the middle of February 1943, she lived quietly in the hospital, slowly regaining her health.

When the news of Madame Chiang's presence in America became known, great numbers of Americans swamped us with messages and inquiries. In 1942, the Generalissimo and Madame Chiang had strongly gripped the imagination of the American people. They were anxious to honor China's gallant fight against the common enemy by paying tribute to our First Lady. Our mailbag reached 1,000 letters a day. I found it necessary to set up a special secretariat just to handle the letters and phone calls. All Chinese offices in both Washington and New York were swamped.

Such unprecedented interest in China was a challenge to us in the International Department to get China's story across to the American people. Madame Chiang recognized that she could perform a major service to China by accepting some of the speaking invitations to her from every part of the country.

American interest was heightened by her White House visit of a week immediately after leaving the hospital. In Washington she met the press at a joint news conference with President Roosevelt and captivated the capital press newspaper fraternity. She was next invited to deliver successive addresses to the United States Senate and the House of Representatives. In both of these appearances, she proved a brilliant spokeswoman of the Chinese point of view. American goodwill toward China probably reached an all- time high during these action-filled weeks of Madame Chiang's 1942–1943 visit.

American groups friendly to China in the important cities organized public meetings for Madame Chiang. We finally narrowed the list of appearances to Wellesley, where she had been a student in her teen years, New York, Boston, Chicago, San Francisco, Los Angeles, and Ottawa in Canada. For six weeks, she was continuously in the public eye. She held a press conference in each city visited. She had a press party traveling with her on the trains. Her speeches were broadcast over a national radio hookup. Madame Chiang had a truly strenuous schedule for a woman just emerged from a hospital. But she stood up magnificently under the strain. The tour ended in April with Madame Chiang in a state of exhaustion. She rested at Bear Mountain while I busied myself with Ministry of Information tasks in New York and Washington. Finally, on July 2, 1943, we took off from Miami and flew back to China.

The Generalissimo had expected me to return to Chungking after his wife's arrival in New York, but when he sent for me, Madame Chiang replied, without my knowledge, that she would release me if he would send her as a replacement an official of equal rank and capability. Interpreting this as her unwillingness to relinquish me, the Generalissimo gave me permission to remain in America until her return, which stretched out into a period of seven months.

After Madame Chiang's great speeches before Congress, Dr. Wei Tao-ming, the Chinese ambassador to the United States, gave a reception at his residence. Among the guests was Claire Booth Luce. In the course of the reception, she took me aside and whispered:

"Holly, do use your influence to induce Madame Chiang to conclude her visit and return to China in a week or ten days. She has reached the pinnacle as an orator. She has captivated the country as a great Chinese woman. If she remains to deliver further speeches, they will be an anti-climax to what she has done. If she returns now to China, the favorable impression which she has made will persist."

I thought over Mrs. Luce's advice for several days before conveying it to Madame Chiang. When I told her, Madame Chiang agreed instantly.

"Of course, Mrs. Luce is right," she said. "But I have already consented to address several audiences. I cannot get out of these commitments without risking bad feeling."

She proceeded with her tour, and after her Wellesley speech, which found me ill; I accompanied Madame Chiang's party from city to city. But there was little that I could do, aside from a few assignments.

While we were visiting in San Francisco, the Press Club announced that it wished to bestow an award, and I was delegated to accept it on behalf of Madame Chiang. The club had a quaint custom of placing a black cat on the table for the speaker to touch as a sign that he had no fear that anything he said would be quoted outside. I enjoyed the informal club atmosphere.

Minister Liu Kai, my principal staff member, Dr. Yu Ming, and I decided to visit a night club, "The Forbidden City." The club was less daring than the name implied. We had intended to visit the club incognito. Unfortunately one of the Press Club members was also at there and passed on the information about our presence to the Master of Ceremonies.

During the introduction of distinguished guests, to our dismay he announced us, explaining that we were members of Madame Chiang's party. For fear that someone might inform her that we had been in such a questionable place, I volunteered the information to her the next morning that we had been to the nightclub and that the name of the club was more menacing than it had really been. She laughed heartily. Later, some busybodies told her that we had been in the Forbidden City, and she told them that she had known the fact from me direct.

Between my services for Madame Chiang, I had been able to direct my overseas offices and the home office at Chungking from the China News Service in New York.

On our way back, Madame Chiang and her staff members nearly became Japanese prisoners. Our plane, after taking off from Karachi, lost radio contact and was flying to Burma under Japanese occupation. A strange signal lulled us on. Our pilot discovered the wrong direction and turned back in time.

Back in China, I had hardly gotten myself resettled in Chungking when I was again called upon to undertake an overseas mission with the Generalissimo and Madame Chiang. It was to Cairo, Egypt, to interpret for the Generalissimo at the historic Cairo meeting with President Roosevelt and Prime Minister Churchill.

The Cairo conference was the only one of the three major wartime summit meetings in which Generalissimo Chiang participated. He was left out of the two subsequent meetings, Teheran and Yalta, through the objections of Marshal Stalin who was not yet technically at war with Japan. Chiang left Cairo with a pledge of territorial integrity for China in the post-war settlement, which his allies dishonored when they met with Stalin later. But at Cairo all was goodwill.

The first meeting of the Chiangs with Winston Churchill was characteristic. In his blunt fashion, Churchill greeted Madame Chiang with three words:

"Well, Madame, I suppose you think I am a scoundrel, a blackguard, and an imperialist, out to grab more colonies and unwilling to part with what we have."

Madame Chiang parried him:

"Why are you so sure of what I think of you?" she asked. Churchill was silent.

President Roosevelt had been host to Madame Chiang in the White House only a few months before, but it was his first meeting with the Generalissimo. Madame Chiang acted as intermediary in all their conversations.

We were only in Cairo four days. I held daily conferences with the American and British press during the visit, giving them background material. The press was preparing its copy and there was a gentlemen's understanding that the official statement issued by the Big Three would not be released in Cairo but would be distributed simultaneously in Washington, in London, and in Chungking.

To my dismay, London had violated the agreement and had released the news in advance of Chungking. I was subjected to harsh words from the correspondents at the press hostel who charged that I had discriminated against them. Later this incident had unpleasant repercussions with my Chungking staff. The North American Newspaper Alliance carried a story from London stating that the leak had occurred through the bad faith of a Chinese newspaperman attached to the Chinese mission who had transmitted the story to Reuter's News Agency in Lisbon, Portugal. The finger pointed to Tommy Chao who had been the Reuter's correspondent in China for ten years. I was indignant over the allegations, but received reassurances of their confidence from both Brendan Bracken in London and Elmer Davis in Washington, my two opposite numbers.

I did not accompany Madame Chiang on her second trip for medical treatment. She left in the summer of 1944, going first to Brazil where she hoped that the warm climate would help her. Later, she decided to return to New York where she could have the attention of the doctors who had formerly cared for her. She lived quietly in New York, seeing few people, and was in the United States when the end of the war came in 1945.

Chapter Thirteen.
Our Propaganda Achievement

Our persistent problem throughout the war was to break through the hard wall of apathy among Western peoples in regard to China. As the focus swung to other fronts, news interest in our struggle in Chungking sagged. It was necessary for our International Department, with its limited resources, to keep China's struggle alive in the minds of our allies.

For this work our top team consisted of (1) H. P. Tseng, who headed the China operations in Chungking; (2) Dr. C. L. Hsia, in charge of North American activities with his office in New York; and (3) Dr. Wen Yuanning, who headed up European operations with his office in London. As Vice-Minister of Information, I was in charge of the whole operation.

Wen, an Oxford graduate and an extremely perceptive man, sent me reports documenting the misinformation about China which prevailed among Europeans. One of the stories which he told was of his visit to a geography class in a school in Birmingham, England. Remember this was in 1944, after beleaguered China had been in the headlines for years. He asked a seven-year-old to tell him the capital of China. After much thought, the child replied "Japan."

Why was China so misunderstood? I concluded that it was largely our own fault. We Chinese had never seriously felt the need to explain China to the Western world. In an age of organized and streamlined propaganda, China had neglected to tell its story. In contrast to China, nations like Japan were conducting elaborate and heavily financed global propaganda activities. We in China had been too preoccupied with war and our task of building a viable republican government to recognize the importance of communicating our activities to the outside world.

War had at last opened our eyes to this need, but even when we understood propaganda, we did it on a shoestring. The United States Information Service (USIS, the opposite number of our China International Department) set up a Chungking branch. By the end of the war, the Chungking USIS office employed a total of 150 persons, both American and Chinese. It was six times the size of our own New York office; our own main office in Chungking never had more than 100 staff members.

During my visit to the United States in 1942–1943, I found the British Ministry of Information spread over several floors of the RCA Building in New York, with 300 employees. Our own office, in the same building, occupied only eight small rooms and a staff of 12 persons.

Besides having little money to work with, inexperienced personnel were a constant problem in setting up our work both in China and abroad. I could count on my two hands the Chinese trained in English language press or publicity work. I drew persons from widely divergent fields, and sent them out to sink or swim by themselves. It is a source of great pride for me that most of them swam, and swam expertly before the war was over.

Dr. Wen, who started our Hong Kong office, had been the editor of a monthly magazine for the intelligentsia before the war. Dr. C. H. Lowe took over the work in Rangoon and later was stationed in Calcutta. He had spent his professional life as a YMCA secretary. Dr. George Yeh, who was Minister of Foreign Affairs, and later ambassador to the United States, headed my Singapore office, then our London office. Dr. C. L. Hsia, who organized and headed the largest of our overseas offices, the one in North America with its five branches, had been a college president and a specialist in international law. None of these colleagues of mine who took charge of our overseas offices had ever been in newspaper, radio, or publicity work of any kind. What they lacked in know-how, they made up in devotion and loyalty.

Hsia's development of the work in America was outstanding. In the early days of the war, I leaned heavily upon two news-trained foreigners for overseas work, namely, H. J. Timperley and Earl Leaf. Timperley, an Australian who had been a correspondent of the *Manchester Guardian* in China, was the only foreigner who joined our anti-enemy committee formed at the beginning of the war in Shanghai. That, of course, was a purely voluntary assignment.

Timperley's suggestions, based on long newspaper experience and on an understanding of the press both in Britain and in the United States, were extremely valuable, and I soon approached him with a request that he join our organization as a regular staff member. I knew that his interest in our work was due to a sincere belief in the rightness of our cause, and I felt we could have no better advisor in our overseas publicity. Timperley agreed to work for us. He first went to America and then to England. In America, he set up a small office in New York and placed Earl Leaf, a United Press correspondent in China, in charge. In London he enlisted the help of Dr. Hsia who was then connected with the Chinese Foreign Office. Timperley did an excellent job for us as roving troubleshooter.

In the spring of 1941, both Timperley and Hsia came to Chungking. Hsia traveled together with Dr. Quo Tai-chi, who had just been appointed Foreign Minister. Hsia had been serving in an advisory capacity to Earl Leaf in New York and had also advised the small information office, the Trans-Pacific News Service. Timperley and I agreed that such an office needed a Chinese at its head, with authority to issue statements on behalf of the Chinese government. Dr. C. L. Hsia was obviously the man. He accepted the appointment and made a fine record, following the line, which Elmer Davis later made famous, that the truth was the best propaganda.

My later experience with Timperley was unhappy. Apparently his early work with our office had given him an exaggerated opinion of his importance. When he learned, in early 1941, that W. H. Donald, the intimate adviser to Generalissimo and Madame Chiang Kai-shek was retiring from his post as counselor, he wrote to Madame Chiang applying for the position. His letter was a curious document, setting as a condition of his employment that a government motor car and a launch be put at his service. His motive, he said, was to help China and to lighten her burdens. Madame Chiang declined his offer, and suggested that, in view of his past experience, he would be most useful working with my office, either in Chungking or abroad.

After this episode, Timperley was a changed man. Our relations became increasingly unpleasant. Shortly after this rebuff, he lost interest in the China problem and went to Australia.

However, in justice to Temperley, I should point out that his exit was not as discreditable as that of another westerner, Bronson Rea, who was a colleague of W. H. Donald. Rea, an American, who had been publisher of the *Far Eastern Review*, was invited in 1916 to work with me in my attempt to prevent Japanese Baron Shibusawa from obtaining a foreign loan to develop Manchuria. He gave good service to China. But later, he changed sides and became a propagandist for Japan. When I asked him why he had done this, he replied, "I am like a lawyer, and am now hired by Japan to defend her case before the world."

Within two weeks after Dr. Hsia's arrival in New York in September 1941, he reorganized the old Trans-Pacific News Service into the Chinese News Service, which he registered with the Department of State as the Official Chinese government news agency. Shortly afterwards, he opened a Chicago branch under the direction of Henry Evans, a publicist and speaker for China who had been working with the China relief groups. Later, we opened a San Francisco office, placing at its head Malcolm Rossholt, former newspaperman who had worked for the *China Press*.

When the Japanese made their sneak attack on Pearl Harbor, December 7, 1941, Dr. Hsia was activating the Western Coast office. Had it not been for his expert and energetic handling of our American office, we would have been ill-prepared for the crushing publicity tasks which were to come after the war began.

Evans and Rossholt joined the American armed forces after Pearl Harbor and we had to find Chinese replacements. Meanwhile, we had opened three more offices in Washington, Montreal and Mexico City.

We made several excellent additions to our staff in the United States. One of the most satisfactory was George Kao, a journalism school graduate who had been a correspondent for the *China Press*. Together with Jean Lyon, an American newspaperwoman who joined us after Pearl Harbor, Kao was soon handling all the press work in the New York office. Later, when we started the magazine, *China at War*, Kao became the editor. His record was outstanding.

We also engaged Lin Lin, an economist who, although lacking in journalistic experience, was extremely helpful to the office in various ways. For one thing, he possessed a photographic memory. When Lin was transferred from New York to the directorship of the Mexico City office, he was replaced by quiet, scholarly H. T. Chu, who made an excellent information officer.

Dr. Lin Mousheng, who had studied both philosophy and political science, had been with us since the Trans-Pacific News Service days. He was an official of the United States. He was assigned the task of putting out a fortnightly bulletin of Chinese opinion called *Contemporary China*. He started the publication in the spring of 1941 and carried it on, largely as a one-man operation, until the end of the war. The bulletin was read attentively by university people and editorial writers and was frequently quoted by press and radio commentators as an authoritative source of Chinese public opinion.

When Dr. Hsia took over our New York office and established a radio station in 1941, he had three able Chinese staff members – Kao, Lin Lin and Lin Mousheng, and three Americans, namely Lyon, Mario Shedd, and Kay Kohan Patrick, who later joined the editorial side of the Press Department and remained with the organization throughout the entire war. All of them were loyal and cooperative. They were dedicated to their work in collecting any information the American press needed, and going out of the way to get pictures. One of the American girls was bent upon getting a picture of a jacket of an American pilot from the famous Fourteenth American Air Force in China with the sign in Chinese on its back. This enabled him to be recognized by Chinese and help him to return to his base if he should fall in remote or even in enemy territory.

As she walked out of the RCA building for lunch, she was started to see walking ahead of her one of the jackets. Without thinking she ran up to the man in the jacket and told him breathlessly that she wanted his picture. He looked properly startled. Thereupon she earnestly insisted that she wasn't trying to flirt with him, but she simply wanted a picture of his jacket for the Chinese government office where she worked, the earnestness of her manner must have convinced him, for he stripped off his jacket and handed it to her. "Lady," he said, "I won't pose for you, but you can have my jacket. Send it back to me at the Waldorf Astoria when you get through with it." She got her picture, and he got his jacket back. The *New Yorker* reported the incident that indicated our American worker's enthusiasm.

Dr. C. L. Hsia later organized a speaker's bureau and invited Dr. Y. C. Yang to head it. Yang still retained the position of the President of Soochow University. Dr. Yui Ming, a tall polished Hawaiian Chinese, was invited to take charge of our San Francisco office and later of the Montreal office. The Washington office was headed by Chen Yih, who had worked in the editorial department of the *New York Times*.

James Shen, who had been head of my writing section in Chungking, was sent to the United States in 1943 and became the head of the San Francisco office until the end of the war. He was a graduate of the School of Journalism at the University of Missouri, and was a good writer and a hard worker. Chen Pao-nan, former vice-consul in New York, joined our Chicago office as its head. His appointment caused criticism by many staff members in Chungking as he had never worked for the International Publicity Department. Later I decided not to engage outsiders and to give preference to deserving staff members in Chungking. This policy worked well.

Above all we kept a listening post at Ventura, California in charge of a local dentist and a ham radio operator, Dr. Stuart. This was necessary due to the interruption of communications by Japanese interference. The listening post cooperated with our 40-kilowatt broadcasting station in Chungking. At one time we provided a service for foreigners who were unable to correspond with their families in America, letting them use our radio facilities to wire radio letters through Ventura for free.

When the war became global, Hong Kong was overrun by the Japanese. My staff in Hong Kong offices made their way to Chungking after having undergone great perils. Z. B. Toong, head of our Hong Kong office, with his wife and four children reached Chungking half a year after Pearl Harbor. I was concerned over the fate of the two officers who had been in charge of our Singapore and Rangoon offices. George Yeh, head of our Singapore office, left Singapore just three days before it fell into Japanese hands.

When George Yeh finally returned to Chungking on March 19 by plane from Calcutta, he had a real story to tell. Before the fall of Singapore, he had organized the Singapore Chinese Anti-Aggression Mobilization Council which helped with the evacuation of Chinese women and children, Chinese government representatives and Chinese businessmen. He helped organize five Chinese guerilla units, and assisted with directing of Chinese labor corps who worked on local defense. He kept a diary during the Malayan campaign, which lasted seventy-three days.

George Yen carried on all these activities in close collaboration with the Ministry of Economic Warfare of the Singapore government. He had collected detailed information on Japanese methods of infiltration in Malaya, and the actual British strength in Malaya. After this experience he was eminently fitted to work with the British, and we sent him to London to head up the London office. Later, he supervised the establishment of the Paris office which was placed under the charge of Robert Liem.

Dr. C. H. Lowe, who had been representing us in Rangoon, left Rangoon ten days before its fall. He traveled to India by ship. He was appointed to head the Indian office. During the next three years the only way to get supplies and literature in and out of Chungking to or from our overseas offices was through India. Lowe helped to facilitate the movement of film and radio equipment and essential magazines, papers and books. We found his office indispensable to our Chungking operations throughout the war.

In the spring of 1942, after our east coast cities had been entirely occupied by Japanese, I sent James Shen to India to make a survey, including possible cooperation with the information office of the Indian government. His observations were illuminating.

He noted that the Sir Stafford Cripps mission had left the Indian people more bitter and disillusioned than ever. Among the common people of

India, he detected a dangerous indifference towards the approaching peril of a Japanese invasion. The renewed support by the Indians of a non-violent and non-cooperation policy was the direct result of bitter disappointment resulting from the failure of the Cripps mission. James Shen noticed the prevailing ignorance of the Indian people about China and its role in the war. He felt that background articles on China should be provided for the Indian papers, and he suggested that we set up an office in India as soon as possible and that we encourage leading Indian journalists to visit China. We did both.

Later we set up one more overseas office, this time in Sydney, Australia, first started by H. J. Timperley, who stayed there for one year, and then went to America to join the United Nations Information office. I then secured Dr. Chau to head the Australian office.

In April 1942, I sent Fabian Chow, a member of our writing section, to Burma to serve as a public relations officer with the Chinese army in Burma. Fabian had worked under me on the *China Press* before the war. He joined me in Hankow in 1937. He was a good writer, and a good newspaperman, and his personality was such that he made friends easily among the foreign correspondents. I felt that during the fighting in Burma we should have a representative working closely with General Stilwell. Fabian was attached to the General's headquarters and was cordially welcomed.

He was actually China's first army public relations officer, helping in the preparation of the Chinese War communiqués issued by General Stilwell and working closely with the censorship officers. When General Stilwell retreated by his long walk out of Burma through the mountainous jungle back to India, we knew that he was with the retreating band. For weeks we heard nothing from Fabian. Two months later, we received word from Calcutta that he had arrived there safely. I asked him to return immediately to Chungking. He wrote several articles on this difficult retreat which was noteworthy since he was the only Chinese newspaperman with the party.

One year later I sent Fabian Chow to Kunming, Yunnan province, to set up a branch office. Kunming had become an important U.S. Army center, and correspondents were anxious to get some of their stories cleared from Kunming rather than from Chungking where they were under Chinese censorship. I wanted Fabian to establish a local censorship office which could handle certain types of stories and also to serve, as he had in Burma, as a Chinese public relations officer with the foreign correspondents. He did his job well, and served as head of the Kunming office until he was transferred to Dr. Hsia's office in America at the end of 1944.

Those who remained constantly throughout the entire war at the main office in Chungking deserved just as much if not more credit for their perseverance and loyalty. It was a hard life and the work grew more and more disheartening as the censorship and our publicity work were often criticized by the foreign correspondents and the Chinese officials. We were all a very tired lot of people when Japan surrendered, and it was a wonder to me that nerves were not more frayed and words harsher than they were.

My main bulwark throughout the war was H. P. Tseng. He worked with me for well over twenty years in one undertaking after another. He is a fine Chinese scholar with a reputation for knowledge of the Chinese classics. His whole psychology is that of the traditional "wise man." I very much needed such a colleague to balance my more enthusiastic and rebellious moods. On account of my Western training, I was often torn between Eastern and Western impulses. But in difficult moments, H. P. Tseng would pull me back with a quiet remark or a quotation from the classics. Throughout the entire seven years we were in Chungking, his desk and mine faced each other, and he knew all the developments within the department and constantly advised me.

Two younger men often came to our office for instructions were N. C. Nyi and Jimmy Wei. Nyi became Director of the Chinese News Service in New York and the Counselor of the Chinese Embassy in Washington. Jimmy Wei was managing director of the Chinese Broadcasting Administration at Taipei. Both of us were in my Shanghai office when it first had to go underground. They followed me to Hankow, and to Chungking. Nyi served as my English secretary, preparing reports and weekly confidential letters for our overseas offices. He had an analytic mind, and a cautious temperament. Sometimes it took both Nyi and Tseng to dissuade me from one of my more radical projects. But they both understood the work thoroughly and helped to give me balance.

Jimmy Wei was the most popular man on my staff and with the foreign correspondents. He was my chief censor, and if he could not make up his mind in handling copies, he reported to me for a final decision.

The rest of the Chungking office was divided into sections, such as Russian, Japanese, bookkeeping, writing, radio, contact, and general sections. The contact section was headed by Professor Chi, who had been with me from the beginning of the war. Mike Peng was the head of program at ratio station XGOY. Warren Lee was in charge of our photographic section. Their work took them out of the office most of the time, but they were key men in our department.

There was a period right after the Pearl Harbor attack when the heaviest burden fell on our radio section. For three months, we could not get mail through to the United States. It became necessary to depend entirely on our cable and radio communications. Right after December 8, 1941, I switched the publication of the monthly magazine *China at War* from Hong Kong to New York. I cabled Dr. Hsia to prepare the January 1942 issue. The Hong Kong office had published the December 1941 issue just before the Pearl Harbor attack, and copies had been shipped out on the last boat leaving Hong Kong.

Among other foreign newspapermen who worked for us were Melville Jacoby, Israel Epstein, Leonard Allen, George Grimm of the U.S. State Department group, and George Alexanderson of the *New York Times,* who was also under the State Department. Epstin became a communist working in Red China.

Chu Fu-sung, another important staff member, combined well a scholarly approach with a good sense of news and feature values. He prepared the annual *China Handbook* which our office put out. I could always depend upon his material to be accurately checked, and well organized. Journalism was not merely a passing interest with Chu. He absorbed in the whole field of modern literature, such as the current plays and novels, as well as with the lore of the Chinese newspaper world. His wife was also a valued member of our staff.

Through the selfless and dedicated work of my colleagues, we succeeded in writing a memorable story of achievement of the International Department during the wracking war years. The true story of the International Department is the chronicle of men and women with high goals who did its unsung tasks.

Chapter Fourteen.
Problems with Correspondents and General Stilwell

My No. 1 task during the Chungking days was to build a friendly informational bridge between our beleaguered Chinese nation and the confused outside world. My principal medium in this effort was the group of foreign correspondents who were interpreting Chungking to the world.

During the early Chungking days, we of the International Department and the correspondents were a close-knit family. Most of the correspondents had been with us through the trying days of Shanghai, Nanking and Hankow. They had experienced with us the fearful bombardments from 1939 to 1941 in Chungking. There was a camaraderie which bound us together amazingly well; we were fellow-workers in a common cause.

I took especial pleasure in going beyond the usual information office procedures to make the foreign correspondents comfortable in their life and work. My staff was all trained to provide tireless service to all correspondents when they were in pursuit of a story. I myself was at everyone's beck during those emotion-packed days.

One venture in which I took particular pride was the construction of the Press Hostel. No newspaperman or woman who stayed in this picturesque hostelry has ever forgotten the experience. Because we were making history in those years, the stellar figures of the American and British newspaper and magazine world passed through its portals.

The Press Hostel was originally built to provide for the steadily increasing number of newspapermen and women who were drifting into Chungking. It became a center for friendships that sprouted during the war years – a sort of anchor to which correspondents could tie their shared experiences in wartime China.

One of the unpleasant discoveries after our retreat to Chungking in 1938 was that the city was ill-equipped to provide quarters for Western newspapermen. The idea of a press hostel came to my mind. I had little or no money and so I was forced to forage for funds. At a dinner which Dr. H. H. Kung, Minister of Finance, gave to foreign newspapermen, I stated the problem. Dr. Kung, without hesitation, asked me how much I needed to put up a hostel. I modestly asked for $10,000. He agreed to find the money. I quickly secured a contractor who agreed to put up a 13-room structure within my budget. I was the architect myself. Before the building was completed, I was able to secure another $10,000 from Dr. Kung for furnishings. We were in business in mid-July 1939.

Correspondents began to write home about this new establishment which soon began to be referred to irreverently as "Holly's Hotel." One of these was Randall Gould, former editor of the *Shanghai Evening Post and Mercury*, who was now covering Chungking for the *Christian Science Monitor*. In his story June 1, 1940, he wrote: "Free China's new capital, in the remote Szechwan hinterland, offers journalists the nearest thing to free 'keep' of any spot in the world today. Accredited newspaper folk can board at the recently opened Press Hostel for slightly more than one American dollar a month. Room will set them back just under $3."

Gould did not exaggerate. Exchange rates (the Chinese dollar had sunk to 17 to U.S. $1) gave the correspondents the edge. Board, consisting of a western style breakfast and two Chinese meals a day was only $20 a month (Chinese currency). Room rent was $40 (Chinese).

The reception to the Press Hostel was so immediate that General J. L. Huang of the New Life Movement and I persuaded Dr. Kung to provide money for a larger hostel, to be build on the banks of the Chialing River, to provide accommodations for non-newspaper visitors. This larger hostel could house 40 guests and had a dining room which could take care of 150 to 200 guests.

The bombings of 1940 and 1941 played havoc with the Press Hostel on which the Japanese fliers seemed to have their sights. We were in constant process of rebuilding. But to my delight, no correspondent was injured in all the long series of raids.

Midway in the war, this cherished enterprise of mine began to turn sour. In the beginning, when we were all in intimate groups, the idea of housing all the correspondents together seemed a good one. It saved time and duplication to have all our news-distributing facilities in one place.

But later, when trouble making journalists, enemies of the Nationalist government, began to trickle into Chungking, the concentration of them at the Press Hostel led to dissension. Even friendly correspondents began to be infected by the critical spirit.

The first sign that the correspondents were prepared to take control out of my hands came on May 18, 1943, while I was away in America with Madame Chiang. The Press Hostel guests organized the Foreign Correspondents' Club. The officers of the club included: *New York Times'* Brooks Atkinson, president; Tass News' Mike Yakshamin and *Time* Magazine's Theodore White, vice-presidents. They were critics of the Chiang Kai-shek administration. The Club eventually assumed the authority to act as representative of all correspondents dealing with the government, which usually meant me. There were 25 foreign news organizations represented in the club. The old cordial relationship between my office and the newspapermen dissolved in controversy.

What sharpened relations was the rankling controversy between General Joseph W. Stilwell and Generalissimo Chiang Kai-shek, Allied Supreme Command of the China and Burma theaters. Stilwell persistently asked to give American Lend-Lease aid to the Chinese Communists, which Chiang adamantly refused. Chiang was certain that Mao Ze-dong would use these weapons against him after the war. In 1944, Stilwell also demanded the command of all Chinese troops. In September 19, 1944, President Roosevelt, most likely at the urgent of Stilwell, sent a telegram to Generalissimo Chiang with a blunt demand that Stilwell be given the full command of all Chinese armed forces, which Chiang was not willing to do. In response, Generalissimo Chiang asked President Roosevelt for Stilwell's recall.*

Stilwell's demand was strange and absurd; if a foreign general demanded to have a complete command and control of all U. S. armed forces, it would be utter foolishness.

In 1942, Japanese conquered Burma after defeating the British and seven Chinese divisions commanded by Stilwell. It was a disastrous rout. The Japanese occupied Rangoon, the major coastal city. Then they pretended to march north along the central railway, but their real thrust north was along the east flank near Thailand. They captured Lashio, the beginning of the Burma Road to China in the north. Stilwell was trapped;

---

* See pages 333 to 339 of the book *The Stilwell Papers*. It was based on Stilwell's diary and letters, edited by Theodore White and published by William Sloane Associates, New York in 1948.

the only way out was to walk through the mountainous jungle to India to the west. His army disintegrated and all heavy equipment was abandoned. Through much hardship, the remnants reached India where Stilwell was in charge of training Chinese troops.

In his book, *The Stilwell Papers*, Stilwell blamed Chiang Kai-shek for his defeat. A fair-minded person who read his book would conclude otherwise. In the book, Chiang asked him to concentrate troops in the north at Mandalay near Lashio, but Stilwell wanted to fight 200 miles in the south and to finish off the Japanese at Rangoon. In view of Japanese superior air power and ground force, this was unrealistic wishful thinking, which contributed to the defeat. It is the responsibility of the field commander to make sure that his only supply and retreat route is not taken by the enemy.

Stilwell redeemed himself in the second Burma campaign. In 1944, he led Chinese and American soldiers to retake northern Burma. He lived with his troops during the campaign. He won the nickname of "Uncle Joe" among Chinese soldiers. The retake of north Burma allowed the building of a new road from India to the existing Burma Road, known as the Stilwell Road. The road was completed in January of 1945, thus reopening China's only land route to the free world until the end of the war in September 1945.

Stilwell served under Chiang Kai-shek as chief of staff. He was also the top commander of the U. S. forces in China and Burma theaters under the supreme commander Chiang. Most of the correspondents, taking their cues from the American officers, who were Stilwell's men, believed that Generalissimo Chiang had mishandled the war. The correspondents failed to perceive the larger issues in this controversy. In the closing years of the war, Stilwell was given a legendary buildup by them, while Chiang became the target of embittered criticism. My staff and I worked tirelessly to stem this tide of unfair American press, but our efforts were not enough.

General Stilwell also won another nickname of "Vinegar Joe" among the American military because of his brusque manner. He was contemptuous and used derogatory language against many people including Chiang Kai-shek. In his book *"The Stilwell Papers,"* he referred to Chiang Kai-shek as the Peanut, or the bastard. He also wrote that Chiang should be shot. Considering that Stilwell served directly under Chiang Kai-shek, his attitude was one of blatant insubordination. Stilwell considered Chinese Communism to be some kind of agrarian reform and socialism. He thought that if Chiang could be gotten rid of, China's problem would be solved. Stilwell had a strong influence on General George Marshall and

Presidents Roosevelt and Truman. He played a key role in the intriguing policy change to "No Significant Support" for China after World War II, which most likely led to the Communists' victory on mainland China.

What were the consequences of the loss of mainland China? One consequence was the Korean War. Before the war, the Communist North Korean leader obtained a promise from Mao Ze-dong to help him if the invasion of the South ran into trouble. Should Free China have retained the mainland, most likely, the Korean War would not have happened, or would be a much smaller conflict. Communist China's help to North Korea prolonged and intensified the war. The loss of mainland China was a disaster to Free China and Korean War was a burden to the United States.

Many factors caused the free world press to shift against Chiang Kai-shek in the closing years of World War II. Communism, after the Russia's victory at Stalingrad, was riding a wave of incredible popularity in Washington and American press. The part played by Chinese Communism in this reversal was one of the cleverest impersonations of their "Liberalism" and "Democracy" during World War II. Many writers, some Communists and their sympathizers, worked to implant a stereotype of an innocuous Chinese Communism in the mind of the free world. It is not often that publicity can turn black into white before the unsuspecting reader's eye, but it was done in China in the 1940s. Many writers such as Agnes Smedley, Anna Louise Strong, Edgar Snow, Owen Lattimore, Harrison Forman, Ilona Sues, Gunther Stein, Israel Epstein, Theodore White, Brooks Atkinson, and others poured out books and magazine articles misrepresenting and praising the Chinese Communists as needed 'agrarian reformers' and 'democratic.' But were they?

They believed Mao Ze-dong was independent of Stalin and if he ruled China, he would work for the good of the Chinese people and be friendly with the United States. These concepts were implanted in the American mind. Communist representative Chou En-lai maintained headquarters in Chungking throughout the war talking democracy, and cleverly cultivated friendly contacts with the liberal and left-wing writers who passed through the city. They accepted the Chinese Communists in their pretended liberal and new democracy guise. It did seem natural when Washington elites began to chatter about the necessity of admitting of the Communists into a coalition Chinese government. Later events showed that Mao Ze-dong was a more orthodox Communist and more war-like than Stalin.

Chiang Kai-shek was not fooled by all this masquerading. But the idea of a post-war partnership between Russia and the United States was accepted in the United States after the Teheran Conference. It was politically dangerous to reject the gratuitous advice, which was coming to us from Americans. The most Chiang could do at the height of the communist popularity was to block such suicidal ideas as providing Lend-Lease weaponry to the Communists, now in open rebellion against him in North China. He was also against giving the Communists a veto power over the post-war Chinese Constitution.

Some correspondents continually demanded security clearance from me to visit Yenan, the communist capital, to report the communist side of the war. For a long time, I had been able to sidestep the issue. In October 1943 Liang Han-chao was appointed Minister of Information, and my immediate superior. The new Minister, disregarding my advice, stepped into this explosive issue and, at a press conference, told the correspondents that he would grant permission for a party to visit Yenan.

Having made this blunder, the Information Ministry had to proceed with a conducted Yenan tour. Israel Epstein, Harrison Forman and Gunther Stein succeeded in going. The Communists put on a tremendous show. All three later wrote books praising the communists. Later, Theodore H. White and Brooks Atkinson received permission to go. A third group was denied permission, with an aftermath of ill feeling. Having thrown open the communist question for discussion at press conferences, Minister Liang's meetings with the correspondents degenerated into ugly scenes of trick questions and constant wrangling. Tempers flared up and the goodwill which I had so laboriously cultivated with the correspondents over the years disintegrated into distrust.

The issue of censorship began to be batted back and forth. China was at war – desperate war – and we had hitherto followed a policy of preventing news of Communist dissension within China from being radioed to the outside world. In April 1944, the correspondents drew up a joint communication, signed by all the members of the Foreign Correspondents Club, asking the Generalissimo to relax the censorship. This put him in an embarrassing position as it was not polite for him to give his real reasons for discouraging pro-Communist dispatches at this period of nominal coalition. As usual, I found myself in the middle of this unhappy squabble, and I came out of it with a sadly lessened influence in the correspondent fraternity.

In August 1944, the controversy with the correspondents broke out in renewed bitterness. A sternly worded protest, over the signature of Brooks Atkinson, of the *New York Times* was sent to Minister Liang, itemizing the censorship practices which the correspondents resented.

Liang, when he met them, only infuriated the protesters more. I tried to relieve the situation by printing a translation into English of the official Central Executive Committee censorship regulations. Unfortunately, some of these rules were vaguely expressed, and when I tried to interpret them liberally, I was in constant danger of being overruled by the Central Executive Committee. Altogether there were twelve regulations, most of them applying to military news.

It was under this preheated atmosphere that the news of General Stilwell's recall broke in November 1944. Brooks Atkinson was a partisan of Stilwell. When he could not clear a bitter series of articles defending Stilwell and deriding Chiang Kai-shek, Atkinson returned to New York and released his story there. Featured in the *Times*, which has been traditionally friendly to the Chiang Kai-shek administration, the series did us much harm. Other American newspapers handled the Stilwell case even more caustically.

While I was being buffeted by these controversial storms, I was able to undertake an educational project, which gave me much satisfaction. As one of the few American trained newspapermen in China, I had long been conscious of the appalling need of China for modern journalists. Only the most rudimentary facilities for newspaper training existed in China before the war. I conceived the idea of setting up a school of journalism in Chungking to train young men and women. In 1942, before taking my trip to America with Madame Chiang, I asked the Generalissimo's permission to start such an institution. He granted permission, provided I could secure competent teachers in America. In New York, Dean Carl Ackerman and the Columbia University, jointly sponsored the school. He helped me to recruit an inspiring staff, headed by Dr. Harold Cross of Columbia University, who served as Dean, and including Rodney Gilbert, Richard Baker, Anthony Dralle and Floyd Rodgers. I arranged for all of them to live in the Press Hostel. I secured some finances for the school, and the budget was met in part by the Kuomintang (Citizen's Party). The school was a part of the Central Political Institute of the Party. The institution flourished for two years, and students eagerly flocked to its classes. Altogether, we graduated sixty young men and women from the school. I felt that I had made a worthwhile contribution to my country's journalism. I owed this to Dean Carl Ackerman who got financial aid from his friends and gave me support and encouragement.

The end of the war came at last after eight years of struggle. Victory that once seemed so remote to China finally rewarded my people. The last year of the war had been an American show. The island by island advance of the Americans toward the heart of Japanese power, the massive bombardment of Japan's cities, and finally the crashing A-bombs over Hiroshima and Nagasaki pronounced the bitter knell to the Empire of Japan. There was always the danger of a final resistance by Japan's continental armies, sprawled over China, but this danger flickered out after their emperor's speech. When the surrender came, the Japanese armies in China submitted without any final gesture of defiance.

But it was a clouded triumph for China because, in halting Japan, our allies, through the Yalta Conference, had admitted another and even deadlier enemy to China – the Russian Communists. In less than four years, this enemy was to torment resurrected China.

For me, V-J Day, August 15, 1945, meant the end of a long assignment. I wished never again to live upon such an exalted plane of danger-filled service to my country as I had experienced in the eight taxing years since 1937. Now I was looking toward to an era of peace. The end of the nightmare found me wearied of governmental jobs and responsibilities, and eager for a return to the civilian life, which I had known before the war. I made plans, but little did I know that these plans would not materialize, and that China was not to know peace. After a short interval, I found myself back in Free China's service. This time, her enemy was not Japanese militarism, but Communist domination.

Chapter Fifteen.
I Quit Politics

Now comes a period in my life which it will be difficult for me to make understandable to most readers. At the age of fifty-eight, I tried to find a new way of life.

Living for eight years of war, surrounded by ever present danger, with nerves taut by the tasks of my hard assignments, I came out of the war wearied in mind and body. Life suddenly became flat and meaningless. As long as I was needed in Chungking, I swallowed my disappointments and worked on. But now that the war was won, I felt a great longing to get out of political life, with all its pettiness and its insincerities.

I was influenced in this attitude by an unpleasant experience in the Information Ministry. A vacancy occurring in the Minister's office at that time, I was the logical choice. Instead, I found myself being punished by some higher influence in the government which resented an action of mine in protecting the wife of a friend who had been away on a government mission. To embarrass me, a junior official, K. C. Wu, was surprisingly appointed as Minister over my head. Since I questioned the suitability of Wu for the office, I had no other choice but to resign.

The Generalissimo thereupon appointed me to the membership on the Far Eastern Advisory Commission which was then stationed in Washington and later moved to Tokyo. At first, it was understood that I was to be chairman of the Commission, but when some of the cabinet members in Chungking decided that the head must be a military man, this plan was dropped. I found it unendurable to remain any longer in Washington.

I resolved to get away and to learn a trade that would permit me to earn a living with my hands. I enjoyed working with my hands and would be free of the whole distasteful political rat race. I realize now that the plan was doomed from the start, but at the time it seemed logical. I decided to learn automobile mechanics. I felt that with the ever-growing automobile industry's hunger for trained men, I would never be at a loss for a job once I had become an expert. I remembered how, during the years 1909 to 1913, when I had been in the United States as a student, the horse and buggy age was still predominant and the automobile was new. I had seen this huge industry growing up in my lifetime. I wanted to be a part of it, however humble my function.

To acquire the needed skills, I left Washington for Los Angeles and enrolled as a student in a school of automotive engineering and refrigeration. At the school, I told them that I was forty, although actually I had passed fifty-eight. I left no word of my whereabouts in Washington, and to avoid discovery by the Los Angeles Chinese consular officers, I changed my name. I lived in a small hotel near the school and tried to adopt the life of a normal student. A few Chinese friends knew where I was, but they were not curious and did not give me away.

Shortly before Christmas 1945, the Generalissimo, with his painstaking attention which he gives to all reports, had noticed that my name was missing from the periodic briefings which Ambassador Wei Tao-ming sent to Chungking. He supposed that I was in Washington performing my duties on the Far Eastern Commission. Learning of my absence, he gave orders to find me. The ambassador found me in Los Angeles. The Generalissimo thereupon ordered ambassador Wei and me return to Chungking for consultations. There was no alternative for me except to comply.

Together with Ambassador Wei, we made the long trip to Chunking on a military plane. It had been only four months since I had left the city, although it seemed much longer. Already, everything in Chungking had changed. Sally had already left with our two sons and daughters-in-law for Shanghai, where we had a house.

My private status was soon interrupted. The Generalissimo requested me to accompany Madame Chiang on a trip to Manchuria (or the Northeast Provinces, as we ordinarily called it) to extend greetings to the Russian military forces which then occupied it. This was the ostensible mission, but the actual purpose of the trip was to convey the hope that the Russians should make an early withdrawal. Madame Chiang bore with her a large number of gifts for the Russian commanding officers, which were carried in a second plane.

We were seen off by President Chiang at the Chungking airport on January 20, 1946. After a flight of six hours, we alighted at Nanyuan, a landing field just outside Beijing. General Li Tsung-jen, garrison commander at Beijing, and an imposing party of military and civilian officials greeted us at Nanyuan. The same evening Madame Chiang received Walter S. Robertson, then Minister of the American Embassy, who was later Assistant Secretary of State for Far Eastern Affairs. Mr. Robertson, a good friend of China, briefed Madame Chiang on the Communist situation.

We left Beijing on January 22 on a plane to Changchun, our destination point. We were met by several hundred Chinese and Russian officers. Russian Marshal Malinovsky, who was to have met us, had conveniently departed for Moscow to attend a party meeting. Madame Chiang presented in the name of the President the highest Chinese decoration to Malinovsky, which was accepted by his chief of staff. It was quite obvious to us that the Marshal had deliberately avoided the meeting with Madame Chiang. It was the first public indication of the rift that was to widen so soon between Russia and China.

The Russian control of the city was undisguised. Madame Chiang was assigned a luxurious Cadillac during her stay. The car had formerly belonged to the Emperor Henry Pu Yi, the last of the Manchu Emperors, who had been made a Japanese puppet when they set up Manchukuo (Northeast Country). The car was driven by a Russian soldier and accompanied by two Russian guards. I had the privilege of riding with Madame Chiang in this historic vehicle. The Russians excused their watchfulness by pointing out that it was the duty of the Russian occupation authorities to assure the safety of their distinguished visitor.

In accepting the decoration, on behalf of Marshal Malinovsky, the chief of staff uttered these words:

"This decoration symbolizes the approval by the Chinese people of the Red Army's military achievement. The Red Army, under the leadership of Marshal Stalin, not only defeated Germany's aggression in the West, but together with our allies defeated our common enemy, Imperialist Japan. We drove out the Japanese aggressors from China's northeast, and liberated the people of the area, and thus enabled them to return to China."

Russians occupied the Manchuria after a short war of five days against Japan that had already been broken by the United States and China.

A farewell dinner was given to Madame Chiang and her party on the evening of January 24. The Marshal, who had promised to be back from Russia in time to appear, did not arrive. We listened to ten wearisome Russian speakers, all of whom repeated the same refrain – praise of

Russian-Chinese cooperation and pledges of its continuance. Madame Chiang said that she wishes a true and equal cooperation between Russia and the Nationalist government of China. Our trip to Manchuria concluded with stopovers at Mukden and several other cities. Everywhere, great applauding crowds greeted her. But there was an undertone of uncertainty giving us gloomy thoughts.

Another mission awaited me on my arrival at Chungking. The Generalissimo sent for me and asked me if I would go to Honolulu to visit W. H. Donald who was an old friend of the Chiangs. He was in the Naval Hospital there dying of cancer. During the war, Donald had been taken by the Japanese and confined to a concentration camp in the Philippines. Fortunately, he was able to conceal his identity throughout.

American authorities brought him from a Tahiti hospital to Honolulu where he could have the best of treatment. There it was discovered that he had an advanced case of cancer. His returning to Shanghai in this condition was considered by the doctors as too hazardous. I remained in Honolulu for three months, waiting for Donald to regain his strength sufficiently for the journey. Then, on the Generalissimo's instructions, I went to Washington to arrange for an American naval hospital plane to transport him to his home in Shanghai.

During his stay in the Honolulu hospital, Donald was approached by Earl Selle, a former staff member on the *China Press*, with a request that he be permitted to write his biography. I distrusted this arrangement. Despite my close relationship with Selle, I did not consider him qualified to write the biography of a man who had played such an historic part in China's politics. Selle was practically blind, and had to depend upon his wife even to read newspapers to him.

I believed that only someone who had known Donald closely for at least thirty years could write an appropriate life of this remarkable man, so much of whose career had been veiled in deep secrecy. I knew of only three possible biographers who were qualified: F. L. Pratt, a fellow Australian, who had been associated with me for twenty years in newspaper work in China; Robert Gilbert of the *New York Herald Tribune*, who had authored several notable books on China; or me.

However, Selle was badly in need of money. Donald had received a check for $5,000 from Dr. H. H. Kung, to pay his hospital expenses. He was anxious that his life story be written before it was too late, and he was persuaded that Selle could do the job. Throughout my stay in Honolulu, the determined biographer held daily sessions with the sick man at the hospital.

Finally, Donald's physical condition bettered so that it was feasible to fly him on the 5,000-mile journey to Shanghai. I accompanied him on the sad homecoming. In Shanghai, he was under the personal care of General J. L. Huang, director of the New Life Movement. I saw him frequently at the Shanghai hospital, and then I was called away to America. During my absence, I learned of his death on November 9 from cancer of the lungs.

Later, in 1947, when Selle's biography, *Donald in China*, was brought out by a New York publisher, my worst fears were confirmed. The book was repetitive with objectionable references to China personalities. I was certain that Donald, had he lived, would have drastically edited it. However, Selle, although he allowed me to see the book in galley proofs, was adamant against any of my suggestions to make it more accurate.

I shall never forget my last meeting with this great man with whom my own life had been interconnected for more than three decades. A brave man, the tears rolled down his cheeks, as he said "goodbye." The doctors gave me some hope that he would be alive when I returned, but it was not to be.

My trip to the United States was necessitated by Sally's serious physical condition. She was suffering acutely from gallstones. Our Shanghai doctors advised against an operation in China since Sally's condition was aggravated by diabetes.

I arranged for Sally to be admitted to the Medical Center in New York, where Dr. Loeb, Madame Chiang's physician, took charge of the case. His care was expert and unsparing. Under his treatment, my wife's gallstones were removed and she made a comfortable recovery.

I was still deeply interested in automobile mechanics and I decided to pass the period of my enforced wait in New York to improve my knowledge. On November 25, 1946, I enrolled myself in the YMCA School in New York under the name of S. K. Tong. My teachers were Messrs. Pease, Delmar and Martin. I kept elaborate notes and, in looking over these old records, I found the following phrase, obviously dictated to me by one of my instructors: "The man who knows how will always have a job, but he will always be found working for the man who knows why."

I followed a regular routine during this period, which continued for more than five months. I reported at the school at eight in the morning, ate a sandwich lunch at noon, and returned to my hotel at four in the afternoon. My first weeks were devoted to electrical principles, my second weeks to mechanical principles, and my final two months to the repair of motor cars. At the close of my course, I received a certificate of completion. I found that there was a real satisfaction in my accomplishment. Before I left New York, I bought a complete set of tools for $400, fully intending to set up an auto repair shop in Shanghai on my return.

That ambition was never to be realized.

Chapter Sixteen.
Called Back to Government Information

When she was sufficiently recovered, Sally and I drove to Key West, Florida, for a rest. While there, we flew to Cuba for an overnight visit.

It was while we were in Key West that the call came to me to rejoin the government. General Chang Chun, who was also in New York at this time for a physical checkup, was appointed by the Generalissimo as Prime Minister. General Chang offered me a position in his Executive Branch, or Cabinet, as Director of the Government Information Office, a newly created agency. When I interviewed him in New York, he explained to me the grim necessity that China should have a better world press, in the face of the worsening communist problem. Although I had some hesitation about returning to government service, with all its frustrations, I could not refuse this call.

The government had now returned to Nanking. We flew back to China and on May 2, 1947, I assumed my new office. It was not difficult to reconstruct an organization, as I was able to assemble virtually the same staff that had worked with me in the International Department throughout the war years. H. P. Tseng and Teng Yu-teh became my vice directors and ably relieved me of most of the detailed work of the office. My other department heads were all men who had worked with me before, and who had the know-how to administer an efficient organization.

I returned to Nanking just in time to say farewell to F. L. Pratt, who had worked with me as a close colleague for twenty years. He had been my assistant editor at the *China Press*. He also joined me in the censorship office in 1936. He had attended to personal correspondence for Madame Chiang on behalf of my office, and as my adviser in the International

Department, he had accompanied me to New York in 1942 when I escorted Madame Chiang when she sought medical treatment.

The first press conference for American visitors held after my appointment came on June 24, 1947. I assigned Charles C. H. Wan, head of the writing section, to interpret for President Chiang. The visitors included Mr. Helen Reid, the publisher of the *New York Herald Tribune*, Roy Howard, publisher of the Scripps-Howard Newspapers and Mr. Moore, representing *Time* and *Life*.

Mr. Howard brought up the pressing question of the situation in Manchuria. The Generalissimo's answer was prophetic, in the light of subsequent developments. He said:

"The Communists have already started a large-scale offensive in the Northeast (Manchuria). If we cannot uphold the Northeast, it will be a serious blow to the whole world. However, I wish to assure you that the Chinese government will do its utmost for sovereignty in the Northeast and will fully cooperate with other nations for the maintenance of peace. If international treaties are not honored and if the Charter of the United States is not observed, no nation can hold its own alone. The situation in Manchuria is very serious."

During the rest of the year 1947, American press attitudes toward China deteriorated rapidly. One of the worst offenders was the *Washington Post*, edited by Herbert Elliston who had worked for the Chinese government between 1925 and 1927, but who did not see eye-to-eye with the Chiang Kai-shek regime. On December 26, a particularly objectionable editorial appeared:

"The correspondents in China are inhibited by the tightest censorship at the source in the world, not including the Soviet Union."

Such a charge was so unfair that I disposed of it in the following statement:

"China has no censorship except that which has been imposed at Mukden where military hostilities are now in progress. The Government has made a full statement to the world press explaining the Mukden news restrictions. Aside from the single military area, there are no 'inhibitions' on the gathering or transmission of news in China. Representatives of the foreign press in China enjoy full facilities for the gathering of news, and are completely unrestricted in the copy which they send to their respective publications. This editorial in the *Washington Post* is not fair play: it is a blow below the journalistic belt."

Since I had known Elliston in China, and could put it on a personal basis, I wired him the gist of my statement. On January 2, 1948, I received his reply. He stressed that he had said "censorship at the source" which meant censorship in the dispensation, not the transmission of news. He closed with the words: "I remain, as I was in China, a sincere friend of China, where many of my lasting friendships were formed."

The Elliston case was only a manifestation of the curious blindness concerning the historic decisions, which were about to be made on China. With the fall of mainland China only a little more than a year ahead, many American newspapers could find nothing to discuss on China except the alleged "corruption" of the Chiang Kai-shek government, or the alleged waste of American aid to China, and the mishandling of the war against the communists. Such comment alternated with the repetition of the stale lie that the Chinese Communists represented the real "democratic" hope for China. I did not have the facilities to answer all these misrepresentations, so they continued to pour out through the years 1947 and 1948 in a poisonous stream to misinform the American public the true natures of the Nationalists and the Communists in China. This anti-Chiang Kai-shek tone of the majority American press during those years was a decisive factor in the later decision of the United States government not to aid Free China when the showdown came with the Communists by the end of 1948.

To influence the American opinion in favor of the Chinese Communists there came into existence at this time the so-called "Committee for a Democratic Eastern Policy." This committee was backed by the millionaire Communist Frederick Vanderbilt Field, who was also an angel for the Institute of Pacific Relations. Field was later to go to prison for his defiance of a Congressional investigation committee. It contributed to the mental confusion which gripped many Americans as Free China's darkest hour approached.

Fortunately, we had friends. One of the most active of these was Alfred Kohlberg of New York, a wealthy manufacturer with China interests, who, beginning in 1947, devoted the major part of his time to refute of the pro-Communists' false propaganda and to supply American editors and legislators with the facts. He launched the American China Policy Association which, at first, was headed by Clare Boothe Luce. An example of his work was the circulation to all editors at the end of 1947 with a draft of his Association statement to Chairman Styles Bridges of the Senate Appropriations Committee, recommending: (1) the appropriation of reasonable aid to China; (2) an immediate grant of surplus arms and ammunitions; (3) further arms, ammunition and training as may seem desirable; and (4) removal of State Department personnel sympathetic to the Communists.

Another headache for the Government Information Office was the persistent unfriendliness of the United States Information Service (U.S.I.S.) which had offices in Nanking, Shanghai and Beijing. The U. S. I. S, in addition to issuing a digest of the American press, beamed a daily broadcast to the Chinese people. It included in these broadcasts the repetition of some of the worst slanders against the Chinese government. It seemed to make a point of picking out for broadcast editorials hostile to the Nationalist China from American magazines and newspapers. I protested against this bias to W. Walton Butterworth, then the Director of Far Eastern Affairs in the State Department. My protest was unavailing.

Some years later, a distinguished foreign diplomat let me read a copy of the official report which he sent from China to his government in July 1947. The section in his report which recounted a conversation with an American newspaperman will throw a revealing light upon the difficulties which confronted me in my information work during the final period of Free China on the mainland. I reproduce it.

"He told me that he kept in close touch with the American military group here. Leading American officers have told him within the last week or so that they were literally amazed at the frank and outspoken criticism of the Generalissimo which they find in the upper ranks of the armed forces, particularly outside Nanking. These military leaders have expressed the opinion that it is futile to solve the issue by military means. . . . My informant is of the opinion that when the smoke clears away, the Chinese Communist movement is gong to be in control of all China and not just those sections north of the Yellow River."

He continued:

"To my amazement he (the newspaperman) also took the ground that under a communist administration, things could not be any worse than they are under the present government and he seems definitely of the opinion that they would be better. He seems to feel that the communist movement is the only virile movement in the country capable of bringing order to China and making necessary reforms. He thinks that the American government should be thinking along these lines and adjusting their actions to what he believes to be the inevitable outcome of this struggle.

It is his opinion that you can differentiate between the so-called Chinese communists and the communists of the Russian variety. He says that Russia could never control this country through the communist Party."

As this confidential report reveals, China was in a demoralizing state of defeatism in 1947 and 1948. The only thing that could have shaken the masses of our people out of this disheartened mood would have been some strong demonstration by the government of the United States for its support of the Free China government. But precious months passed and Washington gave no such sign. The corrosive effect of the left press in America had done its work too well.

An atmosphere of creeping defeatism is the most difficult one in which to conduct a government public relations operation. Although I did all that my limited budget would permit to fight back against the rising tide of misconceptions, we were a steadily losing ground.

I nailed the "Chinese Communists are independent of Moscow" lie in a statement to the correspondents, saying:

"The action of the Central Committee of the Chinese Communist Party on July 12, 1948 condemning Tito's course in Yugoslavia and rubber-stamping the Moscow-dominated Communist International shows the true colors of Mao Ze-dong." I said. "When Moscow snaps the whip, Mao Ze-dong obediently falls in line. This should put an end to the silly talk about the Chinese communists being Chinese patriots. But many so-called American liberals have deliberately blinded themselves to this truth. An amazing example is our old friend Owen Lattimore. Right after Tito's break with Moscow, Mr. Lattimore burst into print with the assertion that there was a "general similarity between Yugoslavia and the Chinese Communists" and with the repetition of his old contention that "the Chinese Communists are deeply rooted in nationalism."

Mr. Lattimore's words were scarcely printed before the Chinese Communists left him out on a limb by snapping into line behind Moscow and against Tito. Other chronic American critics of the National Chinese Government have found themselves similarly embarrassed. The Chinese Communists, by their obedience to Moscow, made it extremely hard for their overseas publicists to keep up the pretense that they are a bona-fide Chinese political party. What I said, as proved by later events, fell on deaf ears in the delirious mood of wishful thinking which prevailed in America in 1948.

Shortly after the capital returned to Nanking, Chiang Kai-shek called a large National Assembly to formulate a democratic constitution giving power back to people. On April 21, 1948 Generalissimo Chiang Kai-shek was elected as China's first President under the new constitution by a vote of 2,430 out of 2,770 in the National Assembly. As General Chang Chun's cabinet was a caretaker one, it resigned *en bloc* to give President Chiang a clean slate to reorganize the executive branch of the government. As Director of Government Information, I resigned with them. Dr. Wong Wen-hao, a graduate of a university in Belgium, and a geologist, was invited by the President to form a new cabinet. His nomination was approved by the Legislative Branch on May 24. Upon his repeated insistence, I was persuaded to continue to serve as Director of the Government Information Office, and additionally held the position of a Minister without Portfolio.

In the midst of political turmoil, I welcomed the diversion of being chosen as the lay chairman of a committee to organize a church in which both President and Madame Chiang could worship weekly. On August 1, I authorized the issuance of a statement by the Government Information Office as follows:

"President and Madame Chiang Kai-shek this morning dedicated their residence in Nanking at the Little Red Hill near Dr. Sun Yat-sen's mausoleum to the worship of God in the presence of nearly 200 Christians, working in various government offices. At the beginning of the service, the President explained in a brief announcement that, on August 1937, he together with Madame Chiang made the vow that one day they would build a church on this site if China should emerge victorious from the war which Japan had forced upon her. Two years ago they had returned to the capital from Chungking and they then decided that they would convert the new building into a church. In October of 1947 upon completion of all repairs to the structure, he had named it the Triumph Church and said that Madame Chiang and I are happy to have fellow Christians today join us in this dedicatory service.

The statement continued, "The President urged all not to be weary in accordance with the highest conceptions of God. He pointed out that the difficulties and hardships which confronted Moses in his endeavor to liberate God's chosen people were many times greater than those which we are facing in rebuilding this nation today. He reminded those present of China's triumph of confidence during the last eleven years and expressed the hope that the faith of the

Chinese people in a greater future will not be shaken by present seeming dangers around them."

Rev. Luther Shao, Secretary-General of the Church of Christ in China, preached a sermon on faith, hope and love upon which he said this church was founded. Following the service, he, assisted by Mr. Yu Wei-ning, pastor of the Methodist Church in Shanghai, who was my teacher in 1899 at the Anglo-Chinese College in Shanghai, conducted a communion service in which both President and Madame Chiang joined. Among the Christians who attended the dedication ceremony were many government officials and I.

To control rampant inflation, by a presidential mandate the government adopted a new currency, the gold yuan, price control measures, control of gold and foreign exchange. These were ill-conceived measures of desperation which cost the government much popularity. The measure meant the surrender of all gold in private possession, as well as of foreign exchange which had to be turned over under the penalty of confiscation plus other severe punishments. There was little which the Government Information Office could do to sell the idea to the people. Its principal staff members realized only too well that the Government was on a downward slide.

China's situation now became desperate. During a cabinet meeting held in the residence of President Chiang on November 26, 1948, Madame Chiang came down from upstairs and called President Chiang out for an urgent consultation. Later we learned that she had had a long distance telephone conversation with General Marshall, who was then Secretary of State. She had told him that she wanted to see him before he entered the hospital for medical attention and that she would be willing to leave China immediately. She would get the decision of the President before she hung up the phone. The President hastily decided to let her go to America to submit the Chinese case for American aid personally through General Marshall.

Before the meeting was over, she called me out and said that she had requested that I accompany her to the States but the President had refused on the ground that my services were too badly needed in China. She wished to know if I wanted to go with her, in which case she would speak to her husband again. I expressed my great appreciation for her kindness and trust in me, but said that I would not like to go against the President's wish. On November 28, 1948, Madame Chiang left Shanghai for Washington DC accompanied by General S. M. Chu, former head of the Chinese Military Mission in Japan, and others.

Upon her arrival, Madame Chiang had a number of conversations with General Marshall at Walter Reed Hospital. She was for nine days the guest at the home of Secretary and Mrs. Marshall, in Leesburg, VA, thirty-five miles from Washington. At Blair House, the temporary Presidential residence in Washington, a tea was given in her honor, those present being President and Mrs. Truman and their daughter, Margaret, and Mrs. George C. Marshall. After the tea, Mr. Truman had a private half-hour meeting with Madame Chiang. The White House later issued a brief announcement that the President had listened "sympathetically" to his visitor. At the time, Communist divisions had already pushed southward to the approaches of Pengbu, only 100 miles north of Nanking.

On December 15, 1948, the *New York Times* published an editorial, which was truly characteristic of the great tradition for fair play of that newspaper. No stronger advocacy of justice and fairness for China could have been uttered than was contained in this editorial. I quote:

"The Government of the Republic of China has asked the United States for a declaration of policy. The Chinese have presumed that such a declaration would be a declaration of sympathy and support. Since the United States was a signatory of the Nine-Power Pacific Treaty supporting that Government, and since the United States was the source of countless assistance to China in the war. We needed China, and the current Chinese government would never go against us.

The wife of the President of China has had a reception in Washington that by no stretch of the imagination could be called cordial. The total amount of United States military aid to China in the past eighteen months has been less than one-third of that dispatched to Greece and Turkey. The chief of the United States Economic Cooperation Administration has just made a statement in Shanghai which was promptly interpreted in China to mean that the United States has "written off" the present legally constituted government in Nanking. A further conclusion drawn from this statement was that the United States would continue its aid program to a "coalition" government in China, if and when the present government is forced out, provided that such a replacement government preserved essential freedoms.

The Chinese are left with the impression the "writing off" Nanking and extending American aid for a "coalition" government in China have been considered by at least one official United States agency. This must be somewhat confusing, not merely to Chinese, but to Americans. Certainly American taxpayers are entitled to ask: 'When and where has there been a coalition government with communists that had any regard for essential freedoms?'

The Chinese, of course, are asking another question. They want to know if an American Administration that urged large sums of money for Greece to keep the Communists out, is veering toward a policy of agreeing to large sums of money for China only if the Chinese let the Communists in. Since what happens to China is important to every American, we ought to have a clear and authoritative statement of American policy directly from Washington."

On December 15, I received reports from my overseas offices that shortly before General Marshall entered the hospital, he told Washington editors and press representatives that Chinese Nationalist troops had lost no battles owing to the lack of equipment. In a recent three-month period, Nationalists lost 236,000 rifles, 14,000 guns, 26,000 submachine guns, huge ammunition dumps, and even arsenals which they failed to destroy. The equipment lost was said to be sufficient for at least 200,000 men. These figures were now appearing in print all over the United States.

In the meantime, the Treasury Department quietly released to the press the estimate that in the United States, the traceable Chinese holdings were worth $600,000,000, adding that, undoubtedly, other huge Chinese assets in this country had been salted away. One hostile commentator took pains to point out that Chinese assets in America had risen sharply since the beginning of the current crisis.

On December 9, 1948, Dr. Sun Wen and General Wu Teh-cheng, Secretary General of the Kuomintang, wired to the Chinese Ambassador at Moscow, Dr. Fu Ping-hsiang, requesting him to approach Premier Molotov for assistance in bringing the Chinese Communists and the Nationalist government together for cooperation. Mr. George Yeh, acting Minister of Foreign Affairs, refused to sign the telegram, but it was sent nevertheless. The reply from Ambassador Fu was that Premier Molotov would be glad to render the assistance requested, but he wanted to stipulate as the condition that China should first eliminate American and British influences before Moscow used its good offices in arranging an acceptable relationship between the Chinese Communists and the Nationalist government of China.

Following the receipt of this message, Acting President Li Tsung-jen sent a representative to see Ambassador Stuart to urge him to persuade Washington to issue a statement in support of Chinese-Soviet understanding.

During the same period, General Chang Chih-chung and Shao Li-tse both urged that China shift her orientation from America to Soviet Russia.

On December 20, 1948, Premier Dr. Wong Wen-hao resigned, and we all resigned *en bloc*. His cabinet was succeeded by Dr. Sun Wen, who took up his office on December 23. I left government service in sadness, and returned to Shanghai to join Sally, who during more than a year and a half of my official life, had refused to move to Nanking as a silent protest against my rejoining government service. In 1949, when the situation became worse we moved to Taipei, Taiwan. We returned once more for the last time before Shanghai fell into the hands of the communists. We all knew that President Chiang would step down sooner or later, due to the tremendous pressure being exerted upon him by Chinese and American officials. He announced his retirement on January 21, 1949.

I had found my eight years as Vice-Minister of Information during World War II vastly more satisfactory than my year and a half as Director of Government Information in 1947, and Minister without Portfolio in 1948 as a concurrent position. In both periods, I was interpreting the same China to the world. In the first period, while China was at war, she had been praised to the skies. In the second period, praise had turned to calumny, and she had been left to perish for lack of the comparatively little aid which might have saved her. I knew that there was worse to come.

Chapter Seventeen.
Taiwan Years

In February 1949, Sally and I sadly boarded a ship for Taiwan to establish a new home. Shanghai was still in government hands, but there was little doubt in the minds of any of us that the city was doomed. It was not important that I remain to the zero hour since I had been only a private citizen. It would be extremely difficult to obtain transportation out of the city if we waited until the end; it seemed the wise thing to leave while we could.

We were sent off at Shanghai's Bund by our relatives. We did not anticipate returning; we brought with us everything which was movable, even including a piano. It was a sad moment when the boat pulled out and our relatives were left behind, waving to us from the pier when darkness fell. For eight years, during the Japanese occupation, we had been separated from our family; now, we were to be severed again. It was difficult to restrain the tears.

We were also leaving behind our modest life savings. Before the war, we had invested what we had in two houses in Shanghai, and some real estate in Tientsin. During the war, we had been unable to collect any rentals. Our property in Tientsin had gotten into the possession of a gang of crooks who refused to be evicted even though I had won a court action to oust them. By February 1948, the Communists had occupied Tientsin, so there was little choice but to give up this property as lost.

Actually, since 1937, we had had no permanent home. During the war, I lost my books and manuscripts which, to me, were our most precious possessions. Finally, all that we had been able to salvage was contained in a few trunks, which followed us wherever we went. When friends asked me, where was my home, I used to reply, "It is wherever my wife is."

On our arrival in Taiwan, we stayed in a hotel, and then purchased a small Japanese-style house for about $1,000, which we remodeled at the cost of another $2,000. So anxious were we to see our relatives once more, before the Communists arrived, that we took a two-week trip back to Shanghai. After our return from this visit, we settled ourselves in our new Taiwan house for good.

I was now faced by the problem of earning a living. I had not given up the idea of an automobile repair shop of my own, and I explored the possibility of starting one in Taipei. But inquiries revealed that, in order to make a profit in motor repairing in Taiwan, a shop owner would have to engage in some under-the-counter practices with the chauffeurs of his customers. It was the prevailing custom. I had never engaged in shady practices yet, and I did not intend to begin at my age.

Since I was determined not to let my New York-acquired skill become rusty, I applied for a job with the Ford agency in Taipei which was run by a personal friend, an alumnus of Lowrie High School which I had attended. I offered to work for him without pay and he readily accepted. But no sooner was I installed than the regular employees went on strike. The manager warned me that, although I wasn't involved in the controversy, I would be beaten up if I remained on the job. After this walkout, a series of further strikes assailed the unfortunate Ford repair plant. Realizing that the odds were against me, I finally gave up. My dream of being the owner of a motor repair shop was abandoned. As a gesture of abandonment, I even gave away my greasy overalls. I determined that, for the future, I would make my livelihood in newspaper and writing field.

To my pleasure, I found that most of my old Information Department staff members had found their way to Taiwan, and were in the process of getting settled. Some of them established the *China News*, a daily bulletin in English. So many foreigners were arriving that they were lamenting the fact that there was no English-language newspaper to keep them informed. My former colleagues scraped together a small amount of money and launched the *China News*. Lack of capital prevented us from getting out a real newspaper, but we made shift with what we had. But at the end of a few months, a fire destroyed the publishing building. It was revived in new quarters with some difficulties.

After the collapse of resistance to the Communists in South China, President Chiang Kai-shek took up his permanent residence in Taiwan. One of the first things which he did was to set up a provisional information office, and he asked me to head this office with my old friend Shen Chang-hua as assistant. So I found myself back in government information work again.

On July 6, 1949, the Generalissimo gave his first interview to foreign correspondents since his retirement at the end of 1948. A slight complication developed. My associate had arranged to give Clyde Farnsworth of the Scripps-Howard newspapers an exclusive interview. Madame Chiang was in New York and through Major Kung, her nephew, had promised the International News Service (INS) an exclusive. The INS sent Howard Handleman from Tokyo to conduct this interview. Both Farnsworth and Handleman insisted that they should have the interview.

The Generalissimo was much disturbed and asked me how we could extricate ourselves from this mix-up without antagonizing one or other of these powerful news agencies. I told him that our only chance was to tell the truth to both correspondents and to offer to give them a simultaneous interview. Because of its news importance, neither would decline this offer, and I believed that both men would accept the situation philosophically. It required a lot of persuading, but the interview was finally arranged on this basis.

Since the Generalissimo's statement gave a rather complete picture of what had happened since the Communist occupation of the mainland provinces, I will paraphrase Mr. Handleman's dispatch.

Handleman first described the simplicity of the Generalissimo's life in Taiwan. He found him living with his eldest son, Chiang Ching-kuo at Tsaoshan, ten miles out of Taipei. Lack of security guards, wrote Handleman, showed the confidence with which Chiang lived among the Formosan people. After their talk, Handleman related, the Generalissimo walked with them unguarded down the mountain road, followed by photographers.

Handleman found Chiang still confident that the fight against Communism in the Far East had not been lost. He gave as a reason the fact that in 1938, one year after the Japanese attack, the Japanese had conquered more Chinese territory than the Communists have done to date. He declared that the rank and file of the Chinese people hate Communism and submit to it only under its terror. Despite the ruthless Communist rule, he cited the fact that the people have staged uprisings in some areas.

He emphasized the Russian role in the rebellion by pointing out that Russia had violated its treaty agreements with China, made under the Yalta Pact, which should have secured Manchuria for China and quickly returned it to the Nationalist government. But a delay in its return to China and allowing the Chinese Communist to gain control first, it became the springboard of the communist engulfment of mainland China.

Handleman decried the talk that Chinese Communists are different and declared that the hope that a "Tito" type leader could arise among them was unwarranted. He stated that Chinese communists follow orthodox communism.

Chiang expressed himself as especially appreciative of a message from General Douglas MacArthur, Supreme Allied Commander of the Pacific, which Handleman brought from Tokyo. MacArthur expressed his conviction that the Generalissimo will never give up his resistance to the Communists.

The two interviews had good coverage and conspicuous placing in the American press. Coming as they did just on the eve of the release of the State Department White Paper, their timing was perfect. But there was an aftermath of bitterness on the part of the International New Service regarding a violation of the promise Madame Chiang had made to them. The Generalissimo was influenced by this attitude and called Shen Chang-hua and me to Tsaoshan. He administered a mild rebuke, telling us that we had wrongly advised him. Both Shen and I were in a mood to resign our honorary posts, but after a talk with Chiang Ching-kuo, we accepted the situation and determined to remain. This was no time to question the Generalissimo's leadership, while the actual existence of the Chinese in Taiwan was hanging in the balance.

The cruelest blow to Free China was the issuance of the State Department White Paper in July 30, 1949. There is no requirement to issue a White Paper on any country at all. This action is equivalent to cutting the lifeline to a drowning man.

The State Department, now headed by Dean G. Acheson, was determined to wash its hands of any responsibility for the fall of Free China. To do this, Acheson decided that the American people should be told that Chiang Kai-shek, and not the United State was solely responsible for the fall of China to communism. For six weeks, a large staff in the State Department, under Phillip S. Jessup of the Institute of Pacific Relations coterie, was assigned the task of compiling all the documents that blackened the reputation and judgment of the Generalissimo, accusing him of corruption and incompetence. On July 30, 1949, the White Paper, a document of 1,054 pages, was published.

After it appeared, Alfred Kohlberg, chairman of the American China Policy Association, issued a point-by-point analysis showing the great number of important documents that would have presented Chiang in a favorable light were deliberately omitted from the Paper. It was an astounding tally of slanted editorial selection.

Chiang Kai-shek, knowing that the White Paper was in preparation, urged the Washington authorities not to publish it because of its potential consequences. His request was coldly ignored. The White Paper was given to the world press. It is apparent now that Acheson and Jessup overreached themselves. The report was so obviously biased and one-sided that fair-minded men everywhere seriously questioned the good faith of the State Department.

Within a year of the publication of this infamous paper on July 30, 1949, the communist North Korea invaded the South Korea on June 21, 1950. This shocked the American government into a complete reversal of its policy by supporting war against the communists in Korea and deploying the Seventh Fleet to protect Taiwan. Phillip Jessup, under a storm of criticism, retired permanently from the Government. The Korean War changed everything; no more talk of democratic communism that misled many Chinese and Americans alike. Everyone needs to be on guard against false information and deception, especially news reporters and governmental officials. A misstep could cause immense suffering of the people.

Within three weeks of the publication of the White Paper, the Generalissimo sent me to Hong Kong to confer with the commander of the Seventh Fleet, Admiral Badger. I was instructed to ask the Admiral to use his influence in asking Washington to pledge its military and economic support to Taiwan, should the communists attack it.

Admiral Badger assured me that he would support the plan which the Generalissimo gave to him through me. He added that he had discussed the question of the defense of Taiwan with General MacArthur, who had already recommended to Washington that Taiwan must not be allowed to fall into Communist hands, and he would add his weight to the words of the General.

For fear of publicity that can be disadvantageous to us, I went to Hong Kong incognito. Upon my arrival at 4:30 p.m., I was met at the airport by a lieutenant in plain clothes who escorted me to Admiral Badger's flagship. I left by the same quiet means, returning to Taipei by plane the next day. Admiral Badger wanted me to explain to the Generalissimo that he had been instructed by Washington not to visit Taipei for good reasons. If he should confer with the Generalissimo, the Congress and the relevant departments might conclude that he had been unduly influenced and what he had to say on behalf of China would be less meaningful. I agreed with his logic.

Admiral Badger said that he would concentrate on making the strongest possible plea to President Truman; Mr. Johnson, the Secretary of Defense; and the Joint Chief of Staffs for immediate and adequate aid to China. He admitted that the White Paper was a regrettable document, but he said that both sides had made mistakes, and that the best policy at this critical time was to refrain from mutual recrimination.

Admiral Badger felt that Washington had given China enough war materials, but the mistake, as he saw it, was that the material was sent unintelligently. Much of the material received proved useless for a war against the Communist rebels. He blamed the Chinese in part for this in accepting war material indiscriminately. There was a lack of coordination and of specifying definite objectives.

Admiral Badger described the frightful waste of war supplies sent to China. He said that, perhaps, ten percent of the supplies received from U.S. surplus were actually used. Indeed, China did not even have experts to sort them out in the supply pools. The confusion was understandable. For instance, Chinese supply officers would find heaps of rods in the stockpiles, but would have no way of ascertaining whether they were automobile or airplane parts. There were no adequate inventories accompanying the surpluses. This, and not corruption, was the basic reason for the Chinese waste of supplies and the Admiral promised to tell Washington that fact.

I presented to him on the behalf of the Generalissimo our position in regard to the legality of the Chinese Communist government. We maintained that the Nationalist government was still entitled to recognition as the lawful government of all China under the terms of the Cairo Agreement, signed by President Roosevelt and Prime Minister Churchill. Nationalist China would not accept any change by the three great powers in the Cairo stipulations. What the Generalissimo requested of Washington was a declaration that the United States would support Free China in Taiwan if it were attacked. Such a declaration would be a powerful morale factor among the anti-Communist Chinese. The Generalissimo instructed me to convey that the Taiwan authorities would be willing to consider any form of cooperation with America's military and economic aid leading to the development of Taiwan as a model in Asia.

Admiral Badger indicated to me the strategic plan, which he believed the Nationalist government should now adopt. It should use Taiwan as a base from which to harass the enemy along the Chekiang and Kiangsu coasts. It should use Hainan Island from which to harass the enemy along the

Fukien and Guangdong coasts. These operations should be supplemented by three or four guerilla activities on China mainland; one in Hunan or Guongxi under General Pai Chung-xi; one in the Northwest under the two General Mas; and one in Shangtung under General Li whose 7,000 veteran guerrilla fighters had impressed him. These commanders should be asked to submit plans to be accomplished within six months. Also, he hinted that various guerilla leaders had approached him independently of Taiwan asking for aid under the $125,000,000 American grant and he had asked his staff to prepare a plan based upon their requests from separate resistance forces.

Turning again to the White Paper, Admiral Badger said that too much blame had been laid upon the shoulders of the Generalissimo. He said:

"The Generalissimo and I came to unpleasantness in our discussions of plans. Sometimes I was angry with him, but he impressed me as a very sincere man. He was determined to carry out a number of things and he would not give them up until he had encountered tremendous difficulties, such as the lack of materials. I am going to testify this to my government. I know the Generalissimo and his ideas well. He is too good, and too faithful to his subordinates. He is always ready to accept the responsibility and blame which should be assessed against some of his subordinates. To foreigners this is incomprehensible.

Later I learned that the two General Mas, who were waging guerilla resistance in the Northwest, were dissatisfied with the amount of arms promised them by the Generalissimo. General Pai Chung-xi had been promised twenty planeloads of munitions. He sought an interview with Minister Clark of the American Consulate, and Clark immediately wired his requirements to Washington. U.S. government seemed to encourage direct dealings with those Chinese officers who had been fighting the Communists and bypassing the central government. Pai was promised war materials if he could hold up the Communists. He was promised aid even if he had to retreat to Yunnan province, which would be a logical place for his army if he should fail to hold Hunan and Guongxi.

The April 3, 1948, a grant of $125,000,000 war aid by Washington had arrived too late to help us hold the mainland. The first shipments of war materials under this grant did not reach China until the later part of November, 1948. The shipments did not use the price for war surplus, but were billed under the new replacement cast, which was much higher. This seriously reduced total quantity.

Being in charge of publicity and government information, I was given an insight into these Chinese generals' backstage scrambling to bypass the Generalissimo in their contacts with the Americans. It was the same disunity which had contributed heavily to the collapse of the Nationalist government before the Communists. This interview with Admiral Badger, who was a sincere friend of China, reveals some of the crosscurrents which faced us in Taiwan in those danger-filled months of 1949. To me it was a saddening experience.

After the summer of 1949 and for two years thereafter, although I had no official position in the government, most of my time was taken up in tours to America, Japan and Europe as a confidential envoy of the Generalissimo. It was desperately important that the Generalissimo, isolated in Taiwan, should have sources of information about the attitudes of the outside world. I tried to supply them to him. Increasingly, the Generalissimo saw China's struggle against Communism as a part of the global struggle. He realized that China's ability to keep up the resistance would be closely connected with the Free World's struggle against the aggression of world communism.

Chapter Eighteen.
Overseas Trips, 1949-1951

The end of the year 1949 saw the Free World in a state of confusion in regard to the Far East. Mainland China was definitely lost and Chiang Kai-shek and the followers of the Kuomintang leadership had retreated to Taiwan. General and Vice President Li Tsung-jen had become acting President of China since the retirement of the Generalissimo on January 21, 1949. Li negotiated with the Communists throughout 1949 but failed. He quit China for the safer retreat of Riverdale, New York, where he attempted to carry on intrigues with the Truman administration for his installment as an American-backed shadow ruler. He had become the center of a new wave of anti-Chiang publicity in the United States. The British were in the process of recognizing Mao Ze-dong's regime while the United States, then largely swayed in its Far East policies by Secretary of State Dean Acheson, was still uncommitted to a definite policy. There were ominous signs that Acheson and the International Public Relations group were seriously contemplating following the British lead and repudiating Taiwan.

It was in this dark diplomatic atmosphere that I was asked to sound out American public and relay their opinions back to Chiang in Taiwan. I conducted a large number of talks with important Americans during these months between the fall of the mainland and the outbreak of the Korean War. Some of these talks were off the record and even now I do not have the permission of the parties to report them. However, I can convey their tenor. A review of some of these 1949-1950 conversations throws some light upon the opinions which agitated the United States during that disheartening time.

I talked with one important public man, who must remain nameless, about the curious course which General George Marshall had followed in the discouraging months of 1948 and 1949 when resolute action might have saved China. He agreed with me that the General Marshall, having taken the mistaken "coalition with the Communists" policy in 1946, was influenced by motives of face-saving in refusing to budge from this position after it had been discredited.

"The General Marshall is a patriotic man," my interviewee told me, "but perhaps he has reasoned that if he should reverse his non-aid-for-China policy now, it would be asked why so late. Why did not Marshall reconsider his position while Manchuria was still in Nationalist hands and could have been saved?"

This man told me of a friend who had recently talked to President Truman and had told him that he believed substantial help should be given to Taiwan. The President, who expressed great respect for General Marshall, did not care to inaugurate a policy which Marshall disapproved.

"I personally called on Marshall and asked him to reconsider his China policy," my informant told me. "He was unbending. He said that there was no reason to help the Generalissimo unless he realized his mistake in refusing to cooperate with the Communists. When I called attention to the fact that events had proved that the Generalissimo was right, and that the Communists did not genuinely desire to form a coalition government, General Marshall showed notable anger. He then asked me why the Generalissimo had not withdrawn the government troops from Manchuria when it became untenable. I pointed out that the morale effect upon China of an outright withdrawal from Manchuria would have been shattering. Moreover, once Manchuria was lost it would have been extremely difficult to hold the territory in the northern China. The General was unmoved."

The picture of the Truman administration at that time was of a President overshadowed by a great military man who refused, even when the facts were presented to him, to face the fact that he had committed a colossal diplomatic blunder in his policy to China.

I asked an important Chinese to talk with Acting President Li Tsung-jen, then in New York after a break with the Generalissimo. He saw Li on January 4, 1950. He found the General eager to make contact with the Washington officials, looking for American aid. My friend warned Li against the bad advice which he had been receiving from Albert Chow and Kan Chia-how. Li showed him a letter which he had received from General

Pai Chung-xi which also warned against Chow's mistaken intrigues. Nevertheless, he indicated that he would continue to use Chow and Kan as contacts with Washington. Li, despite his efforts to persuade Washington to accept him as an alternative to Chiang, made little progress.

From another influential American, I obtained a good picture of President Truman's attitude toward aid to China. He told me:

"The President is inclined to be favorable to China aid, but when a sharp difference of opinion developed in his administration between the Defense Department and the Joint Chiefs of Staff, on the one hand, and the State Department on the other, he declined to take a stand and decided to leave the issue to Congress. The Defense Department favored aid, while the State Department was firmly against it. The China aid question has become a political issue, which causes men to take stubborn and inflexible attitudes."

The State Department, he told me, was hinting on every appropriate occasion that aid to Taiwan might prove to be an economic quagmire, and that the United States couldn't afford it. Moreover, the Department spokesman argued that further American involvement in the Far East might draw us into war, maybe even World War III.

On another occasion this influential American said that the Joint Chiefs of Staff and Secretary of Defense, Johnson, who were then touring in Japan and Korea, all favored sending a military mission to China and giving limited military aid. But the State Department strongly opposed this program. The main argument of the State Department was that the people on Formosa hate the Nationalist government. A revolt on the mainland was bound to happen sooner or later. It would be futile for the United States to offer any assistance to Taiwan in such circumstance. The other argument was that assisting Formosa militarily would provoke the Russians to release some of their submarines and to give other military help to communist China. He pointed out:

"If you can show the world that the people of Formosa are for the Government, and if you can also show that your soldiers have the will to fight as they did on Quemoy Island, I believe things will change for the better for China in this country. Military aid is not hopeless. Congress may be able to do something. Meanwhile you can engage military and economic advisers with your own money. This will not be opposed by our government."

I replied, "The moral value of American government aid is lost in such transactions. What we need most of all is the psychological factor." I inquired what was the latest attitude of American leaders like General

Marshall towards the Generalissimo, and if their attitude had anything to do with the present deadlock. My friend said:

"I must be frank with you. This Government still does not like the Generalissimo. People at Washington consider him as the discredited head of Chinese government. He had his success in the past, but in the last three years he had repeated failures. One of the new disappointments in this country is that the Generalissimo did not halt the Communists at the Yangtse River. People think that new leadership is needed in China. Chiang's presence on Formosa is a handicap to you in winning American assistance."

I reminded him,

"There are many misconceptions about the Generalissimo which the Communists have deliberately planted. We do want a new leader to lead us, and it is not possible to find such a leader. The Generalissimo, with more than twenty years of leadership behind him, is the best man to lead China at this critical time. We have tried Li Tsung-jen, but he has failed us. Without the Generalissimo, Formosa will become absolutely hopeless."

My friend said:

"I know all this. He is very important in the minds of many Chinese, but the unfortunate thing is that the people in Washington do not share that view. In pointing out the foregoing, I intend only to convey to you a true picture of the thinking in Washington."

On January 7, 1950, I saw an American official of ambassadorial rank who had formerly served in China, and one of his former staff members told me the following:

"I had a conversation with General Marshall discussing Chinese affairs. I can say positively that General Marshall has not changed his mind regarding aid to China. If he is right, he will stick to this, and if he is wrong, he will also stick to it. He has not spoken any words in favor of the Generalissimo. Madame Chiang has been misled by the belief that General Marshall has become the Generalissimo's friend again."

During this critical period, among the American legislators who stood by Free China were Senator Knowland, Congressman Judd, Congressman John W. MacCormack, Senator Scott W. Lucas, Vice President Barkley, and others. They had done everything possible to secure American aid to save Taiwan from a possible fall into the Communist hands. One American legislator pointed out that

"It is not possible to force President Truman to modify his China policy. As the President of the United States, Mr. Truman has the power to recognize the Red regime. Although the sum of $75,000,000 was voted for China aid, he has the power not to use it as he is now doing. The Congress has no authority to insist that he use the money immediately."

From another influential American I learned that on December 30, 1949, the President told him that there would be no aid for China. President Truman said:

"America had sent 1,000,000 rifles, large numbers of machine guns and trucks, and aircraft to China from Guam. China had lost all of them, while half of the navy and half of the air force had gone over voluntarily to the communist side. China had abandoned without a fight one ammunition dump storing great quantities of arms and materials. It would take at least ten American divisions to hold Formosa against the Communist attacks. This would mean war."

The American who saw President Truman and heard his complaint pleaded that nevertheless China is worth saving. The President replied that Chinese soldiers had no will to fight. He added:

"I know what I am talking about. There is no use for you to argue with me. We tried everything. The visitor suggested that China should be given as much aid as Greece was given. The reply of the President was that we had, but that the Chinese had not made good use of it. What is the use of giving any further aid to China when the result will be the same, the defeat of Chinese on Formosa? He asked argumentatively."

This was not a new idea to me, nor did it surprise me, for I had heard something worse. As early as October 1949, President Truman had been heard to mutter in the presence of a White House visitor, "If we could only get rid of Chiang." On another occasion, the President had told an important person calling on him on behalf of Free China, "I am about to pull the rug away from under the feet of the Generalissimo." That was soon after the release of the White Paper. This was the hostile atmosphere in which the Generalissimo found himself after his retreat to Taiwan in mid-1949.

The nemesis of China during all the years from 1944 to 1949 was this obsessed determination of official Washington to impose a coalition government upon it. The coalition idea bedeviled and soured all the relationships between Chiang Kai-shek and Washington. All too many Americans used this coalition proposal with the Communists as a yardstick by which to test the good faith of Chiang in his American relationships. The test was cruelly unfair because Chiang had never believed in the coalition and only went along with the idea to keep peace with General Marshall and other insistent American advisers. Today, in the light of Czechoslovakia and other countries, no reputable free world statesman believes in coalition with Communists. But in the 1940s, many Washington statesmen believed in the coalition formula almost it was like a sacred cow. Chiang Kai-shek was crucified in world's opinion because he had the political foresight to oppose it.

Another leader who would not permit coalition with the Communists to be forced upon him at this time was Syngman Rhee, President of Korea. The State Department detested Rhee as thoroughly as they hated Chiang. When Rhee took over the civilian government in Korea at the end of World War II, the State Department sent a directive to Rhee through General MacArthur urging a coalition government in Korea with the communists. General Hodges, Allied Commander in Korea, gave him the news. He took time in giving his reply, and then told Hodges:

"You want my reply, and I shall give it right away. To form a coalition government with Communists is just like living with people having full blown smallpox during influenza."

After completing the sentence, he walked out stiffly. General Hodges, who had merely been the conveyer of the directive, was glad that Rhee would give such an answer.

On January 12, 1950, I called on General MacArthur in Tokyo, in company of General S. M. Chu, head of the Chinese Military Mission in Japan. We talked for one hour. I repeated to the General what an American friend of China in Washington had said in regard to the need of exploring the possibility of finding a safe place of refuge for the Generalissimo and some of his close followers in the event of disaster. General MacArthur emphatically said:

"If attention is paid to this question, the cause is lost. For the Generalissimo there is no refuge in the world. If I were he, I would defend Formosa and defend it even unto death. He would be happier being killed on the battlefield than spending his future as a refugee. I do not advise him to do this, but if I were he, I would select the only course left open for me."

I assured General MacArthur of the determination of the Generalissimo to defend Formosa to death, and that he would consider no other course. General MacArthur said:

"Don't expect any military aid from America. Some economic aid may be forthcoming, but it will be small and given as a token. It is true that some Republicans are putting up a fight for Formosa, but I am afraid that they will not be able to help the situation. You should also mention this to the Generalissimo that you can assure him of my friendship."

American military aid was not possible according to General MacArthur. Perhaps he had in mind the report in current circulation in October and November following the publication of the White Paper. To soften the blow to Free China, Washington had been considering sending a volunteer military mission of twenty to thirty retired officers from each service, an economic mission of more than 20 experts, equipment of 6 divisions, 60 speedy vessels and a radar system, if the Chinese government would make formal request for them. Encouragement came from two sources, namely, former Ambassador Stuart and Admiral Badger. The request was presented as indicated, and it was discussed at the meeting of the National Security Council, with President Truman presiding on December 29, 1949. The Joint Chiefs of Staff were in favor of aiding Formosa, but Mr. Acheson was opposed, and no action was taken.

I succeeded in clearing up the facts during the fortnight of my trip to America, and the Generalissimo reconciled himself to the fact that no aid, either economic or military, would be forthcoming.

President Chiang sent me out again on April 22, 1950. I saw Sir Alexander Grantham, Governor of Hong Kong; John Rayner, Regional Information Officer for the Office of the Commissioner-General for Southeast Asia; Lien Ying-chow, the managing director of the overseas Union Bank in Singapore; and others. In Paris, I called on Wong Wen-hao, former Prime Minister, under whom I had served as a Minister without Portfolio and concurrently director of the Government Information Office, in Nanking. He told me of two offers for service in America: One was from the Director of the American Geological Survey to study a secret document for which he was to receive $7,000, but as a former high official he could not accept. Another was from Mr. Raynord, President of the Raynord Company, to be one of seniors members of his company to study aluminum resources in the world.

On May 6, 1950, I saw Mr. Roger Gazzean, President of the Trusteeship Council of the United Nations. He had once been connected with the French Legation in Beijing, France's ambassador in Moscow between 1942 and 1943, and subsequently ambassador to Poland. He summarized the situation as follows:

"The world situation is bad and deteriorating. The United States hesitates to face it realistically. Soviet Russia is winning the cold war. Western democracy is helpless. . . . Mr. Schuman, French Foreign Minister, was so convinced of the soundness of my view that America must give aid to Formosa for effective defense."

From a number of other equally reliable sources, I learned that most thoughtful Frenchmen were thinking in terms of neutrality in the event of a third world war. They were terribly afraid of Soviet Russia. Consequently they did not openly criticize the Russians for fear they would be marked for reprisals when Soviet Russia decided to go to war. In their conversations, they were more critical of Americans than of Russians. During my visit, the editor of *La Matin,* printed an article by a former high French official suggesting that the question of joining the Third World War which would devastate France to such an extent that war is not worth fighting. Such view was being widely spread not only in France but in other European nations which were in opposition to Communism.

In London I visited General de Wiart, who had served as a British liaison officer in Chungking during the war, and Mr. Peter Hume, a former staff member of mine in London. Hume said:

"Great Britain is now in the pocket of the United States. She has been receiving so much economic aid that she has virtually become an American satellite. The British were realistic that they had to depend upon American aid for the maintenance of their prestige and even for their very existence."

I called on some leading British journalists during my stay in London, and learned from them that a conference of the three foreign ministers of Great Britain, America and France, had agreed not to admit Red China into the United Nations but to review the matter in September. England had already recognized Red China with the approval of Mr. Acheson, but America's refusal to do the same was due to public pressure. At first Great Britain urged America not to help Taiwan. When Red China laid down impossible conditions to the British such as support of Red China's claim to the China seat in the United Nations in return for sending a representative of ambassadorial rank to London, British enthusiasm over siding with Red China underwent a decided slump. There was no more talk of putting pressure on Washington to not aid Formosa. France was against recognition of Red China, and was sympathetic with the Republic of China. I saw Prime Minister Ridault on May 17, in his official residence, together with our Charge d'Affairs, Dr. M. L. Tu, and he expressed his sympathy with us.

On May 25, 1950, back in Washington, I saw Mr. John Foster Dulles, adviser to the State Department. He did not hold out any hope of American aid. The impression he gave me in our confidential talk was that the American government had made up its mind that it was now too late to do anything effective and that most American experts felt that Formosa could survive only three to four months longer. His sympathy was with Free China, but there was little he could do to change the situation or the American policy.

The next day I saw Congressman Judd again. He referred to a conversation with Mr. Acheson on the possibility of losing all American trained Chinese administrators in the event of the Communist occupation of the island of Taiwan. He explained that the cream of China's administrative ability was now collected on Taiwan as the rich and the corrupt for the most part had now gone elsewhere. Judd was all for introducing a resolution in the House providing for the removal of this Chinese intelligentsia from Taiwan in the event of Communist conquest, but I dissuaded him from doing so. It seemed to me that such a move, and the publicity, would spread defeatism and discouragement among the defenders of Taiwan. Actually there was no solution but death for the leaders of the Republic of China if the Communists overran the island.

During this trip I called on Senator Knowland; Leslie Biffle, secretary of the Senate; Dr. Leighton Stuart, Mr. William C. Bullitt, Dean Rusk, Assistant Secretary of State; and Mr. Charles G. Ross, Press Secretary to the President, and my former journalism teacher at the School of Journalism in Missouri. In my talk with Mr. Ross, I heard some cheerful news. After telling him of my views concerning Taiwan, and of my belief that Taiwan still had a fighting chance, he replied, "I am glad to hear this. We have been receiving many reports about the situation on Formosa, and the matter of aid to China is being further considered." He was a man of a few words, and what he said must have come from an inside source. On parting I gave him a personal letter which I wrote to President Truman and he said that it would receive his chief's attention.

On June 1, 1950, I called on General Dwight D. Eisenhower, at that time the President of Columbia University. Our conversation lasted three-quarters of an hour. It was arranged by Dean Carl Ackerman, a classmate of mine at the Post-Graduate School of Journalism at Columbia. The General recalled our meeting in Cairo during the war. The number of questions characteristic of a trained mind of a first class military leader included:

"How long can you hold Formosa? What are the forces available for defense? How about the food situation in Formosa? How long can you sustain Formosa economically? How about your war supplies? How about the charges of inefficiency and corruption against the Chinese government, and can the responsibility for these be squarely placed on the shoulders of the Generalissimo? What action do you propose to stop the further deterioration of this situation?"

General Eisenhower revealed an intimate knowledge of Chinese affairs. I answered his questions frankly. He was my University President, and I discussed these questions with a candidness which I did not display on other occasions. General Eisenhower said,

"All these facts and arguments you put forward sound logical. Has your ambassador told our high officials the same?"

I replied in the affirmative. He thanked me and said, "I am glad that you have been outspoken." He promised to do his best to bring these facts to the knowledge of the high officials in Washington when he intended to visit shortly.

On June 5, 1950, Mr. John Foster Dulles phoned me saying that he would like to see me again before my return to Taipei. I saw him again, and he told me that he hoped he had not left with me a false impression that he was not trying to do what he could for China by way of military aid. In fact, he said, he had been doing his utmost for China. He was about to travel to Korea, and then arrive in Japan on June 19. I invited him to visit Taipei and assured him of a cordial reception by the Generalissimo. He did not commit himself for such a trip.

In this second talk, Mr. Dulles declared to me that aid, if it was to be given to Taiwan, must be in sufficient quantity to assure the successful defense of the island. I assured him that a large aid would enable us not only to hold Taiwan, but also to mount an attack upon the seething mainland. I also stressed a successful stand in Taiwan would give to such wavering countries as France much confidence. I told Mr. Dulles about my recent trip to Europe and of the defeatism which I had found rampant. The future Secretary of State was deeply moved. He assured me that he was working on the China problem and would do his utmost for Taiwan.

Before I returned to Taiwan, I perceived an encouraging change in the attitudes of the confused men in Washington. It was apparent in mid-summer of 1950 there was an important difference between the miserable closing months of 1949 and the new determination to halt further communist aggression. I was able to return home with the report that the worst was over in China-America relations.

I was still a discouraged man when I flew back across the Pacific in June. Before returning home, I made another call on General MacArthur in Tokyo. I asked the General for his latest thinking on Taiwan. He admitted to me that he had changed his opinion since our last talk, two months before. He now thought that the situation in Taiwan was very critical. Information which had come to him had convinced him that it was the Russians who coveted Taiwan. The Russians wanted it for a submarine base, to enable them to control the China Sea. To win Taiwan, he understood that Russians were manning air squadrons in Red China.

Secretary of Defense Johnson and General Bradley were then making a tour of the Far East. General MacArthur interpreted the trip of these two high-ranking officials as an indication of the increasing importance which Washington was giving Asia.

On June 19, 1950, in Tokyo I saw Defense Secretary Johnson and General Bradley together. Mr. Johnson was reticent, and this made our conversation rather difficult. He gave me monosyllabic answers. Then there was a moment of silence. I broke the silence by saying that we were fighting the communists with our backs against the wall and that he was in a position to help us and save the situation. Again some silence, and Mr. Johnson finally threw out the sparing remark: "The situation is very serious." I said that if Soviet Russia does not throw in a large air force, we could hold Formosa with difficulty until the next spring. Evidence indicated that Soviet Russia was going all out for the occupation of Formosa.

Mr. Johnson after hesitation, said: "I am not making a statement."

I replied that I did not expect any statement from him as I was not reporting for the press or news agency. What I might learn I would report to the Generalissimo alone. He listened attentively to what I had said about the will of the Generalissimo and most of the people to defend Taiwan to the end regardless of any help from our friends. I continued my talk for some time, and again there was silence.

I realized that Mr. Johnson was in a difficult position and I excused his silence. It was Johnson who had initiated the bill for sizable aid to China in December 1949. When he learned that Secretary of State Acheson, with President Truman's support, had spoken out against this step, Johnson had deliberately absented himself from the National Security Council meetings to avoid a collision with the President. He was very near to his retirement from the Cabinet, leaving Dean Acheson at top.

Shortly afterwards, on June 21, 1950, the North Korean Communists attacked South Korea. Washington was taken by surprise. On June 27, President Truman announced that he had ordered the Seventh Fleet to defend Formosa without previous consultation with the Nationalist government. This indicated the imminence of a communist invasion of Formosa. To us it meant a new lease of life. The North Koreans had made a grave mistake by attacking South Korea misjudging the temper of the American government. The North Korean had been thrown off guard by Mr. Acheson's repeated announcements that the United States would not intervene forcibly in any civil war in Far Eastern country.

On September 27, 1950, President Chiang sent me out, first to Hong Kong, and later to Japan and the United States. I was again to act as eyes and ears for my chief. In Tokyo I again met General MacArthur, this time under happier circumstances. Arriving in America, I met General Yu Teh-wei in San Francisco, and T. F. Tsiang, head of the Chinese delegation at the United Nations in New York. I also conferred with Arthur and Mrs. Sulzberger, publisher of the *New York Times*. I next went to Washington where I met Ambassador Wellington V. K. Koo, Bishop Paul Yu-pin, Dr. Leighton Stuart and numerous others. I learned the good news that General Marshall had a change of heart regarding Free China. The events in Korea had finally convinced him that the dream of Mao Ze-dong to become an Asian Tito was illusory. My reaction was, "better late than never."

On November 2, I lunched at the Cosmos Club with Dr. Stanley K. Hornbeck, former director of the Bureau of Far Eastern Affairs in the State Department. Hornbeck, reviewing the world situation, did not share the current pessimism about the future of China. He said,

"In the first place, the foreign policy of the United States is contradictory and conflicting. It was a 180 degree change when President Truman on June 27, 1950 announced the assignment of the Seventh Fleet to defend Formosa. It was also a 180 degree change in our policy towards South Korea. At one time and on record, Mr. Acheson publicly announced that we would not do anything in regard to Korea if there should be civil war. President Truman changed that policy and ordered the land, naval and air forces to defend South Korea, a complete reversal of policy."

On November 4, 1950, I again saw Charles G. Ross, Press Secretary to President Truman. He asked me to have luncheon with him and he was in a more talkative mood than I had ever found him, even during my student days. I repeated my question,

"Is there any way to improve the relationship between President Truman and the Generalissimo? We are fighting the same battle, and yet President Truman gives aid to us with such obvious reluctance. Is it perhaps because he is receiving faulty information from pro-Communist advisers?"

Mr. Ross told me that President Truman, of late, was thinking more favorably of the Generalissimo. When I asked him if it might not be advisable for Mr. Truman to receive the Generalissimo, Ross replied that this would, in his opinion, be premature. "The Administration is still following a policy of not provoking the Chinese Communists," he said. "A visit by the Generalissimo to the White House would touch off a controversy." He promised to keep me fully informed if there were any changes in policy.

On November 10, 1950, I saw General Marshall. In 1947, I had discussed the communist question with him in the car as we rode to Shanghai airport. He asked me whether our troops could fight. I replied,

"Other friends of China have asked me similar questions and I have given them similar assurances. Undoubtedly, they have in mind our failures in the north. However I have found a more satisfactory answer in the Bible. Chapter five of Romans says, '… suffering produces endurance, and endurance produce character, and character produces hope; and hope does not disappoint us…"

General Marshall replied,

"You know the Bible better than I do, and your answer is satisfactory."

Nothing substantial was touched upon in our conversation, and he did not wish to discuss anything fundamental and controversial.

On November 15, 1950, I saw Dean Rusk, Assistant Secretary of State, and he told me that the situation in Korea was very serious and that 100,000 Chinese Communist soldiers were fighting in Korea as volunteers. Volunteers would not presumably have tanks and artillery, but they had them. He raised the question,

"I presume you are counting on a third world war to get yourself out of the difficult situation in which you now find yourself. Am I right?"

My reply was:

"You are wrong. We would be the greatest sufferers from a third world war. America is not strong enough to defend Asia. According to your repeated public statements, Europe will receive priority in the event of a global war. For awhile your navy would be present in Asian waters, but it would not be able to remain due to the intensive submarine warfare which would be waged by

Soviet Russia. Russia has at least one hundred submarines based in Pacific waters."

Rusk said:

"However I have read quite a number of statements issued by Governor K. C. Wu and other national leaders in Taiwan in which they all predicted that a third world war would come soon and that when it came you would return to the mainland to drive out the Chinese Communists."

I replied:

"These statements were made to bolster the morale of the Chinese people on the mainland. The people constantly appeal to the Nationalist government on Formosa to liberate them from the yoke of the Chinese Communists. The government cannot turn a deaf ear to these appeals, and must say something to keep up their morale. Of course, if world war comes, we will be the first to suffer."

I saw Congressman Judd; Mr. Roy Howard; Dr. T. F. Chiang; Admiral Badger; Bill Gray and John Osborn, of the *Time* and *Life*, and Mr. Singh, India ambassador to the United States. Singh was outspoken in his denunciation of America, England and the United Nations which he said were trying to appease the Chinese Communists. Singh warned that notwithstanding the press reports that President Truman and Mr. Atlee would not appease Red China, they would eventually forsake the whole of Asia.

I stopped off in Japan on my way back to Taipei, and saw General Charles A. Willoughby, Assistant Chief of Staff for General MacArthur. He suggested that we should land troops on the mainland for the purpose of diversion, and he said he had recommended this to his own government, but he had not yet received a reaction.

My next mission abroad was to attend the Moral Rearmament Conference at Mackinac Island, Michigan, from June 1 to 12, 1951. The Generalissimo insisted that I should attend the conference, and with much reluctance I went. The Chinese delegation was the smallest, namely two, Dr. Han Lieh-wu and myself, whereas the Japanese sent the largest delegation of more than sixty. Differences in the treatment accorded to the two delegations embittered me.

Bishop L. R. Roots, one of the two founders of the Moral Rearmament Movement, the other being Dr. Frank Buchman, was a friend of China and a missionary for many years. I knew him in Hankow during the years of 1937 and 1938, and I also know his sons and daughters. To attract attention to our small delegation, I requested permission from the Generalissimo to lay a flower wreath on the Roots' tomb which is on the island. Permission was secured by telegram, and Dr. Buchman was requested to ask the whole conference of twelve hundred delegates to attend the ceremony.

There was a large turnout. I provided all the carriages (no cars on the island) to take the delegates to the tomb. My ceremony took less than half an hour. But at least I had stolen the show over the larger delegation from other countries. I was hurt when a British Moral Rearmament member, an official of the British Foreign Office, tried conspicuously to avoid me although at the end of World War II, he had sought my friendship eagerly. Free China was down in the international scale of things. When I returned to Taipei, my report to the Generalissimo was not too complimentary to the Moral Rearmament movement.

In Taiwan, President Chiang Kai-shek carried out the democratic constitution and many economic reforms. To help farmers, the government purchased farmland from the owners at fair market value and then sold it to tenant farmers on a 20-year mortgage. This measure resulted in a tremendous surge of agricultural products. The government also converted many public enterprises to commercial companies by issuing stock that traded on the open market. Payments to land owners were in the form of these stocks. The privatization of public enterprises spurred industrial growth. The President and Premier Chiang Ching-kuo completed ten major construction projects such as the cross island highway, the North-South freeway, railroad networks, a subway system, a new harbor, reservoirs for power and irrigation, power plants, a major steel factory and so on. In 25 years after 1951, the productivity increase was so great; the average per capita income increased 20 times, and was referred to as the economic miracle of Taiwan.

Chapter Nineteen.
Broadcast and Newspaper Services in Taiwan

Shortly after my return to Taiwan from the Moral Rearmament Conference in 1951, I received an invitation to visit Prime Minister Chen Cheng. Exhausted by overwork, the Premier was resting in his summer home at Tsaoshan.

Following some preliminaries, General Chen Cheng complimented me on the confidential missions which I had performed throughout the world for the President. Then he reminded me that the peace treaty was about to be signed between Japan and the Republic of China.

"I wish you would be good enough to accept the position as the head of Chinese Military Mission in Japan," he told me. "Upon ratification of the peace treaty, you will automatically be appointed the first post-war Ambassador to Japan."

General Chen's invitation came to me as a complete surprise. I had never dreamed of becoming an ambassador. I had accepted the post, three years before, as managing director of the *National Radio Network* in Taipei, and concurrently I was the chairman of the board of directors of the *Central Daily News*, the principal Kuomintang (Citizen's Party) newspaper. Since these were in the line of my life profession, I hesitated to undertake something new. Even my many trips as envoy for President Chiang had seemed to me as news-gathering missions, more than diplomacy.

This was not the first time I had been offered an ambassadorship but hitherto I had declined it. In the autumn of 1945, at the close of the war, I had been offered the post of Ambassador to Canada but I had refused it.

Shortly afterwards, following the conclusion of the first Foreign Ministers' Conference in London, Minister Wang Shih-chieh had asked me to become Ambassador to Turkey. I had again refused.

I told General Chen that I would give his offer my careful thought. I did not consider that an ambassadorship under present circumstances was a post of honor, as in former years. The Republic of China had shrunk to a single province, and since intrigues were in progress to seat Red China in the United Nations, my tenure might be brief. The most distinguished of China's former ambassadors were now living abroad, mostly in the United States. It was low ebb in China's diplomatic career.

Together with most of my former colleagues of the International Department I had elected to stay in Taiwan and share its danger, rather than seek security abroad. It was true that the outbreak of the Korean War had temporarily removed the threat of attack. For this reason, I would not feel like a runaway in going abroad at this time.

While I was deliberating the matter, my old superior, Dr. Wang Shih-chieh, then chief secretary to the President, suggested that I defer my acceptance until the former exchange of ambassadors, which was sometime ahead.

I was glad to win this respite. I devoted my time uninterruptedly to the work of the *National Radio Network* and of the *Central Daily News*. I had gotten into this broadcasting responsibility by request of the President. Finding the network in a state of confusion, he had appointed Chang Tao-fan, later to become president of the Legislative Branch, as chairman of the board and me as managing director of the network. I found Mr. Chang most cooperative and we worked together harmoniously. Sally was away, and I lived in a tiny two-room apartment at the broadcasting station. My presence in the building was helpful as some of our announcers were in the habit of showing up irregularly to suit their own convenience. I soon had this slipshod habit changed.

I had monitors listening to the broadcasts from the Communist mainland stations to find out what they were saying so that we could counteract them. We also received news from the British Broadcasting Corporation and other foreign stations which we rebroadcast to our Taiwan listeners without delay. Such improvement increased the popularity of our stations, and increased the effectiveness of our broadcasts to the Chinese people behind the Iron Curtain. As a check on the reach of our broadcasts behind the Iron Curtain, I stationed reporters in Hong Kong and in Japan to interview refugees from Red China and to learn how widely our programs were heard. We were gratified to learn that many in Red China were using our broadcasts to keep in touch with what was going on in the outside world.

The price which some of our listeners on the mainland were paying to hear our broadcasts was astonishing. A Chinese anti-communist, who had been unable to get out of the mainland before the coming of the communists, was in the habit of keeping his shortwave set turned to our station for several hours a day. To avoid reprisals, his wife would station herself at the door to watch if Communist snoopers approached. One day he came to grief in a way which he could not have anticipated.

His seven-year-old son was asked in school what his father and mother had done the night before. He innocently replied that his father had been listening to the radio from Taiwan. Within two hours, his parents were arrested. The father was given a public trial on the street. When the judge asked the crowd what penalty should be given to this "American spy," some of the Communist agents in the mob gave a loud cry of "Death." The judge pronounced the sentence and the same day he was shot.

The aftermath of this incident was even more horrible. In school, the teacher pinned a decoration of honor on the son and he was praised effusively as a hero and as a trapper of an American spy. For a few days, the impressionable child enjoyed the adulation. But later he became rebellious and was sent to a labor camp. There he heard that his mother had disappeared. After brooding over what had happened, the child killed himself.

This and similar kinds of atrocities happened numerous time under Mao Ze-dong's communist regime. Where were the liberty, the democracy, and the Utopia Chairman Mao promised?

Although such news gave us a pang, it was obvious that the communist masters on the mainland feared our radio, or else they would not have gone to such efforts to frighten the secret listeners. We improved our broadcasting facilities and had the satisfaction of knowing that we were effectively breaching the iron curtain which Mao Ze-dong had thrown up around the Chinese people. Some of the personnel whom we trained in Taiwan were lured away by the American Army Radio station in Tokyo. Since the Americans could pay technicians much more than we could, I could not refuse our staff members the chance to go. I had the satisfaction of knowing that the Army station was also beaming its programs behind the Iron Curtain in mainland China.

Later, I had an unhappy experience with our broadcasting set-up. Some Americans who were sent to Taipei during the Korean War to conduct psychological warfare determined to bring our broadcasting efforts under their control. They asked that part of our program be turned over to a new company which they set up, the Continental Broadcasting Division. The leader of this group was an American named Betrandis who claimed to be a radio expert. Using the name of Chiang Ching-kuo as their backer, the American transferred some of our equipment and part of our operating grant to the Continental. I doubted if Chiang Ching-kuo actually knew the disruptive work which they were doing in the name of supposed improvement. The whole situation was full of headaches for me.

I was also chairman of the *Central Daily News*. Fortunately, I had an unusually able man to back me up – Ma Hsin-yeh, a graduate of the School of Journalism at the University of Missouri. Ma served ably as both publisher and editor.

I found it extremely difficult to run a modern newspaper in Taipei. Officials had little concept of the limitations of a newspaper. Some wanted to use the press as a vehicle to bolster their own prestige and importance. Because of their high positions they insisted that their lengthy statements or articles be printed in full. On the other hand, the Information Office of the Government of Taiwan laid down the rule that a daily newspaper must limit its size to eight pages and no more. How could we publish statements or special articles as long as five thousand words and have space for the news. When we refused, we made an enemy, and sometimes he could be vengeful.

Ma Hsin-yeh and I agreed that if this situation continued, the *Central Daily News* would become so dull that it would lose its circulation. The first thing I did upon assuming the chairmanship was to inform the editorial staff that I would assume the responsibility for the decision not to publish lengthy statements or articles, those of the President and the Prime Minister being excepted. As a result I made many enemies among high officials.

Free China News had a number of capable young Chinese journalists who have received training in America. They have studied journalism either at the School of Journalism at the University of Missouri or at the Postgraduate School of Journalism at Columbia University in New York. An increasing number of Chinese young men and women have flocked to America to study journalism, and this is a good sign when it is remembered that in 1911 there were only two Chinese attending the University of Missouri School of Journalism, namely, Hing Wong and I.

In January 1950, during my first visit to Tokyo, I encouraged Mr. Woo Chia-tang, another Missouri School of Journalism graduate, who used to work under me on the *China Press*, to start a news agency for Asia along the line of the United Press. This was in anticipation of the possible fall of Taiwan into the Communist hands so that Free China might have a news agency to speak for it. Mr. Norman Soong, still another graduate of the Missouri School of Journalism became Woo's partner. Both of them ran the news agency jointly for a number of years. Later Woo became editor of the *Standard*, an English daily in Hong Kong.

Chapter Twenty.
Ambassador to Japan

By one of those strange coincidences, my old friend Mr. Yoshizawa and I became ambassadors for our respective countries simultaneously, after the peace treaty between Japan and the Republic of China was finally signed on April 28, 1952. As diplomats, there was little similarity between us. Mr. Yoshizawa was a seasoned diplomat, who had entered the Japanese Foreign Office in 1900, and who had been Japan's Ambassador to China, France and other countries during a foreign service career a quarter of a century. In contrast, I was a diplomatic novice receiving my first assignment.

Both of us were critical of each other when our appointments as opposite numbers had been announced. Mr. Yoshizawa felt that my pronounced anti-Japanese record before and during the war disqualified me. My reservations concerning him were based upon his own staunch support of the aggression of Japan during the same war.

Friends pointed out to me that there were social as well as intellectual qualifications for an ambassadorship. For example, they told me, Mr. Yoshizawa plays golf and bridge and dances, and is good at all these things. I did none. When I was asked to name my hobbies, my reply was that I was a collector of friends, of jokes and of newspaper clippings. These seemed incongruous qualifications for a career diplomat.

I asked Prime Minister Chen Cheng pointblank why he had selected me, an American-educated man, non-Japanese-speaking and handicapped by a well-known anti-Japanese record, when Chinese of diplomatic experience who were experts on Japan were available. Surprisingly, his reply was that my very lack of these obvious qualifications had induced him to appoint me. He did not elaborate.

Once I decided to accept the appointment, I took mental stock of my knowledge of Japan and its personalities. I found that I knew much more about my future home than I had suspected. I was confident that I would make a good ambassador, justifying the confidence that President Chiang and Premier Chen had in me.

One factor which strengthened my decision was Sally. To relieve her loneliness during my long trips away from Taiwan between 1949 and 1951, she had taken up the study of Japanese. To facilitate her study, she decided that she would like to live in Tokyo, devoting almost twelve hours a day to her studies. Her teacher – an excellent one – was Marquess Maeda whose husband had at one time been Japan's military attaché in London. When Sally went to Tokyo, she had no advance intimation that I was to come to Japan as ambassador.

At first she had been happy in Japan but, in the spring of 1951, she fell on the polished floor while exercising and fractured her spinal cord. For several months, she was forced to lie in a cast. So strapped had been my financial circumstances at the time of this accident that the Generalissimo had given me U.S. $500 for expenses, when I asked his permission to go to Japan to be with her. Out of this I was able to buy a badly needed suit.

As the time approached for my departure for Japan as ambassador, my interest in Japan quickened. I had seen Japanese in many settings, in war and in peace. It was a civilization that had won the admiration of the world. In my mind was the picture of the private, polite, apolitical Japanese, industriously doing his life work and no inner complexes of either superiority or inferiority. This was the real Japan which I deeply admired.

For many years, it had been one of my continuing interests to get to know the Japanese people from books and from personal contacts. In observing Japanese people, I have always been deeply conscious of the factors of their physical environment of an island nation, where 85,000,000 people must struggle to gain their livelihood. Most anthropologists agree that the physical handicaps of man are usually the sources of their strengths and their successes.

My first introduction to the Japanese people occurred when I met Seichi Ikemoto, my schoolmate at Park College in 1910. Living in the same dormitory we had daily discussions about our respective homelands. We both worked on a farm to earn money for our tuition. A few years later, Seichi died of a pulmonary disease, a promising career ended in its inception.

I had known Mr. Yamada, Dr. Sun Yat-sen's loyal Japanese comrade; Dr. Zumoto, a former secretary to Prince Ito; Mr. Sugimura, the distinguished writer on the *Asahi Shimbun,* and its early publisher Mr. Murayama. In the political world, I had known Prime Minister Yoshida, when he was Consul-General in Tientsin, in the 1920s; Mr. Arita, former Minister of Foreign Affairs, when he was the secretary of the Japanese Legation in Beijing; Baron Shidehara, Speaker of the Diet; and a host of others.

Shidehara told me the angry reaction of the Russian Ambassador in the 1920s when Chiang Kai-shek had expelled the Communists after Russia had helped China in its Northern Expedition. The Russian had told him at the time that Russia would never permit such "ingratitude" again.

The war years were especially educational to me in Japanese matters. As head of Government Overseas Information, it was my task to make a close study of the Japanese. After the end of the war, I visited Japan on an average of four times a year, remaining several weeks on each visit. It was with interest and admiration that I had seen Japan's resurrection in seven years from a war-wracked economy to its present level of prosperity. These achievements, I felt, were due to the uncomplaining self-denial of the Japanese masses, as well as to the sagacity of its statesmen.

Armed with this knowledge of Japanese affairs and personalities, I came to Japan in the middle of September 1952. My appointment dated from August 20. Sally had lived in Tokyo for more than two years already, having mastered the Japanese language. She was fond of foreign languages, and studying Japanese had only an intellectual motivation for her. Her knowledge of the Japanese language proved to be of great help to me during my official life in Japan.

Upon my arrival, Sally and I first lived in the home of General Chang Chun, former Premier and Minister of Foreign Affairs, who was on a goodwill tour as the representative of President Chiang. The ambassador's residence had not yet been made ready. General and Mrs. Chang had long been our good friends, and we treated them as our brother and sister. He was most knowledgeable in Japanese affairs. He gave a number of dinners for his Japanese friends in high government positions, and as his guests we had a helpful opportunity to get acquainted with them. Our stay with the Changs was like a honeymoon for us. We had no responsibility for housekeeping, and we felt at home.

This interlude ended after three weeks, and we moved into the residence of the Ambassador, the former Manchukuo (Northeast Nation) Embassy, located in a spacious compound. There we were to live for nearly four years, and we were to make friends among Japanese and people of other nationalities which would truly enrich our lives.

One of the outstanding early events of my ambassadorship was my audience with His Majesty, the Emperor of Japan, for the presentation of my credentials. The Office of Ceremonies sent a well-decorated carriage drawn by a pair of shining black horses with an elaborately uniformed driver. As my carriage proceeded to the Palace, it was preceded by another carriage and four riders. It was an impressive procession. Sitting with me in the carriage was Mr. Korida, the Secretary of the Imperial Office of Ceremonies, and both of us were in morning coats and wearing top hats. As the procession progressed, curious people lined the streets, watching it and peeping through the windows of the carriage. I was visibly embarrassed, and in order to compose myself, I resorted to the recitation of biblical passages which I had memorized in my student days.

I was ushered into the presence of the Emperor, and after making three bows to him, which was returned, we sat down and then I presented my credentials. Afterwards I indulged in some polite talk such as the expression of greetings from President Chiang and the reciprocating sentiments by His Majesty. The ceremony was soon over, and I was on my way back to my Chancellery. There we drank a toast to the Secretary of Ceremonies who had accompanied me back and forth to the Palace. Later I learned that Sally together with a friend of ours, Mrs. Moon Chin, had gone to one of the streets near the Palace to watch our procession with curiosity.

After the audience by the Emperor, I called on the Prime Minister, the Minister of Foreign Affairs, the Chief Justice of the Supreme Court, and the heads of the various ministries. It was a tiring performance. I was accustomed to calling upon persons of importance for interviews that were exciting experiences of intellectual interest, and yielded information of value. But conversations with the Emperor, the Prime Minister and other heads of the Japanese government were of a social nature, and could be boring to both sides. However, etiquette required that we go through them regardless of our personal feelings. After completing this round, I sighed in relief, telling myself that never again would I accept an ambassadorial position.

In contrast to these official visits was my experience with the family of Mr. Yamato, publisher of the *Kaizo,* a popular magazine in Japan. I had met Mr. Yamato at a social function. Talking about tea in our chat, he had told me of his preference for the Chinese Lungching tea. A few days later, I had sent him a bottle of the very tea he liked from Taipei. Before the tea reached him, Mr. Yamato fell seriously ill. Nevertheless, he requested that this tea be served to him at his bedside, spoonful by spoonful. After his death, the tea bottle with the remaining tea and other things dear to him were kept in his room.

His son paid me a visit, and invited Sally and me to dine with him. We called on his mother and brought flowers. It is a simple story of human interest and yet it is through such instinctive recognition of the value and the depth of personal relationships that Japanese and Chinese learn to know each other. To my mind, it is not the exchange of costly gifts or of solemn vows between nations that build real lasting friendships. It is the small things, growing out of human relations; the bonds which arise from such contacts are the real cement of friendship.

On November 3, 1952, I made my first call on Prime Minister Yoshida in my capacity as ambassador. He discussed with me the possibility of the formation of a bloc of free nations in the Western Pacific area to preserve peace. He had instructed Ambassador Yoshizawa to explore the possibility of such an alignment. Such a block, Mr. Yoshida hazarded, should include Japan, the Republic of China, the Philippines, Thailand, Burma and Indochina.

We recognized that the plan should have the support of the United States. He had no illusions about the difficulty of creating such an entente. It is interesting to note that just two years later, a part of Prime Minister Yoshida's hope came to fruition in the formation of the United States-sponsored Southeast Asian Treaty Organization, but minus both Japan and the Republic of China. Moreover, instead of being an entente of exclusively Asiatic powers, SEATO proved to be a body which included three non-Asiatic nations – the United States, Great Britain and France.

The months which followed this meeting were disappointingly unproductive. The high hopes that I had entertained of quick steps to strengthen the ties between Japan and Free China had not borne fruit. On March 15, 1953, I saw Mr. Yoshida again, on the eve of my return to Taiwan for consultation. I told him frankly,

"Although I have now been here five months, I have seen Chinese-Japanese economic and cultural relations advance scarcely beyond the talking stage. Can we not work out a plan whereby China and Japan can help each other, or complement each other, both on the economic and the political level? I am certain that the United States will support such a plan. If this idea appeals to you, I will convey your reaction to President Chiang and later we can turn our attention to top-level discussions for its implementation."

Mr. Yoshida, while expressing his appreciation, saw serious difficulties in the proposal. He pointed out that "before we face the question of a closer link between China and Japan, there must be a refocusing of Free World attention upon Asia instead of Europe." He said he was highly pessimistic about the European situation, for it was mired in indecision. He held that the most counteraction against Communism could be obtained in Asia, and then he proceeded to brief me on what he had done thus far. He said:

"As early as April 1952, I broached the subject of an Asiatic federation or pact to Mr. Alexander, Minister of Defense of the British government, and the Deputy Minister of Foreign Affairs, during their visit to Tokyo. Their reaction was rather cold. The predominant interest of the British was turned toward Red China and its trade possibilities. Later I discussed the matter with Mr. Dulles, Mr. Allison and Mr. Stevenson, representing the United States, and I found them receptive to the plan. Our prime problem is how to reconcile the differences in viewpoint between the British and the Americans. What I have in mind is the establishment of a sort of *cordon sanitaire* stretching through Hong Kong, Burma and Singapore as a first step toward the defeat of the communists on the mainland. I fully agree with you that the objective must be the return of Free China to the mainland. Otherwise, our future will be circumscribed and perilous."

He continued,

"I have sent my Ambassador-at-large, Mr. Shirasu, to Washington to explore possibilities, and now he is in London talking to the British. I am better acquainted with the British than with the Americans as a result of my long service in the Embassy at London, while President Chiang is closer to the Americans. If the President agrees with my objectives, we can work toward them simultaneously from different angles. When the British and the Americans sufficiently understand the importance of cooperative efforts in Asia, we can call conferences to meet in Tokyo, Taiwan, Hong Kong, or Singapore, to discuss possible programs of implementation. It is not enough to have such discussions in the United States or Europe, they should be held on the spot so that the participants may have a closer view of the situation. I hold the Generalissimo in grateful esteem for his generous gesture toward Japan at the end of the war, and I admire his ability to mobilize the Chinese people behind him in his resistance to Communism."

Following this conversation, I sounded out some American diplomats on Prime Minister Yoshida' project of a Pacific pact, and their reaction was favorable, although there was some disposition to be vague. I took up the matter with President Chiang in my reports, and he wholeheartedly agreed with Mr. Yoshida's proposal. He planned a worldwide trip in 1954, and during the trip he promised to explore the project with free world statesmen, so I left the matter in abeyance. From that time on I gave attention to my own proposal to Mr. Yoshida that Japan and Free China should work out a plan for economic and cultural cooperation in expectation of the return of the Republic of China to the mainland. After a year of exploratory talks with Prime Minister Yoshida, I found myself making little progress. One day he told me frankly that a long-range program for cooperation between the two countries was impossible because of the nature of government in his country. He did not know how long he could remain as the head of the cabinet, and if he should resign, any understanding which I might have reached with him would become moot. As to securing the approval of the Diet, that would not be possible because the Conservative Party did not command an absolute majority.

Beginning in early 1954, relationships between Japan and the Republic of China had become less cordial for the following reasons: (1) Our return to the mainland became less likely; (2) Ambassador Yoshizawa during his trip in the Southeast Asian countries found that while President Chiang was friendly to Japan, some of the other important Chinese officials were still hostile; (3) Foreign Minister Okazaki in his follow-up visit to the Southeastern Asian nations told me that he had discovered a disposition among overseas Chinese in Indonesia and Burma to insist that if Japan should refuse trade with Red China, they would withhold their trade with Japan. But in the Philippines and Thailand, he discovered exactly the opposite attitude. Representative Filipinos and Thailanders told him that they would not trade with Japan if it should trade with Red China. However, generally speaking, relations between the Chinese Embassy and Japan during my term of office were amicable.

On December 8, 1954, Ichiro Hatoyama received the mandate from the Diet for the organization of the first Hatoyama cabinet. I knew him well but not as intimately as Prime Minister Yoshida. His Foreign Minister was Mr. Shigematsu, who held me in esteem, for the following reason. When he was the Japanese Minister to China, he was almost killed by a bomb thrown by a Korean in the Honkew Park at Shanghai during a celebration. I was then editor of the *China Press* in Shanghai. Despite the prevalent anti-Japanese feelings among the Chinese, I condemned the violence by pointing out that it would not solve international problems and that the Koreans who had instigated the bombing were unwise. Mr. Shigematsu always remembered my fairness in discussing the bomb outrage.

I introduced one novelty in the chancellery. I had one huge room in which I and all the staff members worked together in sight of each other as in a modern bank. Not all staff members liked this arrangement, but they were unable to change my decision. During my stay in Tokyo, the arrangement for working together in one big room worked well.

The offices of the military attaches and of the Commercial Counselor were also located in the same compound, thereby facilitating close coordination and liaison. I derived much pleasure by cooperating with them, and warm friendships sprang up among us. The military attaches consulted me often, and sought my views and assistance, which were given only too willingly. They always reported their difficulties to me. I knew what they had been doing, and was in a position to check whether they had correctly reported back to Taiwan. I have had long experience in checking certain information.

In January 1954, I had an operation in the American Army Hospital for the removal of my gallbladder containing half a dozen stones which had not yet begun to cause pain. Colonel Mataske performed the operation, and the wife of General Standlee, the director of all the American Army Hospitals in Japan, had her blood tested and stood by to supply blood in the event I needed a blood transfusion. All these acts gave meaning to life. During my stay in the hospital, I reviewed my life and was thankful to God for His many blessings. I made five decisions which I hoped to keep in the year 1954.

These decisions were: (1) never to loose my temper again; (2) to write a book on Japan; (3) to write a book on the Japanese sense of humor; (4) to eat sparingly, and (5) never touch liquor again during the remainder of my life. At the time of my departure for Washington to take up my new post, I made a check to ascertain how far I had fulfilled these promises to myself. I found that I had written two books, thereby fulfilling number 2 and 3; and had been carrying out numbers 4 and 5, but as to number 1 pledge, I had lost my temper six times in 1954, three times in 1955, one time in 1956, and none in 1957, three times in 1958 and none in 1959.

I have a few other minor items to record of the years I spent in Japan as the first post-war Chinese Ambassador. The first one was my promotion of a summer camp in July 1954 for all Chinese students. More than two hundred Chinese students were gathered in a village at the foot of Mt. Fuji and spent ten days there. I was with them a few days, and Vice-Minister

Chang Peh-cheng stayed with them during the entire period. One day I led more than one hundred and fifty Chinese students to climb the Fuji. One third of them were girls. Usually those who climbed up to the top of the mountain stayed overnight in mountain inns and then got up at four o'clock the next morning to make the last ascent as the sun was rising. In view of the fact that I had more than fifty Chinese girls with me, I decided to make the round trip in one day. This meant more than eleven hours of walking over the rugged and difficult mountain paths.

We reached the top of the mountain at five-thirty in the afternoon, and after remaining for less than one hour, we began to climb down. One little girl had to be carried up and carried down by two fellow men students. Upon reaching the foot of the mountain, a roll call showed that two were missing. My anxiety was great since, if they had been lost, it would have a terrible stigma upon me. A search was made, and telephones were kept busy. Two hours later, they phoned that they had been unable to walk further and had decided to stay in an inn for the night. Both of them were men. I told myself that I would not repeat this mountain climbing again.

Upon the completion of my Mt. Fuji climbing, my surgeon complained that I should not have done this, as my operation had taken place only in the late part of January. I had done it and there was nothing to be undone. I was conscious of the danger, but I wanted to impress these youngsters that I was equal to them in endurance. I was glad that I had done it, being the proud possessor of a wooden stick which is the conclusive proof that I had gone to the top of the mountain. I had won the confidence of the students, both girls and boys. From that time on, morale improved.

I was fortunate to have talented staff in Tokyo. They included Vice-Minister Y. C. Young, who was in general charge of diplomatic affairs; Dr. Chang Peh-cheng, in charge of cultural and educational affairs; Sun Yu-shu, first secretary; Chiu Fan-chi, who was the former head of my Japanese section in the Information office during the war; Soong Yu-lung; and Dr. Sherman Chang. Only one of my colleagues turned bad. He was found to be a communist and was discharged. We felt communist intrigue all about us in our work in Japan.

Although I was accredited to Japan, President Chiang sent me to Seoul, Korea, to see President Syngman Rhee in the autumn of 1953. It was an awkward assignment, as the Republic of China was represented by an ambassador in Seoul, namely, General Wang. I was selected for this mission because I knew President Rhee. I was charged with two objectives. One was to persuade President Rhee to return the visit of President Chiang to discuss a Pacific pact. The other was to persuade President Rhee to be friendlier toward Japan. I spent four days in Seoul, and successfully persuaded President Rhee to visit Taipei although he wanted our President to come to Korea again. As to the matter of a Pacific pact, a draft was agreed upon but nothing came of it.

In my first interview, President Rhee pointedly asked me why President Chiang was so friendly towards Japan. I explained that President Chiang first showed his friendliness to Japan in 1945, at the end of the war when he still had more than 3,000,000 soldiers. Hence, his friendship was not due to his weakness but to his strength. President Chiang considered it regrettable that the excess of the Japanese militarism had caused the invasion of China. We could not afford another war, which would be too costly to both countries. Certainly, to avert such a war, we should follow a policy of live and let live. In addition, President Chiang was a devoted Christian, which emphasizes forgiveness.

President Rhee gave it as his opinion that Japan would become an aggressor again, and that China would suffer terribly in the future. I answered that there was little possibility of aggression within the next fifty years. That would be enough for us. We believed that the Japanese had learned the lesson that it did not pay to fight an aggressive war. President Rhee continued to talk about the untrustworthiness of the Japanese military. During my stay I saw him four times, and in the last talk he said that he would go to Taipei to have further talks with President Chiang.

Prior to the Seoul talk, I had met him in Tokyo on January 6, 1953, when President Rhee visited Japan at the invitation of General Mark Clark, who was anxious to restore relations between Japan and Korea as a preliminary to the discussion of a Pacific Pact to safeguard Asia against Communist domination. American statesmen held the view that such a pact would not be effective if Japan did not join it. If Japan were to join it, the relationship between Japan and Korea must be restored. This visit of President Rhee backfired, because Prime Minister Hoshida did not go to the airport to meet him, and only the Japanese Minister of Foreign Affairs greeted him on arrival. Incensed, President Rhee declined the invitation of Prime Minister Hoshida to dinner, and General Clark finally arranged a meeting between them in his headquarters at a tea reception. At the time of my leaving Tokyo there was no sign of an early rapprochement between Japan and Korea.

Chapter Twenty-One.
Ambassador to the United States

Late in December 1955, I received instructions in Tokyo from Foreign Minister George Yeh to return to Taipei as soon as possible for consultations. Mr. Yeh's tone was urgent. Because of the unavoidable Japanese custom of a New Year's visit by all ambassadors to the Palace to extend greetings to the Emperor and Empress, I deferred my departure until January 2.

Back in Taipei, I met Mr. Yeh and General Chang Chun, Secretary General to the President in the Yeh home for briefing in regard to the President's wishes. To my surprise they told me that the President had decided to transfer me to Washington to assume the Ambassadorship to the United States. I explained that I had other plans. My wife and I were thoroughly weary of government service; upon completion of my Japan tour of duty, we were planning to retire to Taichung or some other Taiwan town to undertake Christian preaching and to write. I didn't want to go to the United States.

Both Minister Yeh and General Chang then explained to me that the President had given long consideration to the change. An important publicity plan had been worked out involving a budget of $300,000, and the President felt that I was the proper man to direct it. The present Ambassador, Dr. Wellington V. K. Koo, who had made such a brilliant record in his long diplomatic career, was less qualified than I for publicity situations.

When I called on the President, I repeated my objections to the new appointment. He brushed me aside. After a 45-minute talk, he began to show increased impatience with my refusal. He was getting old himself, he told me, but he was not retiring. We were virtually the same age, and he saw no reason why I should say "no" when the country needed me.

"Do I take it that this amounts to an order from you?" I finally asked him.

"If you wish to consider it as such, there is no alternative for you but to accept the office." He replied.

I recalled on several occasions during the war when the Generalissimo had given me orders which were not arguable, and which I had obediently accepted. I pondered whether I should similarly accept an unwelcome order this time. I realized that in making me the Ambassador to the United States, the President was offering a position of great distinction. We ended our talk with my pledge not to tell anyone that I was going to Washington. Ambassador Koo had not yet been notified and the President was anxious not to hurt his feelings.

Later, Minister Yeh gave me a copy of the publicity plan. I studied it carefully, taking it back with me to Tokyo. To my regret, I noted that the plan had been finalized, and was not subject to change. It seemed to me a mistake to fix the plan in Taipei, thousands of miles from the scene of operation. Whoever was to administer the plan would need a considerable amount of freedom of action and decision if it was to be effective. I put the plan in my safety box in Tokyo for further contemplation.

Following my return to Tokyo, I talked with Shih Chao-ying, former Vice-Minister of Foreign Affairs and later Ambassador to Brazil who, with his wife, was passing through Japan. In our discussion of publicity work in America, he offered the following suggestions which were later put down in writing. I found that his grasp of the public relations problem in America was extraordinary. His statement was outlined as follows:

(1) AIM. The publicity work in the United States must have limited objectives. These do not include the conversion of the *Washington Post* and the *Christian Science Monitor*.

Our objectives should include: (a) closer liaison with American writers and thinkers who have shown sympathy for our cause; (b) closer liaison with Chinese students in the U.S.; (c) closer liaison with our academic faculty in various American universities and research institutes; (d) maintaining contacts with the political aspirants of both political parties.

(2) METHODS. Individual officers should travel around the country to attend conferences where they can do good, or to keep friendly contact with publishers and newspaper editors. This will cost money, and will, at first, show intangible results, but in the long run

it will pay off. The important thing is to maintain warm personal contacts. Some emphasis should be placed on radio and TV, and Chinese should be made to retain the sympathy and support for Free China of such men of importance in the academic world as Dr. Hu Shih or Lin Yu-tang.

A special concern should be to study the reactions of American public opinion to political and diplomatic moves on the part of Taiwan. While we don't want to swing with temporary moods, we should avail ourselves of all information which we can obtain from informed U.S. public opinion. We must not burden ourselves with too big an organization. It should be flexible.

It seemed to me that Mr. Shih's suggestions reflected a correct approach to the American public relations task. I had always found Mr. Shih friendly and cooperative, and his presence in the Ministry of Foreign Affairs had made my Tokyo assignment more agreeable. For that reason, it was a great shock when I learned of his premature death in Brazil later.

Late in January, 1956, V. K. Wellington Koo, Chinese Ambassador to Washington, who had been called back to Taipei by the President for consultations, stopped over in Tokyo, and came to my official residence for dinner. Sally and I accompanied him on a visit to Hakone Lake, which is less than two hours car drive from the city. Then he had dinner with us and some of the senior staff members. Soon after the dinner and before he left for the airport to catch a plane for San Francisco, he confided that he had tendered his resignation to the President, and that the matter was in the President's hands.

In accordance with the President's wishes, I kept silent and expressed my regret over his resignation, asking if it were possible for him to reconsider his decision. He said, "That is not up to me to say," implying that he might reconsider if somebody would urge the President not to accept his resignation. There I left the matter. I saw Dr. Koo off at the airport and I was relieved over this encounter.

Dr. Koo was naturally anxious to receive word of the acceptance of his resignation. One month passed, and nothing further was heard from Taipei. I hoped that the prospect of my transfer had been abandoned. I was genuinely eager to remain in Tokyo for two or three more years, to gain a better acquaintance with the Japanese situation. I had written a book about Japan, and it needed to be brought up to date, although I was under instruction from the Ministry of Foreign Affairs not to publish it until five years after my severance from the diplomatic service.

After waiting for one month, Dr. Koo officially repeated his resignation, and it was accepted. On March 8, I was informed by telegrams from both Minister Yeh and General Chang Chun of the President's nomination of me to be his successor. The die was cast. I replied to both that I faced the future with a trembling heart, and I requested them to convey to the President my appreciation for the confidence that he had in me and my hope that I would come up to his high expectations of me.

I requested Minister Yeh to approve my travel to America by ship instead of air, for I was tired both physically and mentally from my labors in Japan. I recommended Mr. Chu Fu-sun to be Minister in charge of publicity in the Embassy at Washington. Mr. Chu had been my close colleague during the years of the war when I was in charge of overseas information service. He was the director of the Publicity and Intelligence Department of the Foreign Ministry and had been responsible for the drafting of a memorandum on public relations work in America. I felt that he would be a logical person to handle the work in the States.

At the beginning of April, I returned to Taipei for consultations. During the visit I went to the two groups of offshore islands in order to familiarize myself with the problem of their defense and the importance of their retention as the prerequisite for the defense of Taiwan and the Pescadores. The first day, I went to Quemoy by plane, landing without difficulty. The second day, I left before dawn with General Yu Ta-wei, Minister of Defense, taking this precaution since the Chinese Communists might open their land battery against the arriving plane during the daytime light. Together with Minister Yu, I went to the island nearest the Chinese mainland, and with my naked eyes saw two soldiers pacing in front of their gun positions. I returned to Taipei after dark, for reasons of safety.

During this trip to Taipei, I was briefed by the Ministry of Foreign Affairs in regard to the problems pending before the Chinese Embassy in Washington. These included the settlement of the wartime debts, amounting to $100,000,000; the prevention of America's recognition of Red China which might be discussed at the Geneva talks with the Chinese Communist representative; the continuation of the embargoes against trade with Red China; continuance of American military and economic aid to Taiwan; the problem of surplus agricultural commodities; the matter of refugees; the handling of funds deposited with the National City Bank; immigration questions; relations with students going back to the Chinese mainland, and so on. During my subsequent trip to Taipei on May 12, the President asked me to pay special attention to the Chinese students and the establishment of cordial relations with them, as well as the strengthening of the personnel of the consulates and consulate-generals.

I had a foretaste of some of the unpleasantness which might be in store for me in Washington when I began to receive reports from some of the Washington Embassy staff members telling me of irregularities at the Embassy. Some of these reports mentioned extreme laxity among staff members; charged that favored ones were arriving for work at eleven in the morning and departing at four in the afternoon; and alleged that employees were spending office time to engage in stock market speculations, and that requests for speakers or information from American friends were routinely going into the wastebasket, because the staff members were too slothful to answer them. The Embassy was not even maintaining a usable library, although large sums were being spent for books and magazines. It was a disturbing picture of my future office, but worse was to come.

On the eve of my departure for America, Minister Yeh gave me two anonymous letters which had come in from Washington, purportedly from staff members, and which had been sent to President Chiang. The letters charged the embezzlement of funds by Embassy officials, and even directed an innuendo against Ambassador Koo whom they alleged had engaged in speculation with government monies. I have always despised anonymous letters. In this instance, I determined to pigeonhole the reports, and to make a fresh start when I reached Washington. Any other course would result in bad publicity for the Republic of China.

My predecessor, Dr. Koo, had always availed himself of the privilege of taking along with him on his transfer several personal secretaries who had worked with him for some time and who knew his way of doing things. He referred to these secretaries as his "cabinet." I asked for permission only to take my Tokyo secretary to Washington with me, a step which I later regretted when I found myself involved in red tape. I was required to pay the traveling expenses of both the secretary and his wife out of my own pocket. The Foreign Office did not put him on the payroll until he reached Washington.

After I had attended several receptions in Taipei and had been briefed by the President and the Director of the American Department of the Ministry of Foreign Affairs, I left Taipei on the afternoon of May 13, 1956. I saw the President for the last time after a church service. On parting, the President urged me to contact overseas Chinese as often as I could and give them his greetings. I left Tokyo on May 17 with my wife. The President refused to let me go by American ship, but my wife could do so, he said. Naturally she did not wish to travel alone and so she decided to fly together with me.

I wished to sidestep both Honolulu and San Francisco where there were many overseas Chinese. I realized that they would arrange receptions and I would be expected to say something. I did not want to be quoted before assuming my post. Accordingly, I flew to Washington via Seattle. We arrived in Washington, DC in the afternoon of May 17, 1956 and were met by the staff members of the Embassy and our personal friends. We were especially grateful for the presence of General and Mrs. Edward Hull. General Hull was former American Commander-in-Chief in Japan and we knew both of them well in Tokyo.

Before retiring for the night in the ambassador's residence, we knelt down and prayed. Both of us broke down and wept for several minutes when we saw the condition of the mansion. Dirt and confusion were everywhere. The building reeked of the odor of fresh paint. At two o'clock the next morning Sally's face swelled up from a paint allergy. She was sick for more than three weeks.

We attended a cocktail party the first week of June, and the wife of a former American ambassador told Sally, "Your residence is the dirtiest in the whole of Washington. When we are invited to tea receptions or dinners, I dare not sit close to the arms of the sofa, because I find dirt piled half an inch high." What she said was undiplomatic, and Sally was pained to hear this. She determined to make the residence at least clean.

In the main drawing room there were bookcases lining three walls. They contained out-of-date books collecting dust, giving the room a crowed appearance. When Dr. C. T. Wang was ambassador in 1935, he had bought those books from the owner at ten cents a copy for decoration. In all the twenty intervening years, they had remained there. Sally ordered the removal of the bookcases and the purchase of a new one-color carpet for the room.

The bookcases along the fireplace wall remained, and Sally ransacked the house from attic to basement for curios, ancient porcelain jars and other decorative articles to be placed in the remaining cases. Friends noticed them and thought that we had brought them with us because they had never seen them before.

A short while later it rained, and we were surprised to learn that our roof leaked badly. We decided to replace the roof, which had not been changed since the mansion was constructed 90 years ago. The edifice had been bought by the Chinese government at the end of the war, and was government property. Prudence dictated that money should have been spent on its upkeep, but this had not been done. It would cost several thousand dollars to put on a new roof, and I decided to have this work done, although I did not know where I was to get the money.

The *Washington Post*'s social column printed an article written by an American who obviously was not too friendly to our Embassy. She said that all the spoons, glassware, plates, napkins, tablecloths, bed sheets, chairs and even the cook's aprons were rented, the reason being that the Chinese government did not expect to retain the residence long, as it was anticipated that the Chinese Communist regime might be recognized by the American government. That was extremely damaging publicity for the Republic of China, and its timing was unfortunate, as it appeared after our arrival in Washington. Unfortunately, what she said was true. Otherwise we could have denied the report.

I had to provide funds to buy the needed items to make the mansion presentable. The Ministry of Foreign Affairs declined to provide money for this extra outlay. When I received a telegram from the President inquiring how I was getting along in my new position and instructing me to report to him in detail, I explained the situation and hinted that I might have to use my own salary to meet these expenses. In a week, the President sent me a remittance of $10,000, with the order to defray such expenses. I replied that if I could get a covering appropriation from the Ministry of Foreign Affairs, I would return the money. At the end of December, the Ministry granted me the funds and I returned the $10,000.

In my letter to the President, I suggested the introduction of a system under which an ambassador would at most serve two terms of two years each like a military commander-in-chief. I pointed out that when an ambassador served ten or eleven years, he was inclined to feel resentful when he was relieved of office. I expressed a willingness to serve the first term of two years.

During my two years' ambassadorship in Washington, one of the cases which I handled could be considered as important. This was the case of thirty-two Chinese felons imprisoned in the United States. The American government proposed that they be asked whether they preferred to continue serving their sentences in the United States or be sent to the mainland provinces of China. Our attitude was that the Republic of China was willing to take any or all these felons who wished to go to Taiwan provided no representative of India or another neutral country was present when the wishes of the felons were ascertained.

The Indian government acted for the Chinese Communist regime. In allowing a representative of the Indian Embassy to be present when the Chinese felons were to be asked as to whether or not they desired to return to the Chinese mainland provinces, the American government tried to satisfy the Chinese Communist regime as to its impartiality and to show that no pressure was being used to influence their free choice. To this our government objected. The matter was dragged on for some time, and finally it was dropped when the majority of the felons refused to go to Red China and the Indian Embassy showed no interest in sending a representative to the inquiry. Beijing thereupon charged American manipulation.

Other tasks included carrying out of the instructions of the Ministry of Foreign Affairs: to secure American support for the election of Dr. V. K. Koo as the Judge to the International Court at the Hague; to maintain of our position in the United Nations; to insist upon our participation in the Red Cross conference at New Delhi as the Government of the Republic of China; and to remove Americans' misunderstanding over the May 24, 1957 incident in Taipei where a mob damaged the American Embassy; to secure military and economic aid; and to supervise the consular services, and activities.

I tried hard to employ my talents and training to the best advantage. I made more than one hundred and twenty speeches, within a period of twenty months, averaging six per month. I visited more than sixty cities in 37 states of the Union. I have been told that speech-making in the United States is an important part of the duty of an ambassador. The ambassadors of the Republic of the Philippines, the Republic of Korea, Thailand, and some European countries make four to ten speeches a month.

The Foreign Policy Association, with its headquarters in New York, maintains one hundred branches all over the country, and pursues a policy of informing the thinking of the American people on foreign affairs. I addressed many councils on foreign relations in major cities. Some of these councils distributing opinion ballots immediately after my speech. In the ballots the leading questions were, "Should the United States recognize Red China?" or "Should the United States trade with Red China?" Some of their members, particularly women who were usually more frank than their husbands, came to me after my speech and told me that they had come to the meeting prepared to vote "yes" to Red China, but after hearing me will vote "no." So I realized that my speaking efforts made some impact upon American opinion.

It is my conviction that an ambassador who represents his country in America neglects his duty if he holds himself back from speech-making. Invitations come to him constantly from all types of discussion clubs, universities, business and community clubs, women's clubs, and so on.

Frequently, the organization requesting him to speak enlists the help of its Congressman and Senator. To refuse such invitations is to risk the displeasure of these legislators and other powerful groups.

What hurt me most was not the amount of time I spent on speechwriting or the traveling of long distances, but the sheer lack of appreciation from of my fellow countrymen. Foreign Minister Yeh and President Chiang disapproved of my frequent absences and said that I was doing too much public speaking. They thought that I should spend more time and more energy in cultivating the friendship of important persons in Washington. They failed to understand that those who hold important positions in the American capital are usually so busy with their own interests that they accept invitations to dinners or luncheons from foreign embassies only grudgingly. They often resent a diplomat who drops in for a casual chat, unless he has something of major importance to discuss. The winning of foreign friends cannot be done through forced hospitality. It was difficult for people in Taiwan to understand these facts.

It is true that one approach to some American legislators or administrators is to play golf or bridge with them, or to join them in late evening drinking parties. I confess that I have not fitted into this pattern and would not find myself at home in such amusements. While stories are current of some Chinese playing bridge in Washington with important Senators or Congressmen, and dropping hundreds of dollars in an evening of play, I could hardly engage in such "public relations" gestures on my modest salary. If such is the requirement of a diplomat, then I am not cut out for the role.

I was disappointed by the lack of understanding on the part of some of the higher officials of the Ministry of Foreign Affairs in Taipei. The impression seems to be among them that Chinese should be so glad to receive American assignments that they must not expect more than an extremely limited salary. Of course this attitude hindered the development of an efficient diplomatic establishment in Washington, or in the Consulates.

One painful experience which I had was the case of a secretary at the Embassy who earned only $300 a month. He was transferred to the post of Consul in Los Angeles – a promotion. The secretary came to me dejectedly and told me that he could not accept the promotion. He had a family consisting of a wife and three children. Except allowing railway fares for him, the Foreign Office was providing no funds for his family's transportation to California, or for his other moving and apartment-renting expenses. He had great difficulty meeting all his expenses. I was able to give him $1,000, partly from my personal funds and partly from my extra allowance. After protracted negotiations, the Foreign Office agreed to refund railway fares for his family. China's niggardly treatment of her trained diplomats is a short-signed policy. It made my work as Ambassador unnecessarily difficult.

Chapter Twenty-Two.
Headaches in Washington

Taking a backward glance, I believe that the most uncomfortable experience of my ambassadorship in Washington occurred following the May 24, 1957, Taipei riots. I found myself in the unhappy situation of explaining to the American people the violent attack by a mob upon the American Embassy.

The riots were touched off by the acquittal of Sgt. Robert G. Reynolds by a American court martial in Taiwan. Sergeant Reynolds had shot a Chinese citizen, Liu Chih-jan, who, he alleged, was caught peeping through the window at his wife when she was bathing. The Sergeant had pursued Liu with a pistol. His defense was that he shot the alleged peeper only after he had advanced menacingly with a club which, incidentally, was never found.

To understand the passion which the acquittal provoked, I will quote from *New York Times*, June 3, 1957:

"Because Nationalist China and the United States had never negotiated a status-of-forces agreement for the 2,000 American military personnel on Formosa, soldiers in effect enjoy extra-territorial rights. Chinese newspapermen found themselves unfamiliar with army court-martial.

Their feature stories described the rich and sparkling diamond necklace of defendant Reynolds' wife and painted bitter contrasting pictures of the Chinese widow, Mrs. Liu Chi-jan, pale weakened with sorrow, weeping bitterly until her eyes were swollen with sorrow. The army's conduct of the case did little to dispel Chinese suspicions. Both the defense and the prosecuting attorneys had been flown in from Okinawa. They shared the same office...During the trial they conferred together amiably in whispers and continued their comradely discussions during recesses. Newspaper editorials charged angrily that if Reynolds had killed an American, he would not have gotten off scot-free.

Nationalist authorities privately expected that the court would find Reynolds guilty and let him off with two or three years in jail. Instead, the court-martial's verdict on a basic plea of self-defense, was 'not guilty.' By this time, emotions were running so high that Reynolds, his wife and seven-year-old daughter had to be rushed out to Taipei's airport escorted by police, hustled aboard a U.S. Air Force plane and flown off to Manila."

The *Times* then continued to describe the spontaneous outburst of protest that spread among the population.

"Next day, the Chinese widow appeared outside the U.S. Embassy carrying a crudely lettered placard, bearing the inscription, in English and Chinese: 'THE KILLER REYNOLDS, IS HE INNOCENT? PROTEST AGAINST THE U.S. COURT-MARTIAL'S UNFAIR UNJUST DECISION!'

Soon after the widow with her placard appeared before the Embassy, small knots of spectators joined her. Police dispersed them but, as their numbers grew, the police were unable to cope with them. The crowds grew larger, began to stone the Embassy, and eight attaches took to an air raid shelter. Chinese police and firemen tried to keep the crowds back with fire hoses but were greeted with howls of derision. When they turned on the hose, it produced only a feeble spurt of water."

At one time the rioting mob reached a size of 3,000. They took over the Embassy compound, worked their way inside the Embassy building, smashed furniture, and scattered documents. Other rioters attacked the United States Information Agency building, some distance from the Embassy. They then attempted to attack the United States Communications Center in the Sugar Building. President Chiang acted quickly to halt further mob action by sending in the army which promptly restored order.

I got news of what was happening at 6:30 on the morning of May 24 when I received a long distance call from Foreign Minister George Yeh. My first act was to arrange an appointment with Assistant Secretary of State Walter S. Robertson. I saw Mr. Robertson at 11 o'clock and extended to him the official regrets and apologies of the Republic of China. I assured him that a thorough investigation was being made to fix responsibility for the outrage.

We felt immediate repercussions from the riots. Just before leaving my home, an anonymous phone call came. The voice said: "Your people have wrecked our Embassy. We are going to wreck yours." I immediately notified the State Department and we were given police protection.

One week later, I was called upon to face a national television audience to be questioned on the Taipei riots. This was the Martha Rountree press conference. Here I faced, in addition to Miss Rountree, the representatives of the national press corps.

In my opening statement, I pointed out the extremely friendly relations which had always existed between the United States and the Republic of China. I stated that I had no information that the mob action had been Communist-inspired, nor did I believe that it reflected any notable anti-Americanism. I quoted Ambassador Rankin's statement that the riots had been exceptional and that no resentment against American military personnel existed in Taipei. In reply to a question concerning the actual cause of the riots I quoted Foreign Minister Yeh's statement that a possible cause was the fact that all Americans present had applauded the verdict of acquittal. This had angered the Chinese population.

In answer to another question, I placed the blame largely upon the police for letting the situation get out of hand. Our under-staffed Taipei police had become lax. President Chiang had shown that he took this view by his prompt dismissal of three high ranking police officials.

The TV interview lasted for nearly an hour. I felt that I had stood the ordeal amicably.

This appearance was followed by a subsequent half-hour on Lawrence Spivak's "Meet the Press," which enjoys an immense national coverage. The questions and replies were generally similar to those which I had encountered on the Rountree program.

One of the most outspoken speeches which I made during this difficult period was delivered before the International Relations Group of the American Association of University Women of Alexandria, Virginia on September 26, 1957. In this speech I endeavored to explain the curious and unpredictable nature of mob psychology the world over. While expressing sorrow and shame that this outrage had occurred in the Republic of China, I pointed out that it could have happened even in the United States. I cited the student riots at Urbana, Illinois, which had occurred not long before, and which was halted only by the show of force of 200 policemen, equipped with over 150 tear gas canisters. In Urbana the provocation had not been political: the hysteria had been touched off by some passing horseplay. And yet, for a short time, the hundreds of aroused students went into frenzy scarcely distinguishable from mob dementia. It was a similar mood which had gripped the Taipei rioters.

My Alexandria audience received this explanation with evident concurrence. I have always found that American audiences, when appealed to in the spirit of fair play, are consistently responsive.

Throughout the months of September and October 1957, I found myself living with this difficult public relations problem. I accepted every available opportunity to clarify the riots and their actual causes to American audiences. With my long experience as a newspaperman, I realized the need to kill a lie immediately, before it spreads beyond control. I worked with unsparing energy to prevent the Taipei incident from becoming a stumbling block to friendly Sino-American relations. I believe that my efforts, coordinated with the able handling of publicity in Taiwan, were efficacious.

On February 11, it was our pleasure to attend the dinner given by President and Mrs. Eisenhower for diplomats. This had long been an annual function. About a hundred guests attended. I noted with interest a rapt conversation between the ambassadors of Russian and Turkish, with Egyptian ambassador standing by. I kept myself at a discreet distance. Social functions are always fertile opportunities for valuable observations by diplomats.

On March 4, Secretary Dulles invited my wife and me to dinner as guests of honor. Congressman and Mrs. Judd and General and Mrs. Maxwell Taylor were among the guests.

Now that the ice had been broken, we proceeded to entertain Secretary Dulles and his wife. The date selected was just before the departure of Secretary Dulles for the SEATO meeting in the Far East. On this trip, the Secretary was also to visit Taiwan. Other guests were U.S.I.A. Director and Mrs. George V. Allen, General and Mrs. Maxwell Taylor, Congressman and Mrs. Judd and others who were to accompany the Secretary to the SEATO sessions.

In his toast to me, Secretary Dulles graciously recalled his first meeting with me in China.

"You may have forgotten," he said, "but this is the twentieth anniversary of our first meeting in Hankow which was also my first meeting with President Chiang Kai-shek. During the intervening years much water has run under the bridge but the Generalissimo remains steadfast in his global thinking – calm amid the world's tumult and clamor. I have always held him in the highest esteem. At this critical period in Chinese history, China needs a leader of such indomitable will. I propose a toast to his good health."

In my reply, in offering a toast to the President of the United States, I recalled how I had met Mr. Dulles at the Hankow airport and had escorted him to the residence of Generalissimo Chiang Kai-shek. On that occasion, I gave him a copy of my biography of the Generalissimo.

I told of my embarrassment in 1954, when I was Ambassador to Japan, of receiving a request from the Generalissimo to send him the gist of the conversation which he had had with Mr. Dulles in Hankow in 1938 to prime him for a forthcoming meeting with the now Secretary of State. I had acted as interpreter for the Generalissimo on that occasion. Since I had interpreted hundreds of conversations during the war period, I had no notes of this particular occasion. It would be difficult to recall all the interesting social functions.

Mr. Dulles came to my rescue. In his book on *War or Peace,* he wrote:

"I was with Generalissimo Chiang Kai-shek in Hankow in the spring of 1938. Japan had then been fighting China openly and actively for a year; the capital, Nanking, had fallen, and the seat of government had been moved to Hankow. That city was already under heavy air attack; and shortly after, it was captured, forcing the Chinese capital west to Chungking.

The Generalissimo was at the time under strong pressure to make a compromise with Japan. He discussed it with me. Terms had been offered which would have been very advantageous for him and his government. (Note: The Japanese did not agree to a complete withdrawal, but wanted to retain the occupied territory in Northern China, which was not acceptable by Chiang.) He decided, however, to base his policy on the historical friendship of the United States toward China. He had reached the conclusion that, sooner or later, the United States would come into the war against Japan, and he decided that China would resist, even if it meant standing alone, until that day should come. The day came three and a half years later, but only after China had been subjected to a terrible ordeal."

I was pleased by Mr. Dulles's recollection of our first meeting and his meeting with President Chiang twenty years ago, and the impressions he had of our President, on the eve of his departure for the SEATO conference and for the meetings of the American diplomatic representatives at Taipei.

During our stay in Washington, we attended so many social functions that it would not be possible to count them, and met so many distinguished people. There were 84 diplomatic missions in Washington, some of which have had no diplomatic relations with us, but most of them did have. Their representatives changed frequently, and it takes an extraordinary memory to remember their names.

I suggested to the Foreign Office at Taipei that it make certain procedural changes. One of my suggestions was that the Republic of China more clearly defines the respective statuses of the ambassador and the consul-general. Taipei had been following the French custom under which the ambassador and the consul-general or consul are on a par with respect to their official relations. Each reports separately to the Foreign Office.

To prevent the inefficiency which results from such parallel reports, I had recommended, both from Tokyo and from Washington, that the ambassador have the sole relations with the Foreign Office and that the consul-general or consul clear all their activities through him. Such centralization was favored by the United States Department. However, I had not been able to persuade Taipei to make this change.

Another recommendation which had remained unheeded was that the staff members at the embassy and the various consulates be adequately paid. American living costs being what they were, it was impossible to secure competent stenographers in the United States at a low salary. Since requests for more pay had been ignored, the Embassy and Consulates had been unable to get satisfactory work out of them.

As previously noted, I had also requested the President of the Republic to fix the term of an ambassador to two years, renewable if desired for a second two years. In January 1958, I submitted my resignation to the government, effective in May 1958, which would conclude my two years of office.

Before the end of March 1958, I was called back to Taiwan to have a discussion of this proposal with the President. Since he was unable to secure an appropriate successor, he asked me to return to Washington pending the selection of a suitable replacement. Accordingly, I returned to Washington to await his decision.

My replacement was made possible in July when there was a change of cabinets in Taipei. George Yeh had served as Minister of Foreign Affairs for nine years. S. K. Huang, former Vice Premier, was named to succeed him. I sensed that George wanted to come to Washington to succeed me and I wired the new Foreign Secretary Huang, reminding him of my January resignation and suggesting that now would be a good time for the retiring Foreign Minister to come to Washington to take my place.

My suggestion was accepted, and the first telegraphic instructions from the new Foreign Minister asked me to secure an agreement to Dr. Yeh's appointment immediately after Madame Chiang's departure. But three days before she left, I received a second instruction telling me to defer for a week the securing of State Department agreement for Yeh. On the morning of July 25, I was told in confidence that Madame Chiang wanted me to defer for a few days until she could communicate with President Chiang. The implication seemed that the acceptance of my resignation was being reexamined.

An embarrassing situation arose inadvertently when Madame Chiang attended a dinner given for by General Pate, Commander-in-Chief of the Marine Corps, and other guests were high Pentagon personalities. General Pate, in his toast, said among other things that he had learned with very real sadness that Holly and Sally were leaving Washington soon, that they had won a real place in the hearts of Washington officialdom such as no ambassador and his wife had won before. Since this information had not been officially announced, it was an awkward moment for all of us.

When it came to Madame Chiang's turn to respond, she said that she was pleased to know the friendly sentiments of American officials and public towards Ambassador Tong and his wife. She added that they had done much to improve friendly relations between the two governments and peoples. Of course, we remained silent. The wives of the American top level army, navy, and air force officials, when they received confirmation of the news of our leaving, displayed much genuine emotion. For our part, it was difficult to suppress our feelings.

From July 15 up to July 27, 1958, it was an exhausting round of luncheons, dinners and receptions for Madame Chiang by Washington elites. President and Mrs. Eisenhower invited her to luncheon in the White House, to be fol! wed by a reception at our embassy. Others who hosted events for her were: Senator Theodore Green and other members of the Senate Foreign Relations Committee, at the National Press Club for an address, followed by a period of questions and answers; Secretary of State and Mrs. Dulles; Vice President and Mrs. Nixon; Admiral and Mrs. Redford; Assistant Secretary of State and Mrs. Robertson; Representative Church and other members of the House Relations Committee; Admiral and Mrs. Burke; Secretary of the Army and Mrs. Brucker; and General and

Mrs. George Marshall. On the evening of July 27, she attended a reception for more than three hundred overseas Chinese, at which she expressed the concern of President Chiang over their welfare. Afterwards, she boarded an American Airlines plane for New York to visit with her sister, Madame Kung.

Madame Chiang urged me to continue to work with her after I left Washington. I pointed out to her that this would be difficult in view of all the premature publicity which had been given to George Yeh's forthcoming appointment. Moreover, it would be the duty of the Ambassador of China, whoever he might be, to accompany her on her trips to the various cities, and my presence on such trips would be embarrassing both to him and to myself. She saw my point of view.

My best wishes went out to my successor in his new tasks. For me this was my last government assignment. I replaced that with an entirely different timbre: namely, religion, I intended to take up my residence in one of the less frequently traveled parts of Taiwan and carried on some religious activities during the rest of my days. I looked forward to a life of contemplation.

What is my evaluation of the two years and four months which I spent in the Washington ambassadorship?

My term coincided with a period during which there were no major issues at stake between Washington and Taiwan. I did not have a hand in many of the major relations between the United States and the Republic of China. For instance, American economic and military aid to Free China was handled in Taipei between the American Embassy and its various agencies and the interested Chinese government departments, including the Ministry of Foreign Affairs, the Ministry of Finance, and the Ministry of Economic Affairs. As to publicity work in America, it was funneled through Dr. T. F. Tsiang, China's representative at the United Nations, and funds were also handled through him. A speaker's bureau with a monthly budget of $2,500 was placed in my charge. It functioned efficiently under Dr. C. H. Lowe, who once headed my information office in Burma, India and South Asia.

As for myself, I visited more than sixty cities and addressed various important audiences. I wrote more than one hundred and twenty speeches, and delivered as many additional speeches extemporaneously. All these were done in a period of two years. I had indications from all sides that I had done a truly effective job. However some high officials on Taiwan thought that I should not have absented myself from Washington so frequently and that I should have concentrated my attention upon the cultivation of friendly relations with Administration officials and members of the Congress.

The Chinese Central News, which was headed by a former colleague, sent out instructions to its American offices to play down my public appearances, lest the Foreign Office in Taipei would suffer embarrassment over the fact that other ambassadors were not doing similar arduous work. During my return trip to Taipei in March, the President thought that I had over-emphasized speaking activities before American audiences and that I had not done enough contact with Washington elites. In this he was misinformed, as I pointed out. As the matter of fact, during my two years' stay in Washington, I had done a great deal of entertaining. Annually I had invited more than 5,000 guests to my table besides 5,000 or more guests to cocktails. It seemed that my efforts did not please Taipei. I had no other dignified choice but to resign.

One achievement of mine was to enforce more regular and punctual attendance of the staff members at the office. Previously, the earliest arrival had been at 11 a.m. There had been a good deal of irregularity in attendance.

Another achievement was the building up of a library. In the past, several thousands of dollars were spent annually on the purchase of the books, but not a single copy could be accounted for. Now a regular library was established under my direction, and in due course a good working library would be available.

The third achievement was the collection and centralization of research material. None existed before. Having research material within ready reach is a time saver. There is a constant flow of important documents, news clippings, and leaflets which should be preserved and centralized.

The fourth change was the establishment of a central file of all documents in the embassy. When I came to Washington, I found that there was no room for storing files and that they were scattered in individual offices and kept by individuals. During my last trip to Taipei, I succeeded in inducing the Ministry of Foreign Affairs to assign two staff members to collect all the documents together to start the nucleus of a central filing system.

The affection the staff members felt for me during these two years and four months of association is reflected in their requests for my personal photograph as a token of remembrance. I acceded to their requests although it was not my usual practice to do so. They cooperated with me in my desire not to have a farewell party. There was close contact between my staff members and myself. Their wives and family members also saw my wife quite often.

On the whole, the time we spent in the capital of the United States was pleasant and beneficial. I moved on to a more important assignment, namely, doing the work of God as a layman preacher.

We left Washington on September 8, 1958 for Holland to attend the annual conference of the International Council for Christian Leadership. After the conference we visited fifteen countries in Europe and the Middle East. The greatest satisfaction we derived from this world tour was our visit to Israel and Jordan where we were able to see the places where Jesus lived and worked.

After five months of our absence from the United States, we returned to New York in February 1959 on our way to Taiwan. Friends advised us to have physical checkups. Sally needed to undergo some dental treatment, which would take several months to complete. I left New York first and arrived in Taipei on June 20, 1959, to report to my government the completion of my Washington assignment.

After my return to Taipei, I spent half a year collecting material for a book on the development of Christian churches in Taiwan following World War II in 1945. I was invited to preach sermons in churches on the islands. Sally joined me in Taiwan several months later. Thus we began a new phase in life.

Chapter Twenty-Three.
In Retrospect

As I look back on my life, I realize that I have had to choose between four possible careers. The career that I ultimately engaged in – that of officialdom – was unforeseen. It is something that just happened to me.

I might easily have become a farmer in my native Ningpo. My mother wanted me to become a farmer. She had been brought up on a farm, and my father, also, turned to farming before his constructing ventures for a Christian mission. But I resisted the idea and had the support of my father. Thus I escaped a farmer's career and avoided the fate of becoming one of the faceless men in Mao Ze-dong's obscene agricultural communes.

Having escaped the farm, it is sheer chance that I did not become an employee of the Commercial Press for life. Had I not met Paul Montgomery when I did in my Shanghai Sunday school, and had he not inspired and helped me to get an American education, I might never have left the Commercial Press. In that event, the highest summit I could have reached would have been a manager's job.

The third possibility was to have remained permanently in newspaper field. I would have found happiness in such a career. I achieved a measure of success as a newspaperman. I was once a publisher of my own Chinese daily newspaper in Tientsin, and enjoyed a good reputation in Chinese journalism. Had I struck to my newspaper career, I would undoubtedly have gone to Hong Kong or to some other non-Communist area, when the Communists overran the mainland in 1949, and followed my profession.

As a result of an unpremeditated combination of events, I was destined to establish my career as a government official. It is interesting to trace these events and to note how each one drew me closer into the governmental orbit.

The beginning was in 1929. I was then working in Shanghai as a newspaperman, although my family was still living in Tientsin. Sally came to Shanghai to convey the invitation of Admiral H. K. Tu, head of the Chinese Naval Mission, to accompany him as secretary general on an information gathering tour to study the navies of various countries of the world. It was a flattering offer as I would be second in authority on the mission. Sally was strongly in favor of acceptance. I allowed myself to be persuaded and for the first time entered the ranks of officialdom.

Out of this appointment came my renewed acquaintance with Generalissimo Chiang Kai-shek. Not knowing who I was, the Generalissimo asked me to call on him. In our conversation it came out that I had taught him when he was a student at Lung-ching High School in Fenghua, Ningpo. From this meeting dates my life-long close personal association with China's leader.

The Generalissimo invited me to spend a few weeks of vacation with him and Madame Chiang at his country home. Following this, I had frequent invitations from him to call on him in Nanking, usually to discuss international problems. At the time I was editing the *China Press*, an English-language daily in Shanghai. Also, through the Generalissimo's suggestion, I officially became a member of the Kuomintang or the Citizen's Party, although I had worked for the organization as a non-party member as far back as 1913, when I returned from the United States and met Dr. Sun Yat-sen.

Serious sickness forced me to resign the editorship of the *China Press* in 1936. While I was convalescing, I received a telegram from W. H. Donald, Australian adviser to the Generalissimo, asking me to accept the post of Director of the Shanghai Office of the Military Affairs Council. The Generalissimo headed the Council nationally. My duties would be to censor all foreign newspaper dispatches. With much hesitation I accepted the offer. I felt that I was being drafted for government service to do my part in safeguarding China against the mounting Japanese menace.

When war commenced a year later in 1937, I was appointed Vice-Minister of Information and later was acting Minister, an agency of the Citizen's Party. When information became a government function, I was named as Vice-Minister of Information and held the position for eight years during the war with Japan. Under my direction, an international publicity department was established.

At the end of the war, in 1945, I retired from government service for one year only to be called back to head the Government Information Office and later to become a cabinet minister without portfolio. I continued in this office until the retirement of the Generalissimo in 1948.

When the Nationalist government moved to Taiwan, I became director of the National Radio Network. President Chiang sent me to many countries to sound out their attitude toward Free China. From this I stepped into the diplomatic service, becoming China's first post-war ambassador to Japan in 1952. In 1956, I was appointed ambassador to the United States.

It has been my privilege to become acquainted with a large number of Chinese and Americans in many walks of life. I have found that the continuance of friendship usually depends upon the sharing of similar political and social views. Those who differ with me politically seldom remain friends.

From this long experience, certain broad conclusions have shaped themselves in my mind. I have witnessed, in my life, a far-reaching change in the world as I first knew it. These changes challenge us to reconstruct many of our basic ideas.

The most spectacular change has been the shrinking of distance. The miracle of transportation and exchange of information has brought the peoples of the world marvelously together. United, they now face common world problems. The long age of isolation is ended. The development of speedy transportation and science has placed weapons of mass destruction in the hands of many nations.

The economy of the world has made a vast change. One aspect of this change has been the almost universal acceptance of inflation and the permanent cheapening of money. I recall that when I was a small boy, a few cents in Chinese copper coins would buy a large supply of edibles; hence people were content with small earnings. Today, the picture is strikingly different. There is a mad scramble to acquire large earnings. Many of my Chinese friends who have accumulated as much as a million dollars in property are feverishly striving to increase their wealth. On the other hand there have been many instances of the once rich who are now poor. There has been an economic churning process through which the wealth of the world has been redistributed.

The world has seen a rapid expansion of the communism. In 1917, the first communist nation was established in Russia. By 1949 at the conquest of the mainland China by the communists, one-third of world's population lived in communist countries. Communism advocates one party dictatorship and does not allow true democracy. Without democracy, people's freedom and liberty cannot be secured. Communism is a serious threat to democracy.

My career path really was not my choice, but was shaped by the circumstances and world events. The world is changing rapidly and no one knows the future for sure. The only thing that can guide us is the conviction of our humanity. We are definitely responsible to our inner feelings or conscience. The circumstances and changing world events can make or crush us. With much intriguing and deceit, the battle is on. May the righteousness and our humanity win.

Index

A

Abend, Hallet 63, 64, 107
Acheson, Dean 166, 167, 171, 177, 178, 179, 181, 182
Ackerman, Carl 19, 145, 179
Alcott, Carroll 51
Alexanderson, George 137
Allen, George V. 216
Allen, Leonard 137
Atkinson, Brooks 141, 143, 144, 145
Atlee 112, 184

B

Badger, 170
Baker, William 86
Barkley, 174
Bentley, Elizabeth 117
Biffle, Leslie 179
Boothe, Clare 113, 155
Borodin, Michael 35, 36, 37, 38
Boutwell, Lloyd 16
Bradley 181
Brett, George A. 119
Buchman, Frank 184, 185
Bullitt, William C. 116, 179
Butterworth, Walton 156

C

Chang, Chih-chung 162
Chang, Chung-chong 49
Chang, Hsuan 39
Chang, Hsueh-liang 61, 62, 63
Chang, Tao-fan 188
Chang, Tso-ling 33, 40, 61
Chang, Tso-pang 43

Chang, Ying-tang 15
Chao, Tommy 127
Chao, Yi-di 66, 67
Chemanza, Nevada 51
Cheng, Hawthorne 73
Chow, Albert 172, 173
Chow, Fabian 135
Chow, Fu-hai 90, 91
Chow, Tzu-chi 28
Churchill, Winston 77, 112, 119, 126, 127, 168
Clark, Mark 202
Close, Upton 33
Cripps, Stafford 112, 134, 135
Cross, Harold 145, 210
Currie, Launchlin 115, 116, 117

D

Davis, Elmer 127, 131
Denys, L. E. 119
Despres, Emile 115
Donald, W. H. 25, 51, 59, 60, 62, 63, 112, 131, 150, 151, 224
Dulles, John Foster 179, 180, 198, 216, 217, 219
Durdin, Tillman 51, 54, 76, 78, 85, 95

E

Eisenhower, Dwight D. 179, 180, 216, 219
Elliston, Herbert 154, 155
Epstein, Israel 82, 137, 143, 144
Evans, Henry 132

F

Fairbanks, Douglas Sr. 45

Farmer, W. A. 109
Farnsworth, Clyde 165
Ferguson, C. J. 40, 41
Forman, Harrison 143, 144
Fraser, Leon 19

G

Gandhi, Mahatma 111, 120, 121, 122
Gazzean, Roger 177
Gilbert, Robert 150
Goodnow, Frank J. 29
Gould, Randall 72, 140
Grantham, Alexander 177
Gray, Bill 184
Green, Theodore 219
Grimm, George 137
Gunnison, Arch 110

H

Han, Lieh-wu 184
Handleman, Howard 165, 166
Hatoyama, Ichiro 199
Hindenberg, von 46
Hitler 57, 81, 105
Ho, Ying-ching 62, 63
Hodges, 176
Holt, Hamilton 18, 19, 22
Hope, R. I. 24, 72
Hopkins, Harry L. 29, 124
Hornbeck, Stanley K. 117, 182
How, Sui-feng 8
Howard,Roy 110
Howard, Roy 110, 154, 165, 184
Hsaio, T. T. 73
Hsia, C. L. 72, 108, 130, 131, 132, 133, 135, 137
Hsia. C. L. 129
Hsiung, Hai-ling 30, 31, 33, 39

Hsu, Shih-chang 33, 39
Hsu, Yu-tseng 30
Hsueh, Yueh 92, 93
Huang, J. L. 140, 151
Huang, S. K. 218, 219
Hull, Edward 208
Hume, Pete 178

I

Ikimoto, Seiichi 15
Ing, C. P. 17, 18
Ingersoll, Ralph M. 114
Isaacs, Harold 51, 55

J

Jacoby, Anna Lee 114
Jacoby, Melville 109, 137
James, Harold 54
Jessup, Phillip 166, 167
Johnson, Nelson 168, 173, 181
Judd 174, 179, 184, 216

K

Kai, Liu 126
Kan, Chia-how 172, 173
Kao, George 132
Kerr, Archibald Clark 87, 107
King, H. H. 110
Knowland 174, 179
Kohlberg, Alfred 155, 166
Koo, Wellington V. K. 31, 182, 203, 204, 205, 206, 207, 210
Ku, Chu-tung 73
Ku, Hung-ming 28, 29
Ku, Meng-yu 90

L

Lattimore, Owen 116, 117, 124, 143, 157

About The Author

Hollington K. Tong was from a poor Christian family in China. He graduated in journalism from the University of Missouri and from Columbia University in the early 1900s. Upon returning to China, he worked as a journalist and later became the chief editor of a large English-language newspaper in Shanghai. Due to his proficiency in English, and his honesty and abilities, government officers including President and Madame Chiang Kai-shek often invited him to accompany them on their overseas trips. He was appointed Vice-Minister of Information in 1937.

In 1949, the Communists overran mainland China. The Nationalist government retreated to Taiwan, but was in great danger of falling. During those gloomy years, President Chiang repeatedly sent Tong overseas to assess other nations' positions towards Free China. From this he stepped into the diplomatic service, first as Ambassador to Japan, then as Ambassador to the United States. In 1958, he retired at the age of 71. He became an active lay Christian preacher in Taiwan and wrote many books.

CPSIA information can be obtained at www.ICGtesting.com
Printed in the USA
LVOW13s1522260514

387293LV00002B/526/P